MW00451739

OOo Switch: 501 Things You Wanted to Know About Switching to OpenOffice.org from Microsoft Office

Tamar E. Granor

Hentzenwerke Publishing

Published by:
Hentzenwerke Publishing
980 East Circle Drive
Whitefish Bay WI 53217 USA

Hentzenwerke Publishing books are available through booksellers and directly from the
publisher. Contact Hentzenwerke Publishing at:
414.332.9876
414.332.9463 (fax)
www.hentzenwerke.com
books@hentzenwerke.com

OOo Switch: 501 Things You Wanted to Know About Switching to OpenOffice.org from
Microsoft Office
    By Tamar E. Granor
    Technical Editor: Scott Carr and Sam Hiser
    Copy Editor: Nicole McNeish
    Cover Art: "Open Office" by Todd Gnacinski, Milwaukee, WI

Copyright © 2003 by Tamar E. Granor

All other products and services identified throughout this book are trademarks or registered
trademarks of their respective companies. They are used throughout this book in editorial
fashion only and for the benefit of such companies. No such uses, or the use of any trade name,
is intended to convey endorsement or other affiliation with this book.

All rights reserved. No part of this book, or the ebook files available by download from
Hentzenwerke Publishing, may be reproduced or transmitted in any form or by any means,
electronic, mechanical photocopying, recording, or otherwise, without the prior written
permission of the publisher, except that program listings and sample code files may be entered,
stored and executed in a computer system.

The information and material contained in this book are provided "as is," without warranty of
any kind, express or implied, including without limitation any warranty concerning the
accuracy, adequacy, or completeness of such information or material or the results to be
obtained from using such information or material. Neither Hentzenwerke Publishing nor the
authors or editors shall be responsible for any claims attributable to errors, omissions, or other
inaccuracies in the information or material contained in this book. In no event shall
Hentzenwerke Publishing or the authors or editors be liable for direct, indirect, special,
incidental, or consequential damages arising out of the use of such information or material.

ISBN: 1-930919-36-0

Manufactured in the United States of America.

Our Contract with You, The Reader

In which we, the folks who make up Hentzenwerke Publishing, describe what you, the reader, can expect from this book and from us.

Hi there!

I've been writing professionally (in other words, eventually getting a paycheck for my scribbles) since 1974, and writing about software development since 1992. As an author, I've worked with a half-dozen different publishers and corresponded with thousands of readers over the years. As a software developer and all-around geek, I've also acquired a library of more than 100 computer and software-related books.

Thus, when I donned the publisher's cap six years ago to produce the *1997 Developer's Guide,* I had some pretty good ideas of what I liked (and didn't like) from publishers, what readers liked and didn't like, and what I, as a reader, liked and didn't like.

Now, with our new titles for 2003, we're in our sixth season. (For those who are keeping track, the '97 DevGuide was our first, albeit abbreviated, season, the batch of six "Essentials" for Visual FoxPro 6.0 in 1999 was our second, and, in keeping with the sports analogy, the books we published in 2000 and 2002 comprised our third, fourth, and fifth.)

John Wooden, the famed UCLA basketball coach, posited that teams aren't consistent; they're always getting better—or worse. We'd like to get better...

One of my goals for each season is to build a closer relationship with you, the reader. In order for us to do this, you've got to know what you should expect from us.

- You have the right to expect that your order will be processed quickly and correctly, and that your book will be delivered to you in new condition.

- You have the right to expect that the content of your book is technically accurate and up-to-date, that the explanations are clear, and that the layout is easy to read and follow without a lot of fluff or nonsense.

- You have the right to expect access to source code (if applicable for the book in question), errata, FAQs, and other information that's relevant to the book via our Web site.

- You have the right to expect an electronic version of your printed book to be available via our Web site.

- You have the right to expect that, if you report errors to us, your report will be responded to promptly, and that the appropriate notice will be included in the errata and/or FAQs for the book.

Naturally, there are some limits that we bump up against. There are humans involved, and they make mistakes. A book of 500 pages contains, on average, 150,000 words and several megabytes of source code. It's not possible to edit and re-edit multiple times to catch every last misspelling and typo, nor is it possible to test the source code on every permutation of development environment and operating system—and still price the book affordably.

Once printed, bindings break, ink gets smeared, signatures get missed during binding. On the delivery side, Web sites go down, packages get lost in the mail.

Nonetheless, we'll make our best effort to correct these problems—once you let us know about them.

In return, when you have a question or run into a problem, we ask that you first consult the errata and/or FAQs for your book on our Web site. If you don't find the answer there, please e-mail us at books@hentzenwerke.com with as much information and detail as possible, including 1) the steps to reproduce the problem, 2) what happened, and 3) what you expected to happen, together with 4) any other relevant information.

I'd like to stress that we need you to communicate questions and problems clearly. For example…

- "Your downloads don't work" isn't enough information for us to help you. "I get a 404 error when I click on the **Download Source Code** link on **www.hentzenwerke.com/book/downloads.html**" is something we can help you with.

- "The code in Chapter 10 caused an error" again isn't enough information. "I performed the following steps to run the source code program DisplayTest.PRG in Chapter 10, and I received an error that said 'Variable m.liCounter not found'" is something we can help you with.

We'll do our best to get back to you within a couple of days, either with an answer or at least an acknowledgment that we've received your inquiry and that we're working on it.

On behalf of the authors, technical editors, copy editors, layout artists, graphical artists, indexers, and all the other folks who have worked to put this book in your hands, I'd like to thank you for purchasing this book, and I hope that it will prove to be a valuable addition to your technical library. Please let us know what you think about this book—we're looking forward to hearing from you.

As Groucho Marx once observed, "Outside of a dog, a book is a man's best friend. Inside of a dog, it's too dark to read."

Whil Hentzen
Hentzenwerke Publishing
August 2003

List of Chapters

Table of Contents

Section III: Number Crunching with Calc — 119

Chapter 8: Creating Simple Spreadsheets — 121

Acknowledgements

A number of people contributed to making this a better book. My thanks to all of them.

Whil Hentzen, my friend and publisher, comes first for a variety of reasons, starting with his introducing me to OpenOffice.org and asking me to do this. In addition, he provided insight into organization, style, and content throughout the process. Ted Roche reviewed the outline and read drafts of many chapters, offering suggestions and asking useful questions.

Technical editors Scott Carr and Sam Hiser used their superior knowledge of OpenOffice.org to help me get things right and to grasp some areas that were driving me crazy. Copy editor Nicole McNeish cleaned up my writing and typos, resulting in a more readable book.

The OpenOffice.org mailing lists, especially the Users list, have been invaluable as I attempted to learn a new (to me) product so I could explain it to others. Several members of the lists have been especially helpful. Thanks to Robert Black Eagle, Kelvin Eldridge, Solveig Haugland, Andrew Pitonyak, and Jean Hollis Weber. My apologies if I've forgotten anyone.

Of course, thanks to all the volunteers who've worked to make OpenOffice.org a reality.

On a more personal note, this book is quite different from those I've written before, and writing a book about an office suite using that suite while simultaneously learning it was quite a challenge. So my family got to hear a fair amount of grumbling. As always, they've been supportive and helpful, and made the part of my life outside my office a pleasure.

Tamar E. Granor
July, 2003

About the Author

Tamar E. Granor

Tamar E. Granor, Ph.D., is the owner of Tomorrow's Solutions, LLC. She has developed and enhanced numerous applications for businesses and other organizations, primarily using Visual FoxPro, including integrating it with Microsoft Office. She currently focuses on working with other developers through consulting and subcontracting. Tamar served as Editor of *FoxPro Advisor* magazine from 1994 to 2000. She is currently the magazine's Technical Editor and co-author of the popular *Advisor Answers* column.

Tamar is co-author of *What's New in Visual FoxPro 8.0, Hacker's Guide to Visual FoxPro 7.0* (and its award-winning predecessor), *What's New in Visual FoxPro 7.0*, and *Microsoft Office Automation with Visual FoxPro*. She is the Technical Editor of *Visual FoxPro Certification Exams Study Guide*. All of these books are available from Hentzenwerke Publishing (**www.hentzenwerke.com**). Tamar is also co-author of the *Hacker's Guide to Visual FoxPro 3.0* (Addison-Wesley); she contributed to John Hawkins' *FoxPro 2.5 Programmer's Reference* (Que).

Tamar is a Microsoft Certified Professional and a Microsoft Support Most Valuable Professional. She speaks frequently about Visual FoxPro at conferences and user groups in North America and Europe.

Tamar's years of writing, editing, presentations, and community work have given her considerable experience with Microsoft Office. She has been using OpenOffice.org for the bulk of those activities since late in 2002.

Tamar earned her doctorate in Computer and Information Science at the University of Pennsylvania, where her research focused on implementation of user interfaces. Tamar lives in suburban Philadelphia with her husband and two sons. She can be reached through her website **www.tomorrowssolutionsllc.com.**

How to Download the Files

Hentzenwerke Publishing generally provides two sets of files to accompany its books. The first is the source code referenced throughout the text. Note that some books do not have source code; in those cases, a placeholder file is provided in lieu of the source code in order to alert you of the fact. The second is the e-book version (or versions) of the book. We provide e-books in Adobe Acrobat (.PDF) format. Here's how to get them.

Both the source code and e-book file(s) are available for download from the Hentzenwerke Web site. In order to obtain them, follow these instructions:

1. Point your Web browser to **www.hentzenwerke.com**.

2. Look for the link that says "Download"

3. A page describing the download process will appear. This page has two sections:

- **Section 1:** If you were issued a username/password directly from Hentzenwerke Publishing, you can enter them into this page.

- **Section 2:** If you did not receive a username/password from Hentzenwerke Publishing, don't worry! Just enter your e-mail address and a password of your own choosing, and look for the question about your book. Note that you'll need your physical book when you answer the question.

4. An e-mail containing download links for the appropriate files will be sent shortly to the e-mail address you specified.

Note that the e-book file(s) are covered by the same copyright laws as the printed book. Reproduction and/or distribution of these files is against the law.

If you have questions or problems, the fastest way to get a response is to e-mail us at **books@hentzenwerke.com**.

xx

Section I
Getting Started

Chapter 1
What is OpenOffice.org?

If you're reading this book, you have probably already tried OpenOffice.org. However, you may be asking what this product is and where it came from? This chapter answers that and lays out some terminology used throughout the book.

OpenOffice.org (OOo) is an open source office suite. It runs under Microsoft Windows, Sun Solaris, Linux, and Macintosh's OS X.

What is open source software?

The term *software* refers to programs run on a computer. A program is a series of instructions written in a programming language; a process is then applied to turn that program code into an executable program you can run. Traditionally, when you install a program on a computer, you have only the executable result, not the actual program code. The code is considered a valuable commodity and is protected by the software company as intellectual property.

With open source software, both the executable program you install on your computer and the program code used to create the program are available to the public. Open source software is often referred to as "Free Software." In some cases, as with OpenOffice.org, the software may in fact be free of charge, but the term "Free" actually refers to the lack of restrictions on the software, not to its price.

The average user has no need for the program code, but having it freely available often means changes and improvements become available faster than with traditional, proprietary software. Any user is free to change the program code or to hire someone to do so, and can then use the changed code without further obligation. If a user decides to distribute the changes, he or she is required to make the changed program code available, as well.

Where did OpenOffice.org come from?

OpenOffice.org started its life as a package called StarOffice, created by a German company named StarDivision. In April 1999, Sun Microsystems acquired StarDivision and, with it, StarOffice.

In July 2000, Sun announced it would release the source code for StarOffice as open source and would sponsor development of the product as an open source office solution. A website, also called OpenOffice.org, was created to provide a home for the product and for those working on it. Ever since then, people around the world have been both using and improving OOo.

Sun still sells the StarOffice product, as well. StarOffice has all the functionality of OpenOffice.org, and more. The current version of StarOffice is 6.0.

What's included with OpenOffice.org?

Like Microsoft Office, OOo has a word processor (Writer), a spreadsheet program (Calc), and a presentation package (Impress). OOo also includes an HTML Editor (a first cousin to Writer), a drawing package (Draw), and a formula editor (Math).

While OOo doesn't have a separate database component like Microsoft Access, it does have the ability to work with data in a variety of formats and even to create new databases.

Is OpenOffice.org really free?

Yes, you can download, install, and use OpenOffice.org without charge, both at home and at work. You can give copies of OOo to anyone you want.

You may encounter companies or individuals selling OpenOffice.org. Most commonly, these people package OOo with other useful software on a CD or provide support for the software in some way. Sometimes, these CDs include additional documentation or templates.

Why should I consider OpenOffice.org?

There are a number of reasons to look at OOo. For many people, the fact that it's free is sufficient motivation; this is especially true for those who need to outfit many computers on a tight budget, such as universities or school districts.

Many OOo users do so because they want an office suite that doesn't come from Microsoft. In these cases, often, they're attempting to eliminate all Microsoft software from their computers.

A number of OOo users believe in open source software as a political issue. Related to this issue is that OOo uses an open, documented format for its documents. (See **http://xml.openoffice.org project for details.**) This means anyone who wants to can write other software that can operate on OOo's documents.

Finally, one of the strongest reasons to switch to OpenOffice.org is its cross-platform capabilities. You can exchange documents between Windows, Solaris, Linux, and Mac users, and use the same software to edit them on all four.

Why should I stick with Microsoft Office?

Assuming one or more of the reasons above resonates for you, are there reasons for not switching? A few.

Although OOo does a very good job of both reading and producing documents in Microsoft Office format (see Chapter 3, "OpenOffice.org File Storage"), it's not perfect. Some heavily formatted documents may lose formatting in the transfer. In addition, OOo cannot use macros created in Microsoft Office's Visual Basic for Applications. If you have a major investment in custom macros, you may be better off sticking with Office for the time being.

On a related note, while OOo is quite capable and does some things better than Office, there are some areas where it's just not as strong. You'll find some of those items marked in this book with a special "Still waiting" icon.

Finally, OOo is actively in development. The versions I worked with while writing this book have been pretty stable. However, new versions are released quite often, and it's almost always a good idea to install an update when it's released, as each update fixes a number of bugs. If you're the sort of person who wants to install software once and use it forever, switching to OOo may not be for you. (Of course, Office also has updates—called Service Releases.)

What versions of OOo does this book cover?

This book focuses on OpenOffice.org 1.1. Much of the material also applies to OOo 1.0, but some features discussed were introduced in 1.1, and there are quite a few changes to the user interface between 1.0 and 1.1.

At the time this chapter was written, the current released version of OOo is 1.0.3.1. OOo 1.1 is still in beta testing with version 1.1 B2 the current public beta test.

The material in this book was tested in Windows 2000 with Service Pack 2.

Who is this book for?

This book is aimed at users of Microsoft Office switching to OpenOffice.org. The focus is on showing you how to do in OOo the things you already know how to do in Microsoft Office.

So, often the text refers to the way something is done in Office by means of comparison. I also note some places where OOo has a significant advantage over Office, or vice versa.

Finally, keep in mind this book is not a beginner's tutorial on using a word processor, spreadsheet, or presentation package. It assumes you have done these things before and just need to know how to do this in OOo.

What else should I know about this book?

This book assumes you have some computer experience; in fact, it assumes you have used Microsoft Office, most likely under some version of Windows. To level the playing field, however, here are definitions for some terms used throughout the book.

- A *document* is what you create with any of the OOo applications. A text document is a document, but so is a spreadsheet, a presentation, a drawing, or even a formula. In some contexts, "document" may refer only to a text document, but in most cases, the term is used in its generic sense.

- A *shortcut menu* is often called a right-click menu or a context menu. It's the menu of location-specific options you access by right-clicking. Generally, you can open a shortcut menu by pressing Shift-F10, as well.

- When editing a document, the *cursor* is the marker that indicates where you're working. There are two cursors available. The keyboard cursor indicates where text you type will appear; another name for this is *insertion point*. The mouse cursor indicates the position of the mouse. Although the two are independent, they can be at the same place.

- You can *highlight* or *select* text or other items in order to operate on them. Many of OOo's commands apply to the selected item.

- A *dialog* (or *dialog box*) is a window that displays in front of the document you're editing, typically to let you make some kind of choice. Generally, you can't do anything in the application until you dismiss the dialog (usually by clicking OK or Cancel).

- In a dialog, the item where the cursor is positioned has the *focus*. A dotted line usually indicates what has focus.

The toolbars and dialogs in OOo (as in other applications) use a number of different controls. Here's an overview, along with the terms used for them in the book.

- A *button* is something you can "press" to cause an action. You press a button by clicking it or by pressing Enter when it has focus.

- A *checkbox* is for making yes/no or on/off choices. You change its value by clicking on it or by pressing the space bar when it has focus. Checking the checkbox is generally called *selecting* it, while removing the checkbox is *clearing* it.

- A *drop-down list* lets you choose an item from among a list. You open the list by clicking on its downward pointing arrow or by pressing Alt-DownArrow when it has focus. When the list is open, you make a choice by clicking an item or pressing Enter.

- An *option group* lets you choose one item from among a set of mutually exclusive alternatives. The options are presented with a circle to the left of each one. The circle for the chosen item contains a dot. You make your choice by clicking the item you want or moving through the items with the arrow keys.

- A *spinner* is for entering numeric values. The current value displays and there are up and down arrows next to it. You change the value by typing in the new value, by using the up and down arrow keys, or by clicking the up and down arrows.

- A *textbox* lets you enter data directly by typing.

- A *list box* lets you choose an item from a list. To choose an item, click it or press space bar when the list box has focus and the item is selected.

Most controls in OOo have *tooltips*, short descriptions that appear when the mouse pauses over the item.

Much of what you do in OOo involves working with the menu. This book shows menu items in the following format: Menu Pad | Item | Sub-item. For example, File | New | Text Document indicates you should choose the File item on the menu. When it opens, highlight the New item, which has a sub-menu. On that sub-menu, choose the Text Document item.

Often, if there's more than one way to do something, the book mentions several ways. So, many instructions tell you to choose something from the menu or something else from the shortcut menu or yet a third thing from a particular toolbar. For example, you might see a phrase like "choose Format | Character from the menu or Character from the shortcut menu." In such cases, you can use any of the options presented; if the results are different, the book says so.

Toolbars are referenced in this book using the names displayed in their title bars when they're undocked. (See Chapter 4, "The OpenOffice.org User Interface.") The buttons and other controls on toolbars are referenced using the descriptions in their tooltips.

What are those little pictures in the book?

Three different icons are used in this book to help point out key items.

 This icon indicates a note, something that doesn't fit into the general flow of discussion, but is worth knowing.

This icon points out things OpenOffice.org does better than Microsoft Office.

This icon indicates areas where OpenOffice.org needs improvement, often cases where Microsoft Office does something better or more easily.

How is this book organized?

The first part of this book (Chapters 2-5) covers common ground, starting with installation and moving through things that are consistent, regardless of which OOo applications you're interested in using. While you may be able to skip Chapter 2, which covers installation, you're strongly encouraged to read Chapters 3-5 before moving on to application-specific material. Chapter 3 talks about file storage and formats, Chapter 4 covers the common elements of the OpenOffice.org interface, and Chapter 5 looks at styles and templates.

The second section of the book, Chapters 6 and 7, covers Writer, the OOo word processing application. Chapter 6 looks at word processing basics in OOo, while Chapter 7 covers more advanced document handling.

The third section, Chapters 8-10, looks at Calc, OOo's spreadsheet application. As with Writer, the first chapter (Chapter 8) covers basics. Chapter 9 looks at the data handling aspects of Calc, and Chapter 10 covers Calc's graphing engine.

The fourth part of the book, Chapters 11 and 12, covers OOo's presentation application, Impress. Chapter 11 shows you how to create simple presentations, while Chapter 12 digs into the more complex features of Impress.

In the fifth part of the book, Chapters 13-15 cover the other OOo applications, one per chapter. Chapter 13 looks at HTML Editor, OOo's web page creation component. Chapter 14 examines OOo's graphics application, Draw, and Chapter 15 covers Math, OOo's formula building module.

Chapters 16-18, also in the fifth section, look at advanced topics not every reader may need. Chapter 16 explores the master document capability that lets you combine multiple documents. Chapter 17 examines OOo's tools for working with data. Chapter 18 looks at expanding OOo with custom forms and macros, and using OOo from other applications through automation.

Finally, the Appendix lists resources for working with OOo, including places you can get help when you're stuck.

Updates and corrections to this chapter can be found on Hentzenwerke's web site, **www.hentzenwerke.com**. Click "Catalog" and navigate to the page for this book.

Chapter 2
Installation and Configuration

So you want to give OpenOffice.org a try. Now what? How do you get your hands on it? How do you install it? What do you have once you finish the installation?

Before you can use any application, you have to install it. Often it's the most frustrating part of making a change from one application to another. This chapter looks at setting up OpenOffice.org, including the choices you make along the way and the results.

How do I get OpenOffice.org?

The first issue is getting OpenOffice.org. With a commercial application, you generally buy a shrink-wrapped package and stick a CD into your drive. In some cases, you may pay for the product, and then download it. How does all this work for an open source product like OpenOffice.org?

The easiest way to get OpenOffice.org is by download from **www.openoffice.org**. The home page of the site includes a Downloads link. When you choose it, you go to the Download Central page (**Figure 1**). From that page, you can reach the download page for the current version, as well as for the version currently in development. The Download Central page also links to the CD-ROM Project page, which lists distributors of the latest version on CD (available for a small fee).

The download page for the current version includes a "How to Download" link. Click it and it takes you to instructions for downloading the appropriate version for your operating system and language.

When you click the actual download link, a dialog like the one in **Figure 2** appears. Choose to save the file to your computer, and it prompts you for a location. Once you specify the file location, the file downloads and is saved.

Figure 1*. The Download Central page of OpenOffice.org contains links to download the latest version, as well as the version currently in development.*

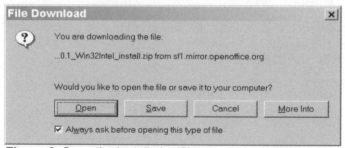

Figure 2*. Save the installation file to your hard drive.*

The file you download and save is compressed. Although the compression format varies with the operating system, it contains all the files needed to install OpenOffice.org. You need to have the appropriate software on your computer to decompress the file.

For Windows, the file is in the ZIP format. Some versions of Windows include the ability to decompress ZIP files, while for others you need a separate utility. (My favorite tool for this task is WinZip, available at **www.winzip.com**.)

For Linux, the file you download is a tar.gz file. With most Linux systems, just type tar -zxf <file>. This extracts the files into an install directory for you. In addition, many popular desktop distributions, such as Red Hat, include a tool called File Roller. One way to decompress the file is to navigate to it using the Nautilus graphical shell file manager, right-click the name of the file, and select Open With | File Roller.

Using whatever tool you have, extract the files, and put them in a separate directory.

How do I install OpenOffice.org?

Once you download and decompress OpenOffice.org, what you do next depends on your operating system and whether you're installing OOo for a single user on one machine or for multiple users on a single machine or on a network. I will look at single user installation first.

For Windows, navigate to the directory where you put the extracted files and double-click Setup.EXE. Single user installation is not recommended for Linux. (Detailed instructions for both platforms are available at **www.openoffice.org**. Look for Setup Guides.)

After a moment, the main installation window (**Figure 3**) displays. Click Next to see the ReadMe information for installation, and then click Next again to reach the license agreement. After reviewing the license, click Accept to move to the User Data page.

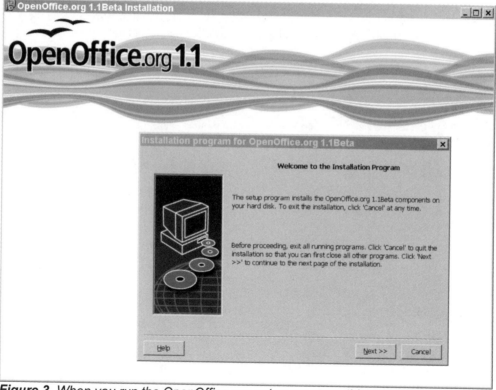

Figure 3. When you run the OpenOffice.org setup program, this page appears to get you started.

OpenOffice.org saves the information you supply (such as name and address) on this page to use within OOo, for example, as the sender for envelopes and labels. (If you choose not to enter any information on this page now or if you need to change it later, you do so by choosing

Tools | Options from the menu of any OOo application.) Click Next to reach the Select Installation Type page.

What choices do I have when I install OpenOffice.org?

The Select Installation Type page lets you choose how to install OpenOffice.org. The choices are Standard, Custom, and Minimum installation. If you choose Standard or Minimum installation, you get no further choices about what installs. The Minimum installation excludes a variety of items, including some of the Help files and some of the filters that convert between different formats. The most significant item omitted is the QuickStarter, discussed later in this chapter. Standard installation appears to install all components and files.

If you choose Custom, clicking Next takes you to the page shown in **Figure 4**, which lists the various components you can install, organized into sections. Click a plus sign to expand a section. (Figure 4 shows the OpenOffice.org Program Modules section and the section for OpenOffice.org Writer within it, both expanded.) Click the disk to the right of an item to change its status. A dark blue arrow indicates the item will install; no arrow indicates it won't install. For items that expand, a light blue arrow indicates some components will install, while others will not. By default, when you reach this page, all program modules are marked for installation. You return to the default configuration by clicking the Default button.

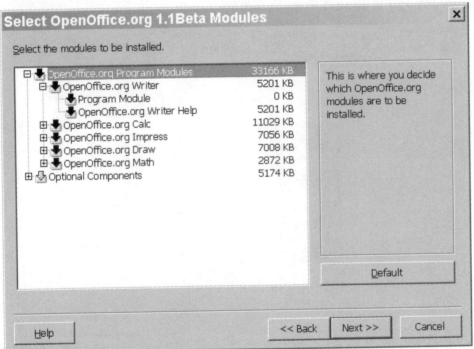

Figure 4. With Custom installation, you choose the components to install.

Once you chose a type of installation and, for Custom installation, indicate what to install, click Next to go to the Select Installation Directory page. On this page, specify the folder in which to place OpenOffice.org. Use the Browse button to navigate to the desired folder; or create a new folder through the Select Directory dialog (**Figure 5**) that appears. (In fact, if the directory you specify doesn't exist, it prompts you to indicate whether it should be created.)

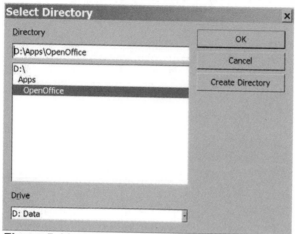

Figure 5. *You can decide where OpenOffice.org installs, even creating a new folder on the fly.*

Click Next to reach the Start Copying page, and if you're happy with the choices you made, click Install. (If not, use the Back button to go back and make changes.) Before actually beginning to copy files, the page shown in **Figure 6** appears. Your choices on this page determine whether the various OpenOffice.org applications become the default programs for Microsoft Office documents (which then display with the OpenOffice.org icon). If these items are selected, double-clicking a Word, Excel, or PowerPoint file in Windows Explorer opens Writer, Calc, or Impress respectively, and HTML files open for editing in HTML Editor. If you prefer to continue editing Office documents using the Office applications or HTML files using FrontPage or a different application, clear these items. You can make a separate choice for each file type.

Figure 6. Your choices on this page determine file associations. When the check boxes are selected, double-clicking on the specified type of document opens it in OpenOffice.org rather than Microsoft Office.

After you click OK, the Java Setup page appears. Click OK to accept the defaults. At this point, the actual installation begins.

When the installation finishes, the Installation Completed page displays. Click Complete to close the installation program.

How do I install OpenOffice.org in a network or multiple user situation?

Installing OOo so users on a network can share the installation or so multiple users of a single computer can have their own settings is a two-part process. Part 1 (called "Phase 1" in the OOo documentation) puts the OpenOffice.org files in a common location and Part 2 sets up the individual users or workstations.

To perform Phase 1, you need to add the "net" parameter when you call the Setup program. In Windows, you do this by using Start | Run, and then type:

```
<path>Setup.EXE -net
```

in the Run dialog, substituting the path to the Setup program as noted. In Linux, you do this by issuing the following command from a terminal:

```
./install --prefix=/opt
```

Phase 1 installation looks much like the single user installation. The same pages appear with the same options, except the User Data page is omitted. On the Select Installation directory page, choose a drive and folder available to everyone on the network. Once you click the Install button on the Start Copying page, installation begins with no further interaction.

When Phase 1 installation is complete, individuals on the network or individual users of a particular computer can perform a local installation. To do so, run the version of Setup.EXE found in the Program folder (a subfolder of the main OpenOffice.org folder) created by the Phase 1 installation.

Individual installation goes through the same series of pages as the other options (including the User Data page) until the Select Installation Type page. This time, the choices are Workstation or Local (**Figure 7**). Choose Workstation if you're setting up multiple users on a single computer (for example, where each member of a family logs in separately to the same computer) or for a network user who runs OpenOffice.org from the network server. Choose Local to make a complete copy of all the OOo files on the machine, as with a notebook computer not always connected to the network.

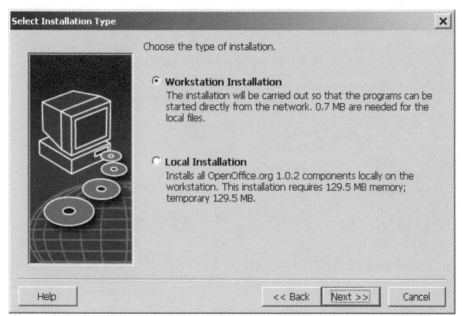

Figure 7. *In the second part of a network or multi-user installation, this dialog lets you determine whether to run OpenOffice.org from the network or install all files on the local machine.*

Once you choose the type of installation, the Select Installation Directory appears for you to specify where to place the files for this installation. For a workstation installation, the only files involved are the user's configuration files. (See Chapter 3, "OpenOffice.org File Storage," for more on this subject.) Be sure not to overwrite the network installation of OOo with a local installation.

After you specify the destination, the process continues as in a single user installation.

What does OpenOffice.org put on my computer?

OpenOffice.org is quite well behaved in terms of what folders and files it creates and where it puts them. It places the bulk of what it creates in the folder you specify for installation and subfolders created within that folder. Of course, with a network installation, OOo may spread its files over multiple drives or folders, but again, it uses only the folders you specify.

In addition, in Windows, OpenOffice.org and its component applications are added to your Start menu, which creates some shortcut files in the Documents and Settings hierarchy. There are only a few changes to the registry. First, a few keys relate to the menu additions. Second, if you chose to make OpenOffice.org the default application for Microsoft Office documents, the registry keys controlling that behavior are changed. Finally, it adds one small set of keys to hold the name and address information you specified.

How can I change what was installed?

If you chose Minimum or Custom installation and later find you need some of the items not installed, it's easy to add them. In Windows, use the Add/Remove Programs applet from the Control Panel. Select OpenOffice.org from the list of programs and click the Change button. The Installation program runs and displays the page shown in **Figure 8**.

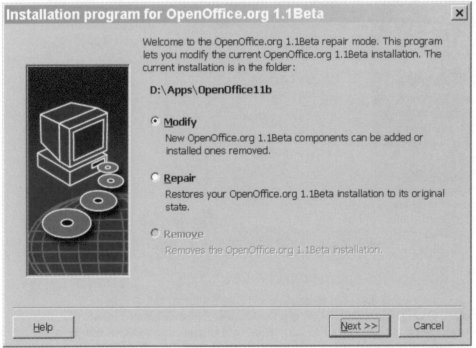

Figure 8. This page displays when you choose to change your existing installation.

Click Next and the page used for Custom installations (Figure 4) appears. Make sure everything you want to install is selected. Items already installed that you want to keep should be selected; if you clear an item already installed, it is removed. Click Install to begin the update. It may prompt you to allow one or more files to be replaced as installation proceeds. In most cases, the correct answer is "Yes."

How do I remove OpenOffice.org?

As with installation, the exact method for removing OpenOffice.org varies with the operating system. In Windows, use the Add/Remove Programs applet in the Control Panel. Choose OpenOffice.org from the list of applications and click the Remove button. In Linux, the technique for removing an application varies with the distribution. In general, an easy way to remove it is to run the Setup program again and choose the Remove option. You have one option in the remove process—whether or not to retain your OOo settings.

Removing OpenOffice.org is remarkably clean. In most cases, it deletes all files and directories (except as noted in the previous paragraph). All it leaves in the Windows Registry is personal information (name, address, etc.), which then fills in automatically if you reinstall. If you want to remove that data from the Registry, look for the key HKEY_CURRENT_USER\Software\Sun Microsystems\setup\recycle.

How do I upgrade when a new version is released?

New versions of OpenOffice.org become available periodically. If the new version fixes bugs you ran into or offers new features you want to use, you will want to upgrade.

You have several choices for installing a new version. You can remove the version you're running and install the new one from scratch, you can install the new one over your existing version, or you can take the middle ground.

Uninstalling and reinstalling has the advantage of cleaning things up. Over time, if you install several new versions on top of each other, you may accumulate files no longer needed. Uninstalling gives you the chance to clean those out and start fresh. The flip side is you lose the various customizations you performed, including settings from the Tools | Options dialog.

Installing on top of an existing installation saves your settings, but at the cost of leaving behind files no longer needed. Also, be aware that updates to OpenOffice.org do not search for an existing installation, so if you installed OOo somewhere other than the default location, you have to point to it yourself. The other disadvantage of installing over an existing installation is the menu items and other shortcuts for the old version are not removed. Fortunately, it's easy to remove them manually.

The third choice appears to be the best. Remove the old version, retaining your settings (as described in "How do I remove OpenOffice.org?"), and then install the new one in the same place. If you do so, you will be prompted about overwriting the various files that contain your settings (choose "No"), but it's a small price to pay for a clean upgrade without losing custom settings.

Is OpenOffice.org one application or many?

Microsoft Office is clearly composed of multiple independent applications that happen to be packaged together. Each has a separate executable file, and you can't open files created with one Office application in another Office application (although there are a variety of ways to use files in applications other than the one that created them).

The picture isn't as clear-cut for OpenOffice.org. In earlier versions, each component of OOo had its own executable (see **Table 1** for a list), but each component allows you to create and open files of all supported types. If you use one component to create or open a file of a type it can't handle, it runs the appropriate program. For example, if you use the File | New menu in Writer to create a new spreadsheet, Calc opens automatically.

Table 1. Each component of OpenOffice.org had its own executable in earlier versions, although each is capable of running the others.

Application	Executable
Calc	OooCalc.EXE
Draw	OooDraw.EXE
Global	OooGlobal.EXE
HTML Editor	OooWeb.EXE
Impress	OooImpress.EXE
Math	OooMath.EXE
Setup	Setup.EXE
Writer	OooWriter.EXE

The main executable program is called SOffice.EXE. The behavior of this program depends on the current state. When any OOo application is executing, running SOffice.EXE sets focus to the running application. If no OOo application is running, executing SOffice.EXE opens Writer.

What is QuickStarter?

QuickStarter is yet another application included with OpenOffice.org; its executable file is QuickStart.EXE. As the name suggests, QuickStarter provides faster start-up for OOo.

Once you run QuickStarter, OpenOffice.org is left running in the background and an OpenOffice.org icon appears in the system tray. Right-click the icon to bring up a menu (**Figure 9**). Choose one of the file types to open the appropriate OOo application with a new file of that type. Use From Template to create a new file using an existing template; again, the appropriate application opens once you make your choice. (See Chapter 5, "Making Life Easier with Templates and Styles," for a discussion of the role of templates.) Use Open Document to navigate to an existing file and open it in the appropriate application.

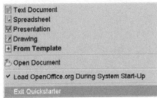

Figure 9. Right-clicking the OpenOffice.org icon in the system tray gives you quick access to most OOo applications.

If you prefer not to run QuickStarter, clear the Load OpenOffice.org During System Start-Up check box. The next time you start the computer, QuickStart won't run. If you change your mind and want to have QuickStarter run at system start-up, change this setting in the Options dialog (Tools | Options) of any of the OpenOffice.org applications (**Figure 10**). Expand the OpenOffice.org section, and then click Memory. Select the check box near the bottom of the page.

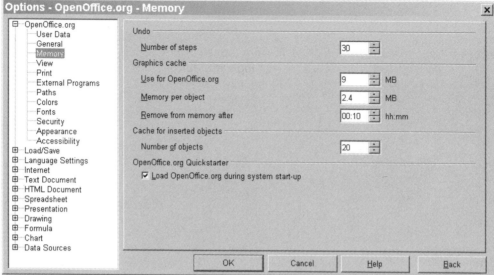

Figure 10. You control QuickStarter from the Memory page of the Options dialog.

Ready to go

Once you install OpenOffice.org, you're ready to get to work. The next chapter takes a look at how OOo stores your files and its own data.

Updates and corrections to this chapter can be found on Hentzenwerke's web site, **www.hentzenwerke.com**. Click "Catalog" and navigate to the page for this book.

Chapter 3
OpenOffice.org File Storage

How does OpenOffice.org store files? Can it read files created in Microsoft Office and WordPerfect? Can I exchange files created by OpenOffice.org with people using other Office suites?

Probably the first issue anyone thinks about when contemplating a change in their office suite is the body of documents they already have. Second on the list is the ability to share documents with others. Microsoft Office is ubiquitous today—you can send someone a .doc or .xls file and feel fairly confident they will be able to read it and even edit it. OpenOffice.org has its own file formats, but it also has the ability to read and write files in a variety of other formats.

Where does OpenOffice.org store my files?

Before looking at how OOo stores files, let's address the issue of **where** it stores them. As in most applications, you can specify the exact location and name of a file when you save it. However, as in Office, you can provide a default location to cut down on navigation.

The Options dialog (Tools | Options on the menu) includes a Paths page (**Figure 1**) under OpenOffice.org. You may want to change several of the items on this page to match your normal working environment. To change any item, highlight it and click the Edit button.

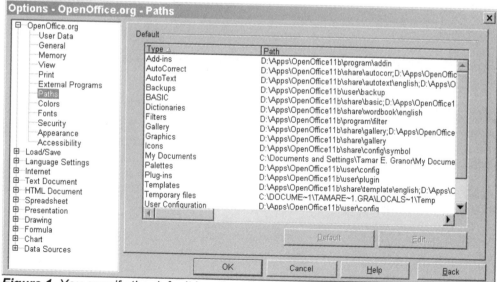

Figure 1. You specify the default location of documents and templates on the Paths page of the Options dialog.

The My Documents item specifies the default folder for documents. The first time you open a document in any OOo session, the Open dialog defaults to that location. (Once you open any document, the Open dialog defaults to the folder containing the most recently opened document.) When you save an unsaved document, the Save dialog defaults to the My Documents folder as well.

The Templates item lets you specify one or more folders that contain templates. When you choose to edit this item, the dialog in **Figure 2** appears. You can add a number of folders to the list. When you choose to create a new document from a template, the templates from all those folders are listed. (For more on creating and using templates, see Chapter 5, "Making Life Easier with Templates and Styles.")

 Microsoft Office limits the locations where templates can be stored. For example, in Word, you specify a single directory tree for user templates and a single one for Workgroup templates. OpenOffice.org lets you specify a list of directory trees containing templates.

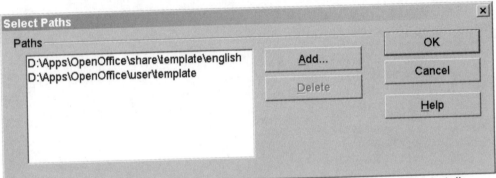

Figure 2. You can store templates in more than one place. Use this dialog to tell OpenOffice.org where to find your templates.

How does OpenOffice.org store my files?

As with other office suites, each of the OOo applications has a "native" format it can create with an extension that identifies its origins. **Table 1** shows the native extension for each OOo application, as well as the extensions used for templates.

Table 1. Each OpenOffice.org application uses one unique extension to identify its files and another for its templates.

Application	File Extension	Template Extension
Calc	sxc	stc
Draw	sxd	std
Impress	sxi	sti
Master Document	sxg	(none)
Math	sxm	(none)
Writer	sxw	stw

However, when you dig inside, it turns out the formats for the different OOo document types are more similar than different. Each file saved on disk is really a compressed file in the Zip format. When you open it with an appropriate tool (like WinZip), you find a number of files inside.

Most of the files found in the Zip use XML, a format designed to carry information about structure as well as content. (For the adventurous, documentation on the structure of the XML files is available at **http://xml.openoffice.org/xml_specification.pdf**.)

The compressed file for a particular document may contain files other than XML files. For example, every picture you use is included.

What types of files can OpenOffice.org read?

Each of the OpenOffice.org applications can read files other than the ones it creates. The Files of Type drop-down list in the Open dialog (**Figure 3** shows a small portion of the list) lists the compatible types.

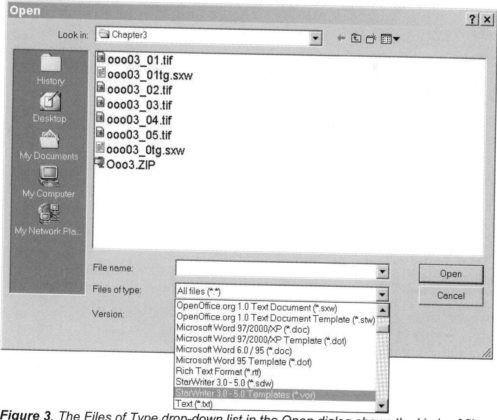

Figure 3. *The Files of Type drop-down list in the Open dialog shows the kinds of files OOo can read. Make sure to scroll through this list to see all the options.*

Most important for those coming to OOo from Microsoft Office is the ability to read Office files, including Word documents, Excel workbooks, and PowerPoint presentations, as well as templates from those products. Most Office files appear unchanged in the appropriate OOo application, although some highly formatted documents may not survive the conversion exactly as originally formatted.

If OOo can't read a particular type of file, consider using the original application to save the file in another format OOo can read. In addition, development is underway for filters to import additional file formats (including, as of this writing, WordPerfect documents—see **http://wp.openoffice.org** for information), so be sure to check at **www.OpenOffice.org** to see whether a newer version that supports your file format is available.

How do I share files with other applications, such as Microsoft Office?

Just as OpenOffice.org can read a wide variety of file formats, it can save to quite a few formats, as well. The Save As type drop-down list in the Save As dialog of each application lists the available formats. **Figure 4** shows part of the list for Calc; as with opening files, be sure to scroll through the complete list of available formats.

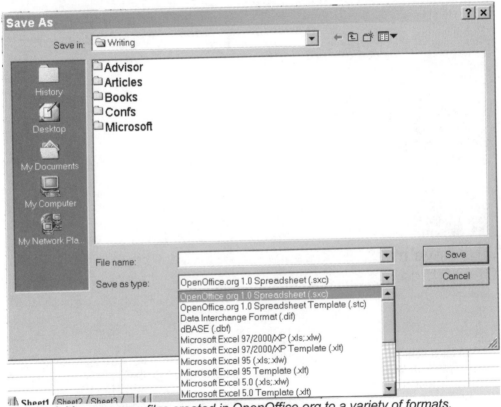

Figure 4. You can save files created in OpenOffice.org to a variety of formats.

If you need to exchange most of the documents you create with Office users (or anyone else using something other than OpenOffice.org) , you can save yourself a lot of effort by setting up default save formats. To do so, open the Options dialog (Tools | Options) and expand the Load/Save section. Click General to display the page shown in **Figure 5**. In the Standard file format section near the bottom of the page, choose a file type from the list on the left, and then choose the default format for storing that kind of file from the drop-down list on the right. Once you do so, any new files you create are stored using the specified format.

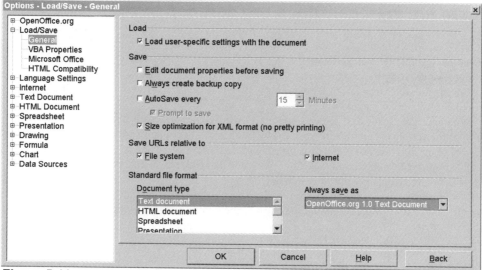

Figure 5. *You can specify the default formats for saving new documents. This is a real time saver when most of your work involves sharing documents with Microsoft Office users.*

It's worth noting that I wrote this book using the native .sxw format. Files were exchanged with both Windows and Linux users in that format. As the original manuscript was completed, files were converted to Word's .doc format and again exchanged with both Windows and Linux users.

Why have my Office files been converted to OpenOffice.org files?

This may be the most frequently asked question by new users of OOo. During the installation process, you can choose whether to use OOo for Office documents (.doc, .xls, .ppt) or not. The wording on that page of the Setup process (Figure 6 in Chapter 2, "Installation and Configuration") is ambiguous enough for many people to misunderstand it.

For each item selected on that page, the file association is changed. That is, when you select "Microsoft Word Documents" on that page, you're telling the Setup process to make changes on your computer so when you open a Word .doc file from Windows Explorer, it uses OOo instead of Word. This automatically changes the icon shown for the file as well. However, the file itself is unchanged and you can open it in Office using the File | Open menu item.

If you allowed the associations to be changed when you installed OOo, but prefer to leave Office files associated with Office, you have a couple of choices. One solution is to uninstall

OOo and then reinstall it, making sure not to select those items. Another option is to right-click any Office file in Windows Explorer and select Open With | Choose Program.... In the Open With dialog, choose the appropriate Microsoft Office application for that file and select Always use this program to open these files. You need to do this once for each type of file you want to re-associate with an Office program.

Where are my OpenOffice.org settings saved?

OpenOffice.org stores settings in a number of files spread across a number of folders. The name of the root folder for the group is User and its location depends on whether a single user or network installation was performed.

For a single user, the User folder resides beneath the root OpenOffice.org folder. For a network installation, each user's User folder is placed beneath the folder specified for that particular workstation installation.

Wherever the settings are located, there are many folders beneath it. Each contains a subset of the settings. The files in those folders use several different formats, but many are either XML or compressed files containing multiple XML files. The key settings for each of the OOo applications are stored in files with names like Calc.XCU and Writer.XCU several folders below the Registry subfolder of User.

In addition to your individual settings, the Share folder (also one level below the OpenOffice.org root folder) contains shared settings and the original default settings.

What's next?

Now that you are reassured about using OpenOffice.org transparently with people you share documents with, the next chapter looks at the OOo user interface, especially the parts common to all the applications.

Updates and corrections to this chapter can be found on Hentzenwerke's web site, **www.hentzenwerke.com**. Click "Catalog" and navigate to the page for this book.

Chapter 4
The OpenOffice.org Interface

While the biggest concern in changing office suites may be file compatibility, the most difficult part of the process is unlearning old habits and learning how the new suite works. Fortunately, in OpenOffice.org, the applications have a lot in common, so once you start learning, much of what you learn applies to all of them.

One of the appealing things about graphical user interfaces (GUIs) is the idea that knowledge is transferable from one application to another. For example, most Windows users expect the first three items on an application's menu to be File, Edit, and View. They further expect the File menu to contain items for creating, opening, and closing whatever objects the application deals with and the Edit menu to include Cut, Copy, and Paste items.

When applications are part of a suite, as with Microsoft Office or OpenOffice.org, users have a right to expect even more commonality. Fortunately, OpenOffice.org delivers. There are many features that work pretty much the same way, whether you're using Writer, Calc, Impress, or even Draw. This chapter looks at the common features of OOo's user interface.

What does the OpenOffice.org interface look like?

Not surprisingly, OOo looks a lot like other applications designed with GUIs. Each application has a title bar, a menu bar, and a number of toolbars. **Figure 1** shows what Calc looks like when you first open it.

One less common feature of the OOo interface is, by default, there's a toolbar docked on the left side. In each case, it's the main toolbar for the application, but the actual contents vary.

Also different from many applications are two floating windows—the Stylist and the Navigator. Navigator is discussed later in this chapter; Stylist is covered in Chapter 5, "Making Life Easier with Templates and Styles."

How do I set things up the way I want them?

OOo offers several ways to configure your working environment. Most settings are controlled by the Options dialog, available through the Tools menu (Tools | Options). This dialog (shown in **Figure 2**) is organized into sections. You move from section to section using the list at the left. Click a plus sign to expand a section and show all the items it contains. Click a minus sign to contract a section.

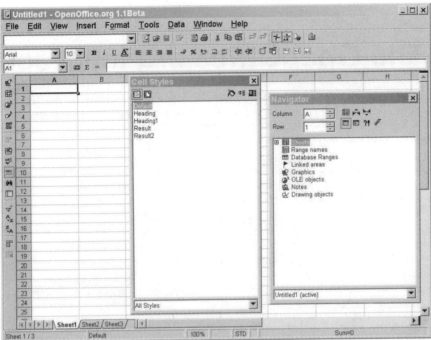

Figure 1. *Like other modern applications, OpenOffice.org applications have a title bar, a menu bar, and plenty of toolbars.*

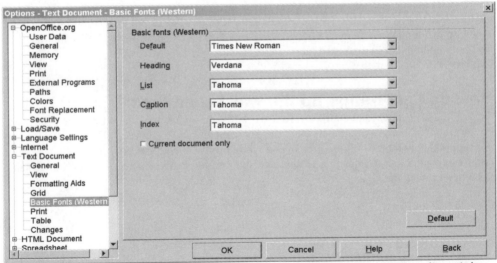

Figure 2. *The Options dialog lets you configure OpenOffice.org your way. It contains a general section that applies to the product as a whole, and specific sections for each application.*

Chapter 3, "OpenOffice.org File Storage," discusses some of the items you can set. Others are discussed in this chapter. Chapters for the individual applications cover even more.

You set up some items, such as customized menus and keyboard shortcuts, through the Configuration dialog accessible through the Tools menu (Tools | Configure, shown in **Figure 3**). Those items are discussed later in this chapter.

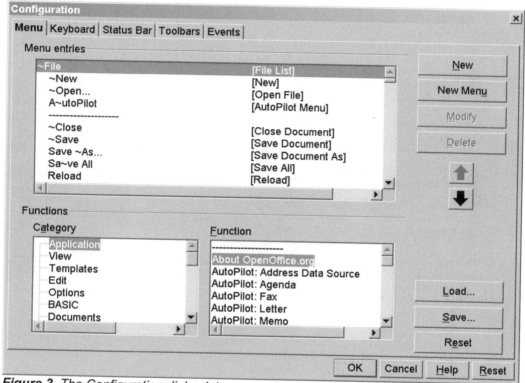

Figure 3. The Configuration dialog lets you customize menus, keyboard shortcuts, toolbars, and more.

How do I make my configuration changes stick?

Almost everything you change in the Options and Configuration should apply for that OOo session and all future sessions. The Basic Fonts page in the Text Document section of the Options dialog is an exception. It includes a check box allowing you to apply the specified fonts to only the current document.

How do I set up custom keystrokes?

Whether you have been using another office suite with numerous keyboard shortcuts or you just prefer the keyboard, you may find you would like to attach actions you perform often to key combinations in order to avoid using the menus or the mouse to access them. You do this on the Keyboard tab (shown in **Figure 4**) of the Configuration dialog.

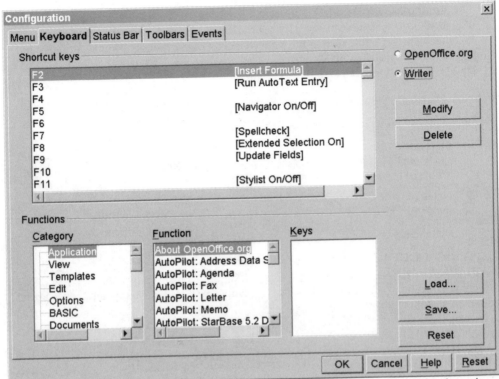

Figure 4. *The Keyboard page of the Configuration dialog lets you set up keyboard shortcuts to speed your work.*

The option buttons in the upper right corner of the Keyboard page determine whether you see keyboard shortcuts that apply throughout OpenOffice.org or only in the application you're working with.

There are very few shortcuts defined for OOo as a whole. Most correspond to commonly used shortcuts, such as Ctrl-A for Select All. If you have certain operations you want to perform in all (or several) of the applications, define them for OpenOffice.org.

Far more shortcuts are predefined for each application. Some of them match the keyboard shortcuts in Microsoft Office. However, many familiar Office shortcuts are not built into OOo. Fortunately, you can create many of them.

To create a new shortcut, highlight the character you want to use for the shortcut. (You can get to it quickly by clicking in the list of characters at the top of the dialog, and then typing the desired key combination.) In the lower half of the dialog, find the command to which you want to assign the keyboard shortcut. The list on the left shows menus and other major groupings. Find the right item there and the middle list shows the items from that menu or grouping. Select the item you want the shortcut to access. At this point, the rightmost list shows all the keystrokes already assigned to that item. Click Modify to assign the highlighted key combination.

Among the Microsoft Office applications, only Word allows you to set up keyboard shortcuts for menu items. (Excel allows shortcuts to be assigned to macros.) In OpenOffice.org, all the applications support custom keyboard shortcuts.

 That said, Word does go one better than OOo in this regard. In Word, you can assign a keyboard shortcut to all kinds of things, including styles, fonts, and even special symbols. OOo supports keyboard shortcuts only for commands and macros. (Of course, you could create a macro to assign a particular style or insert a particular symbol, and then assign a keyboard shortcut to that macro. See Chapter 18, "Macros and Automation.")

To remove a keyboard shortcut you defined, highlight the appropriate command, highlight that shortcut, and click Delete.

How do I customize the toolbars?

For a mouse lover, putting commonly used operations on the toolbars and organizing toolbars is incredibly useful. There are several ways to configure OOo's toolbars; you can even create your own custom toolbars.

The first issue is displaying toolbars. You determine which toolbars are displayed at any given time using the View | Toolbars menu item. Currently displayed toolbars are checked, while hidden toolbars are unchecked.

Each of the built-in toolbars actually includes more items than it displays by default. You determine which items listed are displayed by right clicking on the toolbar and choosing Visible Buttons. **Figure 5** shows the list for Writer's main toolbar. You make an item visible by checking it in the list and hide it by clearing the checkmark.

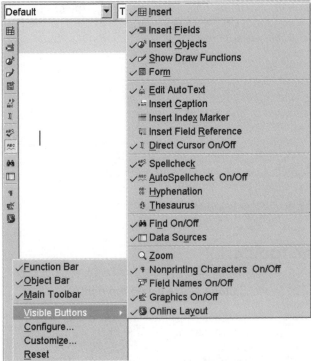

Figure 5. You turn toolbar items on and off using the Visible Buttons command on the shortcut menu for each toolbar.

You can also add and remove items from the built-in toolbars. To add an item to a toolbar, use the Customize Toolbars dialog **(Figure 6),** accessible from the shortcut menu of any toolbar (choose "Customize") or from the Toolbars page of the Configuration dialog (Tools | Configure on the menu).

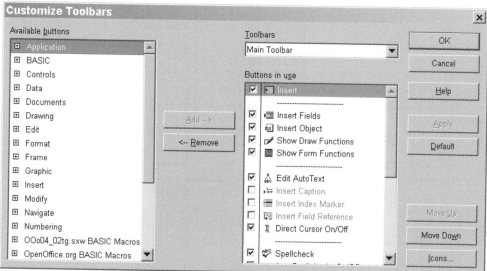

Figure 6. *To add an item to a toolbar, choose the toolbar in the dropdown list and drag the item from the list on the left to the Buttons in use list on the right..*

To add a command to a toolbar, find the command you want in the Available buttons list. Choose the toolbar you are customizing in the drop-down list. Now drag the command from the list into the Buttons in use list in the position you want.

> *The technique for customizing a toolbar is quite different in earlier versions of OOo. In that case, you added a button to a toolbar by dragging it from the Customize Toolbars dialog to the appropriate toolbar.*

You can also use the Customize Toolbars dialog to associate an image with a command. Choose the command you're interested in (by choosing a Toolbar that contains it from the Toolbars drop-down and looking in the Buttons in use list). Click the Icons button and choose the icon you want from the Customize Buttons dialog that appears. Be warned that this associates the icon with that command permanently, not just for that OOo session. It also affects all uses of the button, not just on that toolbar. (You can restore all button icons by clicking the Default button in the Customize Toolbars dialog. You reset a particular command to no icon by choosing the empty icon in the Customize Buttons dialog.)

You can't remove standard buttons, although you can hide them as described above. However, buttons you add can be removed in a couple of ways. To remove an individual button from a toolbar, use the Remove button in the Customize Toolbars dialog. To undo all your customizations from a toolbar (including buttons you have added, hidden or made visible), right-click the specific toolbar and choose Reset.

How do I dock and move the tools?

OpenOffice.org's toolbars can either be docked to the edges of the application or float. Initially, all displayed toolbars are docked, but you can undock them. In addition, the Stylist (see Chapter 5, "Making Life Easier with Templates and Styles") and Navigator (described later in this chapter) can be docked. Toolbars and tools can be docked at the top, bottom, or on either side.

To dock any toolbar or dockable tool, drag the title bar with the Ctrl key pressed. As you drag it to a border, you should see a shaded outline appear showing where the toolbar will be docked. When that happens, release the mouse button.

To undock a tool or toolbar, use Ctrl-drag on any unused space on the toolbar (such as the divider bar between sections or unused space at the end of the toolbar) until you see the shaded outline of the undocked toolbar appear, or double-click it while holding down the Ctrl key.

Once you dock a window once, you can re-dock at the same place using Ctrl-double click. (Actually, there's a bug in OpenOffice.org 1.1 that causes toolbars to dock at the top when you use Ctrl-double click; it's expected to be fixed in later versions.)

Navigator and Stylist behave differently than toolbars in some ways. When you dock them, two small buttons appear at the border with the editing window. The upper or left-hand button (depending on where you docked) allows you to collapse the tool to minimize the area it occupies.

The lower or right-hand button is a pushpin. It determines whether the document window shrinks to accommodate the docked tool or is partially covered by the tool. **Figure 7** shows Calc with the Stylist docked on the right—the pushpin is up, so the Stylist partially covers the spreadsheet. **Figure 8** shows the same set-up, except this time, the pushpin is down and the spreadsheet has adjusted.

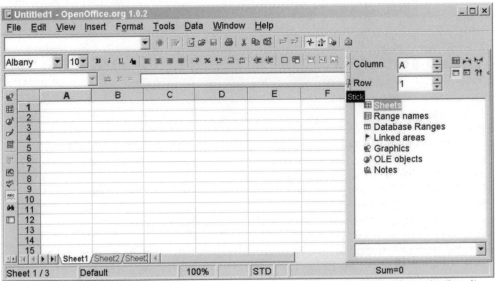

Figure 7. When you dock the Stylist or the Navigator, you can determine whether it covers the document window or the document window shrinks to make room. Here, the spreadsheet window is partially covered by the Stylist.

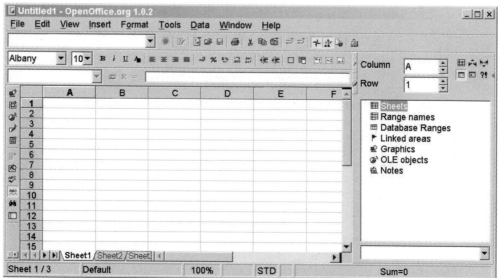

Figure 8. *Pushing the pushpin on a docked tool tells the document window underneath to resize itself to accommodate the docked window.*

You can also resize the Stylist and the Navigator when they're docked, changing the relative sizes of the tool and the document window. Actually, you can resize these windows when they're not docked as well. However, the two sizes (docked and undocked) are independent.

Why do some toolbar buttons have a little arrow?

The OOo toolbars contain several buttons that open submenus or activate other toolbars. All of these buttons include a tiny blue-green arrow in the upper right corner of their icon. If the toolbar is docked horizontally, the arrow points down; if the toolbar is docked vertically or undocked, the arrow points to the right.

If you click one of these buttons, releasing the mouse button immediately, it performs a default action. If you click and hold ("long click"), it opens the submenu or additional toolbar.

For example, by default, the New button in the Function toolbar opens a new document of the type you're currently working on. If you click and hold the button, it offers the same submenu as the File | New option on the menu.

The buttons that open additional toolbars have several other behaviors. First, once you open such a toolbar, you can undock it by dragging it away from the button using its title bar. **Figure 9** shows the Insert button from Writer's Main toolbar, with its additional toolbar docked. **Figure 10** shows the additional toolbar undocked.

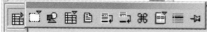

Figure 9. *Some toolbar buttons display additional toolbars.*

***Figure 10**. When you drag one of the additional toolbars away from its button, it undocks.*

When you use one of the items on an additional toolbar, the corresponding button changes to make that item its default. For example, in Figure 9, the default behavior of the Insert item is to add a table. If you use the button to open the Insert toolbar and then choose the Insert Special Character button, the default behavior for the Insert button changes to Insert Special Character. Its icon changes, as well, as shown in **Figure 11**.

Figure 11. When you use one of the buttons from an additional toolbar, the triggering button changes its default behavior.

The additional toolbars are accessible only through the related toolbar buttons. They're not included in the list of toolbars accessed through View | Toolbars.

What is the Navigator?

The Navigator provides a structural overview of your document, as well as quick navigation within the document. It's a first cousin to the Document Map feature of Microsoft Word. It's available in all the OOo applications except Math.

When you first start OpenOffice.org, the Navigator opens automatically. On subsequent uses, it remembers its last state. That is, if you left it open when you closed OOo, it opens the next time. If you left it closed, it doesn't appear automatically.

You open the Navigator by choosing Edit | Navigator from the menu or by pressing F5. There's also a toggle button for it on the Function toolbar (it resembles the image of the compass on an ancient map).

The appearance of the Navigator varies with the different OOo applications. For example, in Writer, it's divided into a number of sections, such as Headings, Tables, and Graphics, with each section listing all the objects of that type in the current document. (In **Figure 12**, the Navigator shows the organization of the outline for this book.) For Impress, the Navigator lists each slide in the presentation and drills down to objects (such as pictures) on each slide. For Calc, there are sections for worksheets, ranges, graphics, and other objects, with each section listing all the objects of that type.

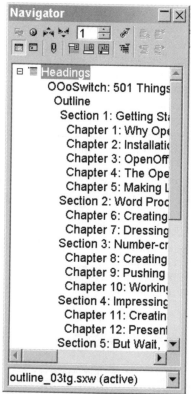

***Figure 12**. The Navigator shows the organization of a document. Use it to move quickly from one place to another.*

Regardless of what structure it shows, the Navigator offers a variety of ways to make editing a document easier. The simplest and most obvious is navigation within the document. Double-click any item in the navigator and your cursor is positioned on the item.

However, the menu at the top of the Navigator offers a lot more options. The two navigation buttons move to the previous and next objects of a specified type. In Writer, Calc, and HTML Editor, you can shrink Navigator to show only the menu portion. (Click the first button in the second row. In Writer and HTML Editor, the button's tool tip reads "List Box On/Off"; Calc uses the same icon, but the tool tip is "Contents.") **Figure 13** shows the reduced Navigator in Calc.

***Figure 13**. A toggle button in Navigator lets you show only the menu portion, providing many navigation options in minimal space.*

You can drag items from the Navigator into the document or another document. The result depends on the current Drag Mode (set using the button that looks like two links of a chain). By default, in most OOo applications, dragging an item from the Navigator creates a hyperlink to that item, which is the Insert as Hyperlink setting. The Drag mode button in the Navigator lets you change that behavior. Insert as Link makes a copy of the specified object, but links it to the original, so it can be updated later. Insert as Copy makes a copy of the specified object at the drop location. (Some of the applications, such as Draw, support only a subset of the choices.)

What makes this tool particularly powerful is the document drop-down list at the bottom. You can switch it to point to another document, and then drag an object from that one into the document you're editing.

In some cases, you need to save the document before you can drag-and-drop items from it.

How do I search and replace?

Search and replace is one of the key functions of any document creation software. OOo's search and replace functionality varies with the application (and is omitted in Math), but in all cases, offers a variety of options that make it possible to find almost anything.

You start the process by choosing Edit | Find & Replace from the menu or pressing Ctrl-F. The Find & Replace dialog displays—which application you're in determines its exact appearance. **Figure 14** shows the dialog in Writer.

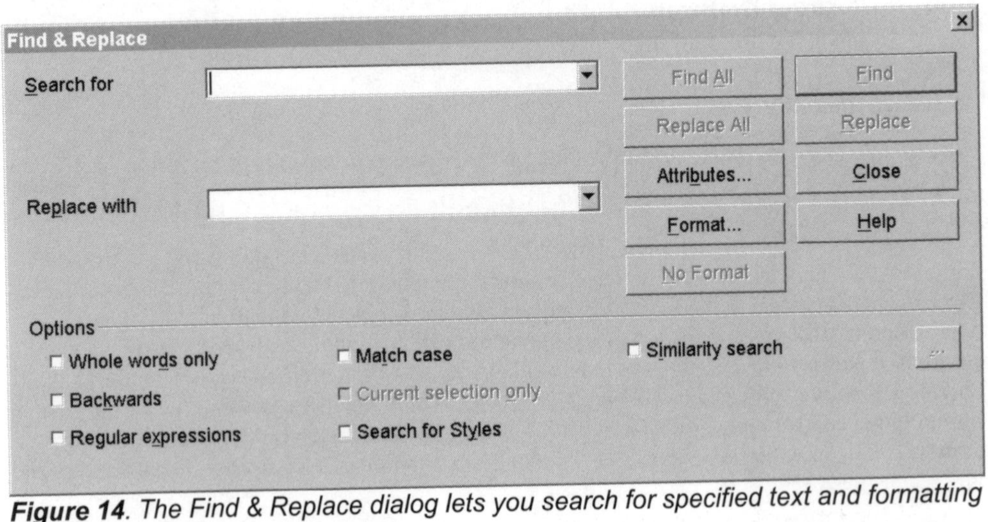

Figure 14. The Find & Replace dialog lets you search for specified text and formatting and replace it with something else.

Regardless of the application you're in, much of the dialog is the same, including the Search for and Replace with textboxes, the Find, Find All, Replace, Replace All, Close, and Help buttons, and the Match case, Similarity, and Backwards check boxes.

A few items in the dialog call for explanation. The meanings of Find, Replace, and Replace All are probably apparent, but Find All doesn't make sense without an explanation. When you click Find All, every occurrence of the search string is located and highlighted. Whether this is useful for you depends on which module you're in and how you use it.

In Writer and HTML Editor, you can search for formatting as well as for text. Use the Format button to open the Text Format dialog to specify font attributes; use the Attributes button to specify other kinds of formatting, such as paragraph information (things like alignment and Keep with next). You can apply the items in the Text Format dialog to both the search string and the replacement string. The string they apply to is determined by the position of the cursor prior to clicking the Format or Attributes button.

Writer, HTML Editor, and Calc also allow you to search for styles. When you select the Search for Styles check box, the Search for and Replace with drop-down lists change to show the list of styles. The Search for list shows only those styles in use in the current document; the Replace with list shows all styles.

If you have bad habits like transposing letters when you type, adding extra letters, or missing letters, take a look at Similarity search. When you select that check box, OOo looks not just for your search string, but for strings similar to the string you specify. Click the ellipsis (three dots) button to set the rules for similarity searches.

How do I find paragraph breaks and tabs?

Searching for punctuation like the end of a paragraph or a tab in a text document is common. In Writer, you do this by selecting the Regular expressions check box in the Find & Replace dialog. To find a tab, specify "\t" (without the quotes) as the search string. To find the end of a paragraph, specify "$" (without the quotes) as the search string. To find blank lines, use "^$" (without the quotes).

Watch out. When you close the Find & Replace dialog and then open it again, the Regular expressions check box is no longer selected.

Regular expressions are actually a very powerful mechanism that allows you to search for things based on complex patterns. If you need to find all strings that fit a particular structure, check out the topic "List of Regular Expressions" in the OOo Help file.

Why does Undo stop undo-ing after a while?

Edit | Undo (Ctrl-Z from the keyboard) is one of the most valuable tools in pretty much any program. It saves you from your mistakes by letting you back up. However, if you use Undo to back up a long way, you may find it stops and no more changes are undone.

You can control the number of steps that can be undone using the Memory page in the OpenOffice.org section of the Options dialog (Tools | Options on the menu). The default is 20.

How do I track changes?

Revision marks are a powerful tool for editing documents, especially when several people are collaborating. They allow you to see what's been changed, by whom, and when. OpenOffice.org supports revision marks in Writer and Calc.

Revision marks were a key tool in producing this book, as various editors marked up the original manuscript. We were able to share documents with revisions across platforms and even document formats.

You turn on revision tracking by choosing Edit | Changes | Record from the menu. From that point on, every change to the document is marked. You control the appearance of marked changes using the Tools | Options dialog. To configure revision marks for Writer, use the Text Document | Changes section; for Calc, it's Spreadsheet | Changes.

As the mechanism for customizing implies, revisions have a different appearance in Writer than in Calc. In Writer, by default, a black line appears in the left margin for any line changed in the document. Deletions are stricken out, additions are underlined, and text with changed attributes (such as bold and italic) is bold. Changes by different authors appear in different colors. (OOo determines the author by looking at the user information, which is a good reason for specifying at least your name when you install OOo.)

The vertical line indicating changes doesn't appear in Online Layout view (View | Online Layout or Online Layout on the Main toolbar).

In Calc, by default, revised cells have a thin colored border with a square in the upper left corner. Calc marks changes to contents, additions, deletions, and movement of data. Changes by different authors appear in different colors.

In both cases, hovering the mouse pointer over a change displays a tool tip describing the change. **Figure 15** shows a portion of a spreadsheet containing several changes, with the tool tip for one included.

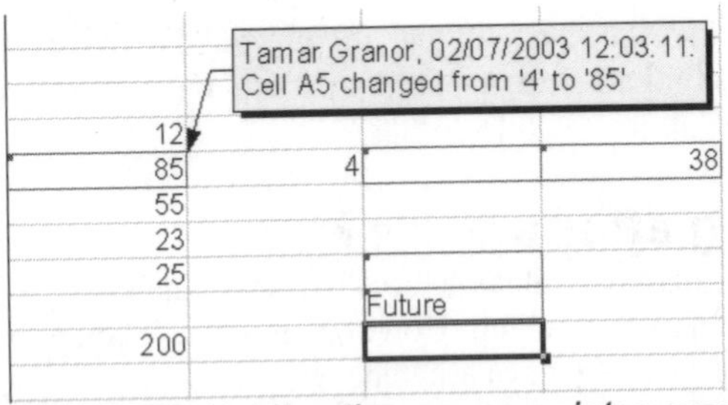

Figure 15. Holding the mouse pointer over a changed item displays a tool tip describing the change.

Once some changes are marked, you have a variety of options for dealing with them. You can determine whether to display changes (Edit | Changes | Show) and you can accept or reject changes individually or as a group. To begin the process, choose Edit | Changes | Accept or Reject. The dialog in **Figure 16** displays, allowing you to see the list of changes and decide which to keep, removing revision marks (accept), which to keep, leaving revision marks (do nothing), and which to undo (reject).

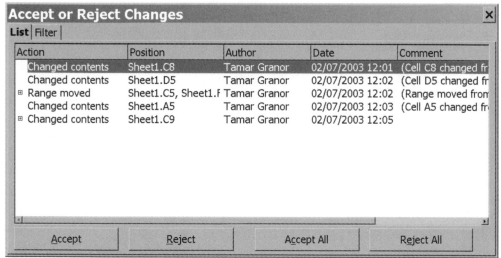

Figure 16. Use this dialog to determine what to do with marked changes. The Filter page lets you limit the list displayed.

The Filter page of this dialog lets you limit the items shown on the List page. You can filter the list based on when changes were made, by whom, the type of change, or the comment associated with the change. Calc generates comments automatically, describing the actual change made. You add your own comments by highlighting the item you want to comment and choosing Edit | Changes | Comment from the menu.

In Writer, you can turn revision marking on and off freely and your changes remain marked (although changes you make with revision marking turned off aren't marked). In Calc, however, turning off revision marking accepts all marked changes. The message in **Figure 17** displays to let you decide whether to accept revisions and turn off revision marking.

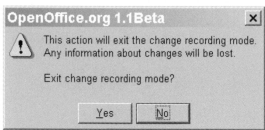

Figure 17. Calc displays this message when you turn off recording of changes without accepting or rejecting all changes first. Choose Yes to accept all remaining changes and turn off revision marking.

How do I compare documents?

Document comparison is a first cousin to revision marking. It's useful when someone has made changes to a document without recording the changes.

 Microsoft Excel doesn't support comparison of spreadsheets. Calc does.

To begin document comparison, open the newer version of the document or spreadsheet. Choose Edit | Compare Document from the menu. When the Insert dialog appears, choose the older version of the document or spreadsheet.

After the comparison is complete, the Accept or Reject Changes dialog displays, showing all the differences between the two documents. Revision marks are added to the document to indicate the changes, as well.

Why does what I type get changed?

By default, OOo has a variety of automatic correction and formatting options turned on. These tools correct a variety of typing errors, as well as make your documents look more professional. However, sometimes these tools get in your way.

The exact set of auto-correct and auto-format options varies with the application. Not surprisingly, Writer (and its alter-ego, HTML Editor) offer the most choices. However, a number of the options are the same across applications, and the applications share the underlying data.

The most important thing about these tools is you can turn off any or all of them, and you can customize those you choose to keep. To modify the settings, choose Tools | AutoCorrect (or in Writer and HTML Editor, Tools | AutoCorrect/AutoFormat) from the menu. The AutoCorrect dialog opens; the exact appearance of the dialog varies with the application. **Figure 18** shows the Options page of the Writer/HTML Editor version of the dialog, where you choose the features you want to use. (The Word Completion tab is present only in Writer and HTML Editor—Chapter 6, "Creating Simple Documents," discusses that feature.)

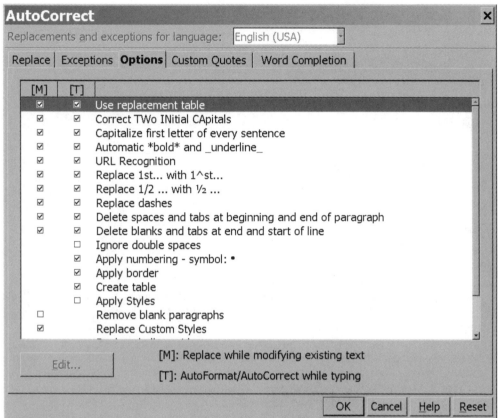

Figure 18. *Use the Options tab of the AutoCorrect dialog to turn the various features on and off.*

In Writer and HTML Editor, you can have two groups of settings, those that apply when you initially enter text (the "T" column) and those that apply when editing existing text (the "M" column). To apply changes while editing (the "M" column), you choose Format | AutoFormat | Apply. (This structure is analogous to Word's AutoFormat as you Type and AutoFormat features.)

There are too many configurable items to cover here, so I will look at just a few. However, the Help file explains the options reasonably well. Choose Help from the dialog itself to get to the right topic.

The first item you're likely to notice is automatic correction of typing mistakes. For example, if you type "withe" (one of my personal bugaboos), it automatically changes to "with". The first item on the Options page, "Use Replacement Table" controls this feature. The Replace page of the dialog (shown in **Figure 19**) lets you configure the actual replacements. It comes with a substantial list of items, but you can remove or modify any of them that are inconvenient for you (for example, I prefer "withe" be replaced by "with the" rather than the default "with") as well as add your own. Consider adding abbreviations for names and terms you type often. Be aware that it does not replace items inside of quotation marks.

Customizing the list of corrections can save you considerable time as you type.

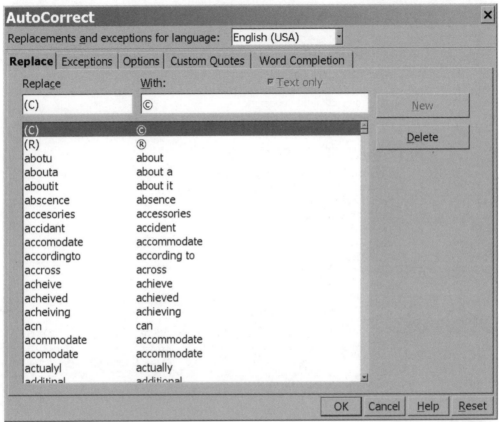

Figure 19. The Replace tab of the AutoCorrect dialog lists the substitutions that can be made automatically.

You can immediately undo a particular replacement by choosing Edit | Undo from the menu or pressing Ctrl+Z as soon as the change is made. In Writer, HTML Editor, and Draw, a single Undo is sufficient; in Calc and Impress, it takes two uses of Undo to restore the original string. Also, in Calc, you can do this only if you're still in the same cell. Once you leave the cell, Undo removes the new string.

The second and third items, "Correct TWo INitial CApitals" and "Capitalize first letter of every sentence" are handy, catching two fairly common typing errors. However, there are places where each behavior is wrong. The Exceptions page of the dialog (shown in **Figure 20**) lets you define exceptions to the rule for each. When the AutoInclude check box for each feature is selected, it adds words to the list automatically when you undo one of OOo's changes.

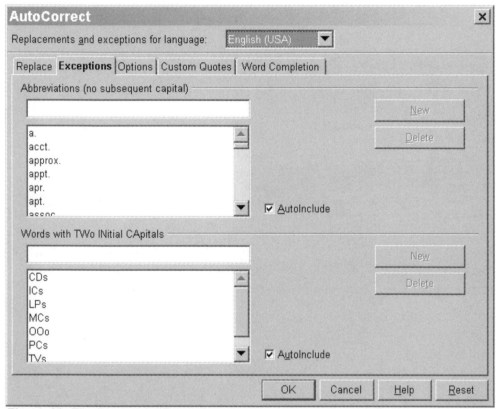

Figure 20. *The lists on the Exceptions tab let you override capitalization after a period and correction of two initial capitals.*

The Custom Quotes page of the dialog (**Figure 21**) controls the feature often known as "Smart Quotes." Normally, the single and double quote keys on the keyboard insert straight quotes (" and ') when you type them. In many situations, curly quotes (", ", ', and ') look better. The Replace check boxes determine whether to replace the straight quotes.

 In Microsoft Office, substitution of smart quotes can be either on or off. In OOo, you can determine what characters to substitute for straight quotation marks. Click the button showing one of the marks and a dialog displays showing symbols. Choose one to substitute for the quotation mark.

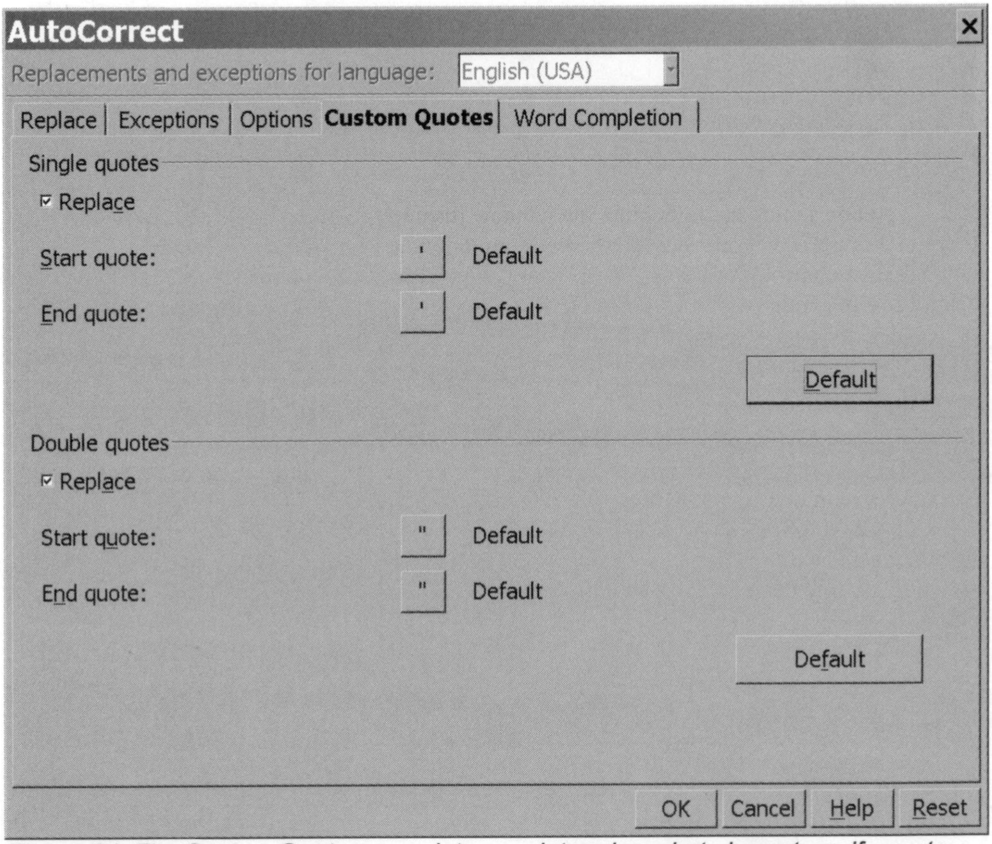

AutoCorrect   [×]

Replacements and exceptions for language: [English (USA) ▾]

| Replace | Exceptions | Options | **Custom Quotes** | Word Completion |

Single quotes
☑ Replace

Start quote: [']   Default

End quote: [']   Default

                              [Default]

Double quotes
☑ Replace

Start quote: ["]   Default

End quote: ["]   Default

                              [Default]

[OK] [Cancel] [Help] [Reset]

Figure 21. The Custom Quotes page lets you determine what characters, if any, to substitute for straight quotes.

Other changes controlled by this dialog include turning pseudo-bold (text surrounded by asterisks) and pseudo-underlines (text surrounded by underscore marks) into the real thing, recognizing URL's and turning them into hyperlinks, and much more. As you notice changes being made to your document, look at the AutoCorrect dialog to understand the change and decide whether to leave that particular feature on.

Why does a "light bulb" window appear now and then?

The light bulb window is the OOo Help Agent, designed to help you learn about OpenOffice.org. Whenever certain actions occur (such as changes due to your AutoCorrect settings), a little window (**Figure 22**) appears at the bottom right of your document. If you click the window, the Help file displays information about the operation that triggered it. This can be a handy learning tool as you're getting accustomed to OOo.

***Figure 22**. This icon appears when OOo wants to tell you about some kind of change it made, or operation it performed. Click it to open Help at the appropriate topic.*

If you don't click the light bulb, the window disappears after a bit. If you let it close three times in a row for the same operation, it will no longer appear for that operation.

You can control the Help agent in several ways. First, you can turn it off entirely by clearing Help | Help Agent on the menu. You can also turn it off in the Tools | Options dialog on the General page of the OpenOffice.org section. That page also lets you specify how long the window remains open when you don't click it.

How do I check spelling and grammar?

Like Microsoft Office, OOo offers spelling checks both as you work and after the fact. The Spellcheck item on the Tools menu controls these features.

Choose AutoSpellcheck to turn on continuous spelling checks. When you do so, a check mark appears next to that item in the menu, and words that aren't recognized display with a red squiggly line beneath. Right-click such a word to display a list of suggestions for correcting it.

To check the spelling in an entire document or a selected portion, choose Tools | Spellcheck | Check from the menu or press F7. If any words aren't recognized, the Spellcheck dialog (**Figure 23**) displays. Make the appropriate choice for each word found.

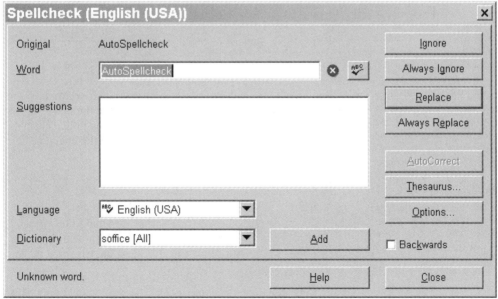

***Figure 23**. The Spellcheck dialog lets you deal with words not recognized by the dictionary you're using.*

The Spelling engine uses a number of dictionaries specified in the Language Settings section of the Options dialog (Tools | Options). The Languages page of the section lets you specify the language you're writing in, so it uses an appropriate dictionary . The Writing Aids page of that section provides lists of specialized terms; these lists include a variety of terms relevant to OOo, as well as those you indicate should be ignored through the Spellcheck dialog. (Note that the same information is available by clicking the Options button of the Spellcheck dialog.) Check the websites listed in the Appendix for additional lists.

As installed, OOo includes a dictionary only for US English. However, you can download some additional language dictionaries from **http://lingucomponent.openoffice.org/download_dictionary.html**. You switch to an alternate dictionary by choosing Edit for the Available language modules section of the Writing Aids page. On the Edit Modules page that displays (**Figure 24**), choose the language for the dictionary you want to use.

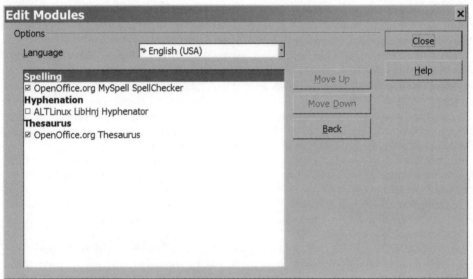

Figure 24. You specify the language to use for spelling checks, hyphenation rules, and thesaurus on the Edit Modules page, accessed through the Language Settings | Writing Aids page of the Options dialog.

OOo doesn't support grammar checking at this time.

What is AutoPilot?

AutoPilot is OOo's answer to Microsoft's Wizards, providing a guide through the initial construction of a document, as well as guidance for some other tasks. A number of OOo document types are supported.

Help refers to each item in the AutoPilot menu as "an AutoPilot," and I will follow that style. To use an AutoPilot, choose File | AutoPilot from the menu. The sub-menu (**Figure 25**) shows the available options. You can create a variety of documents, as well as convert some data from one format to another.

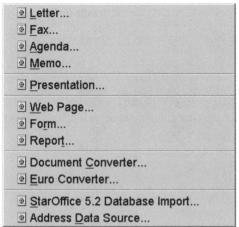

Figure 25. *Choosing File | AutoPilot from the menu offers these options for creating new documents and templates, or converting existing data.*

The AutoPilots provided perform a variety of tasks. The first group (letter, fax, agenda, memo) create both a new template and a new document based on that template. (See Chapter 5, "Making Life Easier with Templates and Styles," for an explanation of using templates.) The Presentation AutoPilot creates a new presentation, possibly based on a template, or opens an existing presentation. (By default, this AutoPilot runs automatically each time you open Impress. You turn that setting off in the Tools | Options dialog.)

The Web Page AutoPilot creates a new HTML document based on a template and a layout style. The Form AutoPilot sets up a Writer document as a form, using specified data. The Report AutoPilot lets you create reports based on data in a database.

The Document Converter provides bulk conversion of StarOffice and Microsoft Office documents to OpenOffice.org format. The Euro Converter converts currency in Calc spreadsheets into Euros.

The last two AutoPilots make data available in a format OOo can work with. In fact, the Address Data Source AutoPilot opens automatically the first time you use OOo.

The exact steps and options involved vary with the AutoPilot. It's worth spending some time experimenting to see what each can do for you.

What is the Gallery?

The Gallery is a tool for organizing graphics to make them easily accessible. To open it, choose Tools | Gallery from the menu. This menu item is a toggle, so choose the same item again to close the Gallery.

The Gallery is dockable. By default, it's docked beneath the Function toolbar. Like the Stylist and Navigator, it includes buttons to let you collapse it and to have the document adjust to it.

The Gallery (**Figure 26**) is organized into themes (categories). Each theme contains graphics from a directory tree (specified when creating the theme). You can filter on the type of graphic image. OOo provides a number of themes, and you can add your own. You can also download themes from **http://www.ooextras.org** or **http://documentation.openoffice.org**.

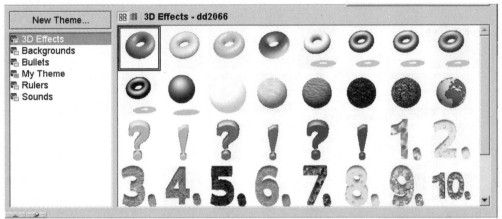

Figure 26. *The Gallery holds graphic images organized into categories called themes.*

To add a theme, click the New Theme button. The Theme Properties dialog (**Figure 27**) displays. Specify a name for the theme, and then switch to the Files tab (**Figure 28**), where you choose the files to add to this theme. First, specify the type of graphic image to include in this theme. The default "<All Files>" includes all types of graphic images. Click the Find Files button to specify a directory tree to search. All the graphics of the specified type in the directory and its subdirectories are listed. Either click Add All to put them all in this theme or choose the ones you want to include and click Add.

Properties of New Theme		x
General Files		

	New Theme

Type:	Gallery Theme
Location:	file:///D:/Apps/OpenOffice/user/gallery/sg104.sdg
Contents:	0 Objects
Created:	00/00/0000, 00:00:00
Modified:	03/13/2003, 15:39:15

OK   Cancel   Help   Reset

Figure 27. *The Theme Properties dialog displays when you add a new theme.*

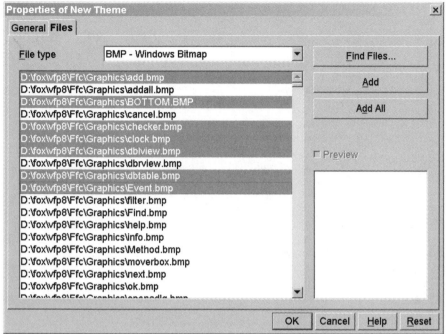

Figure 28. *Use the Files tab of the dialog to specify the graphics to include in the new theme.*

You can drag items from the Gallery into documents to add that graphic image to the document. For more information on adding graphics to documents, see the chapters for the individual applications.

The Gallery can also hold sounds in a couple of formats. As with graphics, you can drag the sound items to a document if the document supports sound.

Summary

Quite a few things work the same way or similarly across multiple OpenOffice.org applications. Learning how to use one of the applications is likely to make using the others easier.

There are two more major features shared by the bulk of the OOo applications: templates and styles. The next chapter explains what they are and how to use them.

Updates and corrections to this chapter can be found on Hentzenwerke's web site, **www.hentzenwerke.com**. Click "Catalog" and navigate to the page for this book.

Chapter 5
Making Life Easier with
Templates and Styles

For most users, uniformity within and across documents is important. OpenOffice.org supports this need with styles that define a group of formatting characteristics and templates that combine styles with boilerplate text to form the basis for new documents.

Seasoned Microsoft Office users may be familiar with both templates and styles; in Office, they're a key to increased productivity. However, many Office users never touch them. In OOo, styles and templates are even more important than in Office, and wise users will become familiar with both the concepts and the details of using them.

What is a style?

A style is a group of formatting characteristics gathered together and given a name. Styles offer a number of advantages. First, they make it easy to apply the same formatting to different parts of a document; just use the same style. Second, they make it easy to change formatting uniformly; change the formatting of the style and everything using that style changes. Finally, because you can save styles in templates (discussed later in this chapter), it's easy to use the same formatting across a whole family of documents.

For example, you may decide to write a document using 10-point Arial for the text and 14-point Arial for headings. If you later decide to change to Times New Roman, with styles, you make the change in two places—the definitions of your body text and heading styles. Without styles, you have to go through and change each paragraph.

OpenOffice.org offers a variety of style types, varying with the application. **Table 1** shows the types of styles available in the various applications.

Table 1. Different types of styles apply to different objects. Each application offers a variety of style types.

Type of style	Applies to	Used in
Cell	Individual cells	Calc
Character	Blocks of text	Writer, HTML Editor
Frame	Inserted objects	Writer
Graphics	Drawn objects	Impress, Draw
Numbering	Bulleted and numbered lists	Writer, HTML Editor
Page	Entire pages	Writer, Calc
Paragraph	Paragraphs	Writer, HTML Editor
Presentation	Components of a presentation	Impress

Depending on the type of style and the application, a style's definition may include such things as font characteristics, paragraph formatting, tab definitions, colors, text wrapping, page size, margins, borders, columns, bullets and numbering, alignment, and more. In other words, pretty much every kind of formatting can be applied to some type of style. (The chapters that cover the individual OOo applications explore many of the items that go into styles.)

OOo includes a large number of predefined styles, usable as is. You can modify the predefined styles to fit your needs. OOo also offers the ability to define new styles of the various types and use them. Defining custom styles is discussed later in this chapter.

For a number of the style types, there's a style named Default. This is the style used for objects of that type if you don't specify a different style. To change the overall appearance of a document, modify the Default style. (See "How do I change the existing styles and create new styles?" later in this chapter.)

What is the Stylist?

The name "Stylist" is a contraction of "style" and "list," no doubt chosen because of the implications of the word "stylist." The Stylist is available in every OOo application except Math.

Open the Stylist by choosing Format | Stylist from the menu, clicking the Stylist button on the Function toolbar, or pressing F11. (All of these actually toggle the Stylist on and off.) The Stylist can be docked. See "How do I dock the tools?" in Chapter 4, "The OpenOffice.org Interface," for details.

The Stylist provides easy access to all available styles, offering options for organizing them, as well as for defining new styles. **Figure 1** shows the Stylist in Writer, where it has the most options.

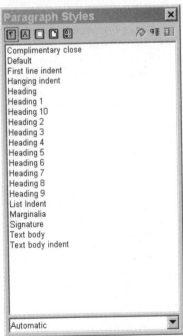

Figure 1. *The Stylist shows defined styles of each type and allows you to apply them, as well as define new styles.*

The left section of the button bar at the top of the Stylist shows the different types of styles available in the application (from the list in Table 1). In Writer, five types of styles are available (paragraph, character, frame, page, and numbering), so there are five option buttons in Figure 1. (The buttons have tooltips to identify the style types.)

The main section of the Stylist is a list of styles of the chosen type. In Figure 1, the list shows paragraph styles. The dropdown list beneath the list of styles lets you limit the list to a particular subset. In addition to "Automatic" shown in Figure 1, the drop-down list includes options such as "All Styles" to show everything of that type, "Applied Styles" to show only those styles in use in the current document, "Custom Styles" to show only user-defined styles, and a variety of others. The items in this drop-down list vary with the application and with the type of Style currently chosen in the button bar.

The buttons on the right end of the button bar provide easy ways to change formatting; they're discussed later in this chapter.

How do I use the styles provided?

There are several ways to apply styles to text and objects, with some variation from application to application. For text, you can generally apply styles either before or after typing. For other kinds of objects (such as graphics and drawings), it's easier to add the object, and then set its style.

You set the style using the Stylist. In Writer, HTML Editor, and Calc, make sure the cursor is positioned where you want the new style, double-click the desired style in the Stylist, and then begin typing. In Writer and HTML Editor, the Text Object toolbar also contains a drop-down list showing all the styles already in use in the current document. You can choose a style from the list (shown in **Figure 2**). Unfortunately, there's no keyboard shortcut to get to the drop-down list quickly as in Microsoft Word. (See "How do I apply a style using the keyboard?" later in this chapter for an alternative.)

Figure 2. The styles drop-down list in the Text Object toolbar includes all the styles in use in the document.

The Format menu provides another way to get to the list of styles. Choose Format | Styles | Catalog to open the Style Catalog dialog (**Figure 3**). Choose a style from the catalog to apply at the insertion point.

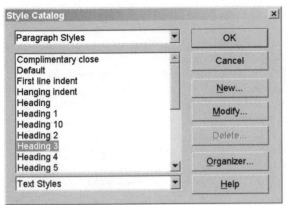

Figure 3. The Style Catalog provides a third way to access the list of styles.

You can also change the style once you enter text. Highlight the text or cells you want to change and choose the desired style from the Stylist, styles drop-down list, or Style Catalog.

When working with objects other than text, and in Draw, you apply styles by selecting the object and then choosing the appropriate style from the Stylist, drop-down list, or Style Catalog.

You can quickly change the style of multiple items using the Stylist. The paint can icon on the right side of the button bar controls "Fill Format Mode"—choose a style, click this button, and then, depending on the application, either select all the objects you want to apply the specified style to or click the objects to be changed. When you're done, click the button again to turn off this mode.

How do I apply a style using the keyboard?

Microsoft Word power users may be accustomed to changing styles using only keystrokes. Word provides a keyboard shortcut (Ctrl-Shift-S) to jump to the Styles list in the toolbar, and allows you to assign keyboard shortcuts to individual styles.

It's not as easy in OOo. There's no keyboard shortcut for the Styles drop-down list, and the Stylist's shortcut turns it on and off, but doesn't land focus there; at a minimum, you have to click in the Stylist before you can use the keyboard there. In addition, you can't assign keyboard shortcuts to styles.

However, all is not lost. You can assign a shortcut to the Style Catalog. (See "How do I set up custom keystrokes?" in Chapter 4, "The OpenOffice.org Interface." The command you want is Templates | Style Catalog.) Once you open the Style Catalog, you can navigate solely with the keyboard.

You can also create a macro that applies a particular style to a paragraph or other selection, and then assign a keystroke to that macro. See Chapter 18, "Forms, Macros and Automation," for details.

How do I change the existing styles and create new styles?

There are several ways to create and edit styles. You can do so directly, defining exactly what you want or you can tell OOo to create or change a style based on formatting in your document.

Editing styles directly

To edit an existing style directly, select it in the Stylist or the Style Catalog, right-click, and choose Modify. (In the Style Catalog, you can click the Modify button, instead.) A dialog displays showing the definition for that style. The exact appearance of the dialog varies with the type of style. **Figure 4** shows the Paragraph Style dialog.

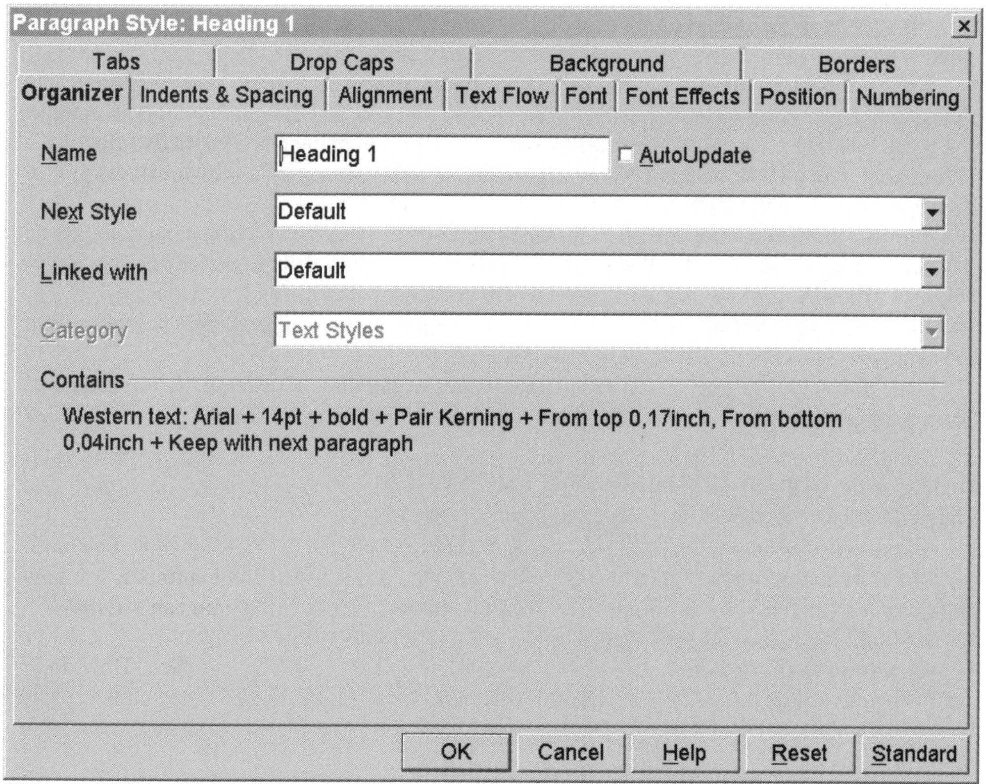

Figure 4. The dialog that appears to edit a style varies with the style type. This dialog is for editing paragraph styles.

Most of the items in the dialog are analogous to things you can change directly through the Format menu. That makes sense because styles encapsulate formatting choices.

Change whatever aspects of the style you want, and then click OK to save the modified style. The changes you make here apply only within the current document. To affect styles across documents, you need to change the style definitions in a template. (See "What is a template?" later in this chapter.)

Creating new styles directly

Creating a new style isn't much different than editing an existing style. Right-click in the Stylist or Style Catalog and choose New or, in the Style Catalog, click the New button. The Style dialog appears as when you modify a style, but the Organizer page is different. In this case, the Name field shows "Untitled1," as does the Next Style drop-down list, if it's present.

For many of the style types, every style (except the Default style) is based on another style and inherits its characteristics from that style. The Linked With drop-down list indicates which style a style is based on. When you create a new style, it's automatically set to inherit from the style selected when you chose New, but you can change that if you wish. (It's actually easiest to first click the style you want to base the new style on, and then choose New.) The important thing to keep in mind is that a style has all the characteristics of the style it's linked to, except those you change explicitly. If you modify a style, any styles linked to it are modified as well.

Assign a name to the style. If the new style should always be followed by a different style, choose the appropriate style in the Next Style drop-down list, if it's available. For example, in this book, heading styles are always followed by a paragraph using a style called "_first paragraph," which isn't indented. Paragraphs using "_first paragraph" are always followed by an indented paragraph that uses a style called "_body text." Setting the next paragraph style as part of the style definition ensures that when you hit Enter at the end of a paragraph, the next paragraph is already set to the appropriate style. (This works the same way in Microsoft Word.)

The Organizer page also lets you choose the category where the new style belongs. That choice affects both the Stylist and the Style Catalog.

Once you set all this up, use the remaining pages of the dialog to set up the formatting of the new style exactly as you want it. When you finish, click OK.

Using the Stylist to create and edit styles

The Stylist offers shortcuts for creating and editing styles.

The middle button on the right side of the Stylist's button bar (with a tooltip of "New Style from Selection") lets you define new styles on the fly. Highlight some text or choose an object, and then click the button. The Create Style dialog (**Figure 5**) appears. Type a name, and then hit OK to save the new style, based on the formatting of the selected item.

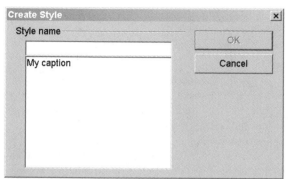

Figure 5. *This dialog displays when you create a new style based on a selected object.*

The rightmost button on the button bar (with a tooltip of "Update Style") lets you change the definition of a style. Select some text or an object, and then click Update Style. The definition of the style the selected text or object is based on updates to match the current formatting of that item. For example, suppose you use the style "Heading 1" for all the headings in a document, and then you decide to make them dark blue instead of the default black. Change the color of one of the headings, highlight the heading, and click Update Style in the Stylist. That changes the definition for Heading 1, which affects all the uses of Heading 1 already in the document, as well as those you add afterward.

As with modified styles, new styles apply only to the current document. You need to define styles in a template to make them available to multiple documents.

What is a template?

A template is a model for a document. It contains basic structure, styles, and macros. Templates make it easy to create multiple documents with the same structure and format.

Every document you create in OpenOffice.org is based on a template. If you don't specify one, it uses the default template for that application. (By analogy, Microsoft Word bases new documents on the Normal.DOT template, if you don't specify otherwise.) The default template is normally an empty document of the appropriate type. (See "How do I change the template used for new documents?" later in this chapter for more on the default template.)

You can download a variety of templates from **http://documentation.openoffice.org/Samples_Templates/index.html**. The templates available provide the framework for such things as a balance sheet (Calc), an invoice (Writer), flowcharts (Draw), and more. There are also templates available at **http://ooextras.sourceforge.net/**.

How do I use a template?

To create a document based on a particular template, choose File | New | Templates and Documents from the menu in an OOo application, or choose From Template in the QuickStarter. The Template and Documents dialog (**Figure 6**) displays. Double-click a folder to open it and see the templates within. Choose the template you want and click OK to create a new document based on that template. (See "Where does OpenOffice.org store my files?" in Chapter 3, "OpenOffice.org File Storage," for an explanation of where templates are stored.)

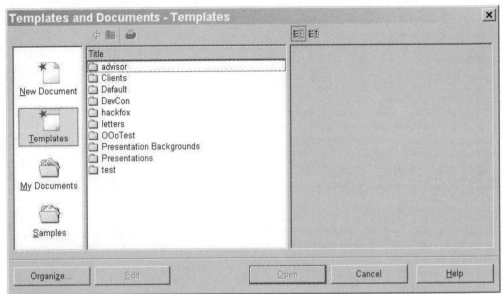

Figure 6. *Choose a template from this dialog to create a new document based on the template.*

You can also create a new Impress presentation based on a template by choosing File | AutoPilot | Presentation. In fact, by default, the Presentation AutoPilot runs when you open Impress, so you can always start an Impress session by creating a new presentation from a template.

The various AutoPilots for Writer documents work by creating a new template, and then creating a document based on that template. Once you run a particular AutoPilot once, you may find it easier to simply use the template for future documents of that type.

When it comes to applying a template to an existing application, OOo differs from Microsoft Office. In most Office applications, you can open an existing document and apply a different template to it to change its appearance. OOo doesn't support this behavior. To change the template for an existing document, you need to create a new document based on the desired template, and then either cut and paste the contents of the original document into the new document, or in those applications that offer it, use Insert | File to put the original contents into the new document.

Can I use Office templates?

Yes and no. Templates created in Office don't show up in the Templates and Documents dialog. However, you can double-click a template in the Open dialog (File | Open) or in a tool like Windows Explorer and a new document is created based on that template.

To use this solution, you have to know where the template is located. If you don't already know, the easiest solution is to search for the appropriate extension (DOT for Word templates, XLT for Excel templates, POT for PowerPoint templates). Once you find the template, if you made OOo the default application for Word files, simply double-click the file name to create a new file based on the template. If not, use Open With from the file's shortcut menu and choose OOo from the list.

How do I create a new template?

Creating templates isn't much harder than creating documents. First, create a new document in the appropriate application. Create and modify the styles you want for the template. Add any boilerplate text or objects you want in the template. (For example, if you're creating letterhead for a company, you might add a header with the company name and address, and set the company's logo as a watermark.) Make sure to position the cursor where you want it to appear when you create a new document based on the template.

When the document looks exactly as you want your template to appear, choose File | Templates | Save from the menu. (Note that this works differently from Microsoft Office, where you use File | Save As and choose template as the type of file.) The Templates dialog (**Figure 7**) displays. Type a name for the new template, and choose a category in which to store it. This list of categories here is the same as in the Templates and Documents dialog.

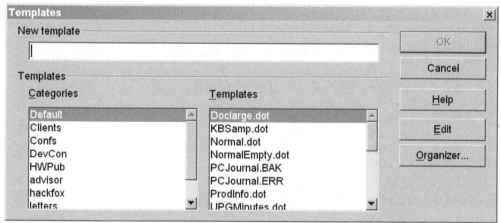

Figure 7. *This dialog lets you save a new template. Choose a category on the left to keep your templates organized.*

How do I change the template used for new documents?

When you choose File | New and pick a document type, or click the New button on the Function toolbar, or create a new document using QuickStarter, OOo bases the new document on the default template for the specified application. This is analogous to Microsoft Word's behavior where new documents are based on the Normal.DOT template unless you choose another. However, unlike Word, OOo doesn't make the default templates available as files you can edit. So, changing the default template isn't as easy as opening the right file and modifying it.

If you want to make changes that carry over to all new documents of a particular type, you need to create a template with the desired settings, and then make that template the default. Create the template as you would any other (see the previous section, "How do I create a new template?"). Once you save the new template, make it the default for the appropriate application using the Template Management dialog (**Figure 8**). You open this dialog by clicking the Organizer button on the Templates dialog (File | Templates | Save, shown in Figure 7), the Organize button on the Templates and Documents dialog (File | New |Templates and Documents), or by choosing File | Templates | Organize from the menu.

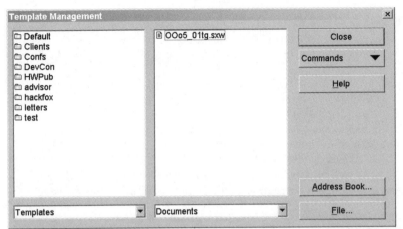

Figure 8. The Template Management dialog lets you set up default templates and much more.

In the left column, navigate to the template you want to make the default. (Double-click a folder to expand it and show the templates within.) With the desired template highlighted in the left column, open the Commands list and choose Set as Default Template. From that point on, all new documents of the appropriate type created without specifying a template are based on the template you set as the default.

If you want to return to the built-in default, open the Commands list and choose Reset Default Template. Choose the appropriate file type from the list.

How do I open a template for editing?

To open a template so you can make changes to it, choose File | Templates | Edit from the menu, and then choose the template you want to edit. Make whatever changes you need to the boilerplate text, the styles, or the macros, and then save it as you would any other document.

You can also open a template, modify it, and save the modified template as a new template. In that case, when you're done editing, use File | Templates | Save to give the modified template a new name.

How do I manage templates and styles?

The Template Management dialog (File | Templates | Organize on the menu) provides a lot more options than just setting default templates. For example, it lets you move styles between templates and documents and move templates from one folder to another.

Each of the lists in the dialog shows either templates OOo knows about or the list of open documents. You can work with the items in those lists to move both templates and styles around.

Copying styles

Sometimes, you have a style in one template you want to make available in another. To do so, find the template that contains the style in one list. Double-click the template name and a Styles item appears. Double-click the Styles item and a list of styles displays.

In the other list, find the template to which you want to copy the style. Again, double-click the template name to show the Styles item; double-click the Styles item to display the list of styles.

Now, you can drag (to move) or Ctrl-drag (to copy) a style from one template to the other. If the target template or document already has a style by that name, you're prompted about overwriting it.

Moving templates

The dialog also lets you move templates from one folder to another. Set both lists up to show folders, and then drag the template from one list to a folder in the other list.

The New button in the Commands drop-down list lets you add a folder for templates. Focus must be on a list of templates for New to be enabled. When you click it, it adds a folder called "Untitled". Type the name for the new folder.

The dialog offers a variety of other options, including the ability to print a list of the styles in a template or document with their descriptions.

Summary

Investing some time developing your own styles and templates will pay off in both the short run and the long run. As you create documents, having appropriate styles defined minimizes the amount of time you spend on formatting. Instead of needing to set a variety of options, you can just choose the right style and keep going. Over the long haul, templates and styles provide uniformity both within and across documents, making your work look more professional and making it easier to apply global changes.

Updates and corrections to this chapter can be found on Hentzenwerke's web site, **www.hentzenwerke.com**. Click "Catalog" and navigate to the page for this book.

Section II
Word Processing with Writer

Chapter 6
Creating Simple Documents

Most of the documents you need to write aren't complicated, but do require some formatting and other features. This chapter looks at straightforward document creation with Writer.

Most people write just a few kinds of documents, letters, memos, reports, and so forth. You don't have to learn all the features of Writer to produce basic documents that look good.

How do I start Writer?

You can open Writer in a number of different ways. If QuickStarter is running, right-click it and choose Text Document to open Writer with a new blank document. Choose Open File from QuickStarter and pick an existing Writer or Word document to open Writer with that document loaded. A third choice with QuickStarter is to choose From Template, and then choose a Writer template; that opens Writer with a new document based on the chosen template.

If you have another OpenOffice.org application open, choose File | New | Text Document or long click (see "Why do some toolbar buttons have a little arrow?" in Chapter 4, "The OpenOffice.org Interface") on the New button on the Function toolbar and choose Text Document to open Writer with a blank document. Choose File | Open or the Open button to open Writer with an existing document.

Finally, depending on your operating system, you may be able to open Writer from a menu. In Windows, choose Start | Programs | OpenOffice.org <version> | OpenOffice.org Writer.

What do I see when I first open Writer?

The first time you open Writer, the Stylist will probably be open; the Navigator may be open, as well. (See Chapter 5, "Making Life Easier with Templates and Styles" for details on the Stylist and Chapter 4, "The OpenOffice.org Interface" for information about the Navigator.) The document is zoomed to fill the entire width onto your screen.

Figure 1 shows the initial layout of Writer.

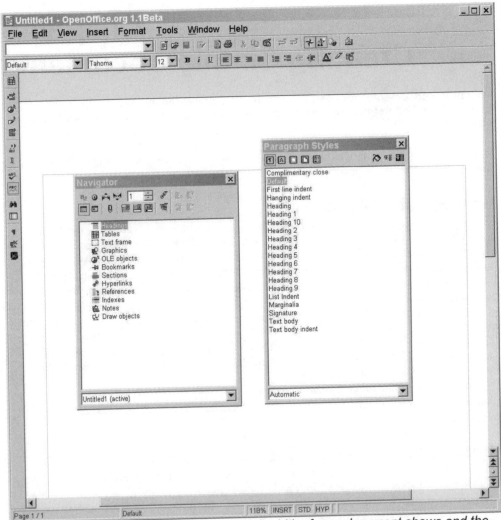

Figure 1. *When you first open Writer, the full width of your document shows and the Stylist and Navigator are open.*

Three toolbars are docked by default. Right underneath the menu is the Function toolbar, which includes buttons for opening, saving and printing documents, cutting, copying and pasting, undoing and redoing, plus a few others. Beneath that toolbar is the Text Object toolbar. This one includes controls to set the style and font of text, as well as to control text alignment, and a variety of other items. The Main toolbar is docked at the left, by default. It includes buttons for inserting tables, graphics, and other items, for checking spelling, and to turn on and off the displaying of non-printing characters (paragraph marks, spaces, and so forth), as well as other items. (See Chapter 4, "The OpenOffice.org Interface," to learn how to move the toolbars around.)

How do I control the way my document fills the window?

Writer gives you choices about how your document displays in the Writer window. The default behavior varies with the version of OOo you're using.

To have the document fill the horizontal space and show as much of a page vertically as possible (the default in OOo 1.1), choose View | Zoom from the menu and then choose Optimal from the Zoom dialog that appears. You can experiment with the dialog to find the setting that works best for you.

The status bar at the bottom of the Writer window shows the current setting. (In Figure 1, it shows 118%.) Click the value for a list of choices to change the view.

In Microsoft Word, you have several options for how to view a document. Writer also offers a couple of options, but they don't map exactly to Word's options (and, in one case, Word has more functionality).

Writer's default view corresponds, more or less, to Word's Page Layout view. You see page breaks, and headers and footers are always visible. Online Layout view (View | Online Layout from the menu or the Online Layout button on the Main toolbar) corresponds to Word's Web Layout view. No page breaks are shown, and in fact, pages are considered somewhat irrelevant. Online Layout is a toggle, so to switch back to the default view, choose View | Online Layout again.

Unfortunately, Writer doesn't offer a view analogous to Word's normal view, which doesn't show page breaks, but does include page information in the status bar.

How do I create new documents?

As described in "How do I start Writer?" earlier in this chapter, you can create a new document in several ways when you open Writer. The same techniques work to create another new document once you're working in Writer.

How do I set default fonts?

Writer defaults to using particular fonts for documents. You can change that setting to provide your own defaults using the Basic Fonts (Western) page in the Writer section of the Options dialog (Tools | Options on the menu, and then expand the Text Document item). **Figure 2** shows this page.

The Basic fonts page is one of the few places where the Options dialog lets you set things for a single document rather than across the application or the entire suite. If you select Current document only, the fonts you choose apply only to the document you're currently editing, not to any others you have open or create later. Use the Default button to reset to the original fonts.

Also, keep in mind that the best way to choose the fonts in a document is by setting styles to the fonts you want. See Chapter 5, "Making Life Easier with Templates and Styles," to learn how to use and define styles.

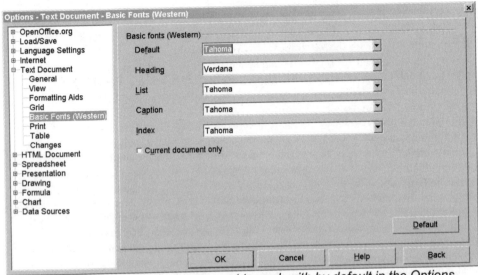

Figure 2. You choose the fonts you want to work with by default in the Options dialog. Select Current document only to change fonts only in the document you're working on now.

> Even when you're using custom styles, changing the Default style (the first drop-down list) in the Basic Fonts page may change the font of the text in your document.

How do I make the ruler available?

Like Word, Writer offers a ruler to show you where things are on the page. However, when you try to turn it on using View | Ruler, you may find the menu option disabled. To make the ruler available, you have to turn it on on the View page of the Text Document section of the Options dialog (Tools | Options).

To make the Ruler available, select the Ruler check box; once it is selected, separate check boxes for the Horizontal ruler and Vertical ruler are available. Select one or both of those. Clicking OK at this point makes the ruler available and displays it. If you want to enable the Ruler item on the menu without displaying the Ruler, clear the Ruler check box, but leave the Horizontal ruler and Vertical ruler check boxes selected.

Once you enable the Ruler, you turn it on and off using View | Ruler. Be aware, though, if you have several documents open, only the one you're editing when you enable the Ruler can use it at that time. Documents you create or open from that point on have access to the ruler.

What the heck is the ruler measuring?

By default, OOo uses inches. If you're in a country that uses the metric system, the first time you turn the Ruler on, you may be very surprised. Fortunately, you can determine what units Writer uses, not just for the Ruler, but in its dialogs as well.

To set the measurement units, open the Options dialog (Tools | Options) and choose the General page of the Text Document section. The Measurement unit drop-down list in the

Settings section lets you specify millimeters, centimeters, inches, picas, and points. The last two are units familiar in the printing and publishing world, but much less well known to the rest of the world.

What's with the text that appears when I'm typing?

You're likely to find Writer's word completion feature either incredibly helpful or very annoying; I suspect few people are neutral on this one. Word completion pays attention to what you type and offers to finish the word for you. Word completion learns as you write, so the list of words it can complete grows constantly (though the total list size is limited).

Word completion is controlled by the Word Completion tab (**Figure 3**) of the AutoCorrect dialog (Tools | AutoCorrect/AutoFormat on the menu). To turn word completion off, clear the Enable word completion check box. If you want to use the feature, but prefer it not learn as you go, clear the Collect words check box.

The item you're most likely to change in this dialog is the Accept with drop-down list. When Writer makes a suggestion, you have to actively accept it to keep the word in the document. By default, pressing Enter accepts the suggestion. However, you can change the AutoCorrect mechanism to use the End key, the right arrow, or the spacebar, instead.

The Min. word length spinner lets you determine what size words are recognized. By default, only words of five or more letters appear on the list.

If you find having the suggested word appear on your typed line distracting, try selecting the Show as tip check box. This makes the suggestion appear as a tooltip (the approach used in Microsoft Word).

Select Append space to tell Writer to add a space at the end of the word when you accept a suggestion. This feature is smart enough to add the space only if you don't add a space or other punctuation yourself. However, when Append space is cleared, you can accept a suggestion and then add additional characters to the word manually. For example, if you type "abb," word completion offers "abbreviate" as a suggestion. If you accept that suggestion, with Append space cleared, you can then add a "d" to form "abbreviated," an "s" to make "abbreviates," or whatever change you need.

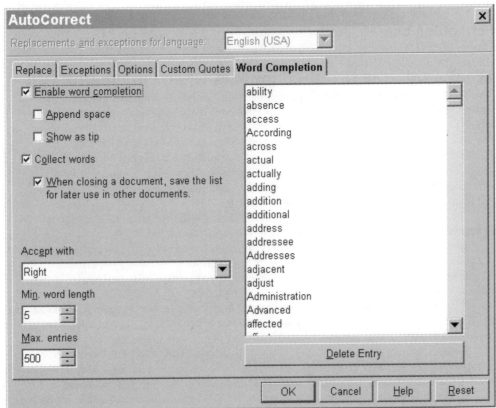

Figure 3. This tab of the AutoCorrect dialog controls word completion. You can choose the character that accepts the suggestion, manage the list of suggestions, or even turn the feature off altogether.

How do I format my text?

This is a big question, but the best answer is brief: Use styles. For both consistency and ease of editing, it's far better to apply an appropriate style to a paragraph, a block of text, or pretty much anything else than to format each separately.

However, saying that styles are the answer requires the follow-up question: How do I set up the formatting for my styles? The answer to both questions is similar, though the particulars vary.

Formatting covers quite a lot of territory. Fortunately, Writer's menu system makes it easy to look at the options. When formatting directly, you can approach things on a character basis, a paragraph basis, or a page basis. The Format menu contains options for each. A number of the most common formatting options (such as bold, italic, underlines, and paragraph alignment) are included on the Text Object toolbar, as well.

Formatting characters

Choose Format | Character from the menu to open the Character dialog (**Figure 4**). It contains choices that affect individual characters and blocks of text, primarily font-related. If text is selected (highlighted) when you open this dialog, the changes you make affect the selected text. If no text is selected, the choices you make affect what you type once you close the dialog. The new formatting remains in effect until you change it or turn it off. (See "How do I turn off character formatting?" later in this chapter.)

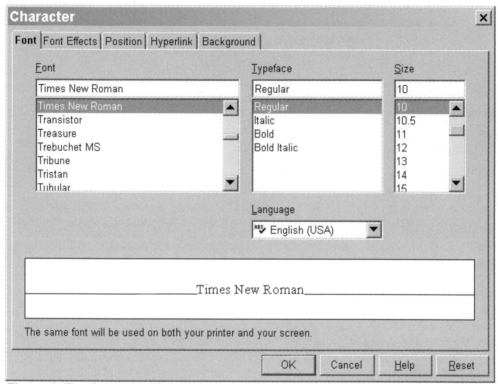

Figure 4. The Character dialog lets you change the formatting of individual characters and blocks of text.

Formatting paragraphs

Not surprisingly, you format paragraphs by choosing Format | Paragraph from the menu, which opens the Paragraph dialog (**Figure 5**). The dialog offers control over a variety of items, including indentation, tabs, and hyphenation. There's a key difference between character formatting and paragraph formatting. Changes you make in the Paragraph dialog affect whatever paragraph the cursor is in, whether that paragraph is highlighted or not.

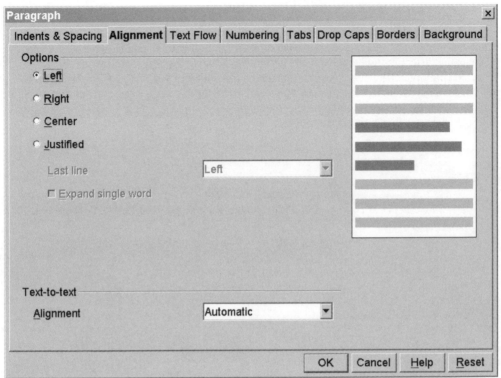

Figure 5. The Paragraph dialog controls indentation, text alignment, hyphenation, borders, and more.

Formatting pages

Page formatting is different from character or paragraph formatting; it works only with page styles, not with individual pages. When you choose Format | Page from the menu, the Page Style dialog (**Figure 6**) opens, showing the formatting for the style used on the current page. Any changes you make affect not just that page, but also the style itself. (For an explanation of styles and how to create them, see Chapter 5, "Making Life Easier with Templates and Styles.")

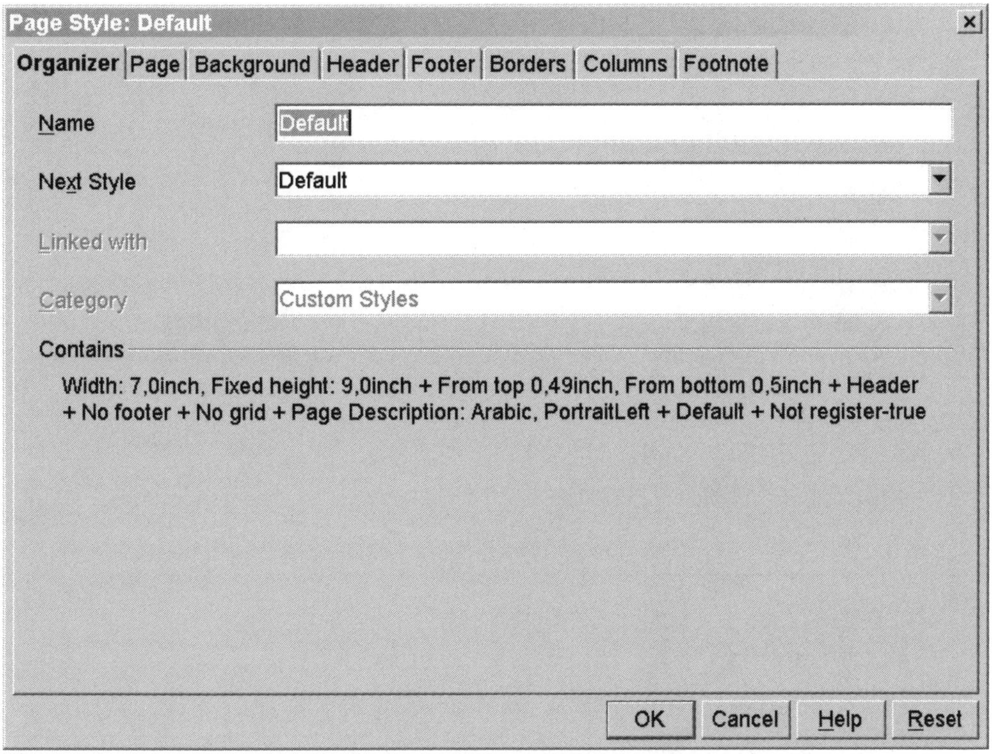

Figure 6. *You can't format individual pages, only page styles.*

The Page Style dialog controls the paper size and type, margins, the presence and size of headers and footers, and more. In order to have pages in a single document use different margins or have different headers or footers, you must use different page styles. This is in contrast to Microsoft Word where you handle that kind of change with a new section.

Formatting styles

Setting the format for a style isn't much different than setting the format for a block of text or a paragraph. Highlight the style in the Stylist or Style Catalog (see Chapter 5, "Making Life Easier with Styles and Templates") and choose Modify from the context menu. The Style dialog opens, showing the appropriate choices for that style.

Paragraph styles have a lot more options than character styles, and in fact, include many of the character style options, such as font settings.

Some specific formatting options are discussed in the sections that follow.

How do I create subscripts and superscripts?

Subscripts and superscripts are character formatting. You set them on the Position tab (**Figure 7**) of the Character dialog (Format | Character from the menu). As with other character formatting, you can change highlighted text into a subscript or superscript or you can turn the feature on first and then type the text that should become a subscript or superscript.

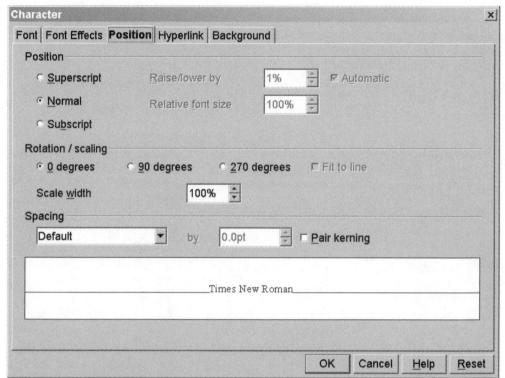

Figure 7. This tab of the Character dialog lets you create subscripts and superscripts as well as rotating text.

> In Writer, you can specify how far above or below the baseline a subscript or superscript appears. Word doesn't include this option.

There are predefined keyboard shortcuts for subscripts (Ctrl-Shift-B) and superscripts (Ctrl-Shift-P).

How do I turn off character formatting?

If you turn on formatting like bold, italics, subscript, or superscript with no text selected, it applies to everything you type from that point on. Eventually, you probably want to return to normal text. To do so, choose Format | Default from the menu. You can use the same menu item to return highlighted text to the normal formatting for the paragraph style. The menu item removes any character style you may have applied and any inline formatting.

In Word, the Ctrl-Spacebar combination is assigned to this task. Be careful—in Writer, that keystroke inserts a non-breaking space. You may want to redefine it to restore normal formatting; see Chapter 4, "The OpenOffice.org Interface," to learn how. (The item to use for this is Format | Reset Font Attributes.)

How do I set up indentation?

Indentation is paragraph formatting, and choices you make here affect entire paragraphs, although you can handle the first line differently than the rest of the paragraph. You can indent a paragraph from the left margin or the right margin.

Set indentation using the Indents and Spacing tab (**Figure 8**) of the Paragraph dialog (Format | Paragraph). The top section of this tab addresses indentation.

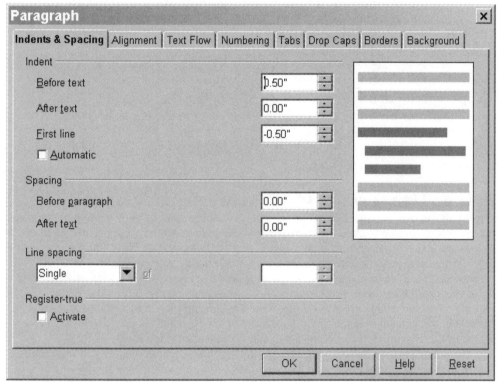

Figure 8. *This tab of the Paragraph dialog lets you determine the indentation of a paragraph, as well as the white space before and after it. The indentation settings shown create a hanging indent in which the first line of the paragraph sticks out farther to the left than the rest of the paragraph.*

As you'd expect, the Before text and After text settings control indentation of the paragraph as a whole from the left and right margins, respectively. Use a positive number to move the paragraph in from the margin and a negative number to set the paragraph outside the margin.

The First line setting controls the left-hand position of the first line of the paragraph relative to the indentation of the whole. When it's set to 0, the first line begins at the same position as the rest of the paragraph. When First line is set to a positive number, that line is indented more than the paragraph itself. When First line is set to a negative, the paragraph has a hanging indent.

Figure 9 shows a variety of margin settings.

This paragraph has no indentation set and extends to the margins on both sides of the page.

    This paragraph has Before text set to 0.5", so the whole paragraph is indented from the left margin. On the right, it extends all the way to the margin.

    This paragraph has both Before text and After text set to 0.5", so it's indented from both the left and right margins. You might use this setting for a long quotation.

    This paragraph has only the first line indented 0.5"; subsequent lines are not indented.

This paragraph has Before text set to 0.5" and First line set to -0.5". That   produces a hanging indent where the first line sticks out to the left. This   type of formatting is often used for numbered lists.

Figure 9. *The indentation settings in the Paragraph dialog let you create paragraphs with quite a few different formats.*

How do I leave white space between paragraphs?

While you can use first line indentation to indicate the beginning of a new paragraph, in many documents, it's preferable to have every paragraph begin at the left margin. In that case, you need space between paragraphs to indicate the break. While you can provide that space by pressing Enter twice at the end of the paragraph, that's not a good choice.

It's better to give the paragraphs themselves (and even better to give your paragraph styles) the appropriate space preceding and following them. You do this on the Indents & Spacing tab of the Paragraph dialog (Figure 8). The Spacing section of that tab lets you indicate how much white space should precede the paragraph and how much should follow it. (In the printing business, this is known as leading, pronounced "led-ing.")

The paragraphs in Figure 9 are all set to have 6 points of leading before and none after. Although the dialog displays these settings in the measurement units you specify (see "What the heck is the ruler measuring?" earlier in this chapter), you can enter values in other units by including the units. So, even with inches displayed, I entered "6pt" in the Before paragraph spinner.

How do I control the position of paragraphs?

Individual lines of a paragraph at the top or bottom of a page with the remainder of the paragraph on the preceding or following page are called widows and orphans. In general, you can use the terms "widow" and "orphan" interchangeably. However, Writer specifically defines them. An orphan occurs at the bottom of a page; a widow occurs at the top.

Widows and orphans make a document harder to read, so it's often desirable to prevent them. Writer lets you control this through the Text Flow tab (**Figure 10**) of the Paragraph dialog (Format | Paragraph on the menu).

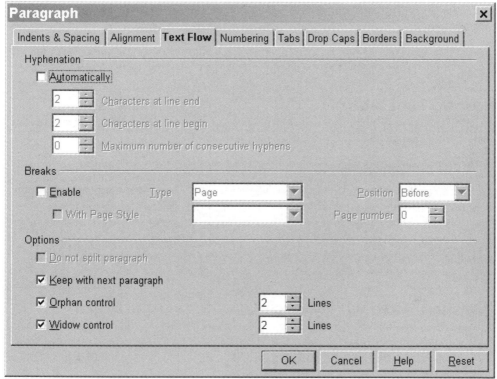

Figure 10. *The Text Flow tab of the Paragraph dialog gives you control over orphans and widows, as well as letting you specify that a paragraph should be on the same page as the paragraph that follows it.*

You can specify not only the prevention of orphans and widows, but also exactly what constitutes an orphan or a widow. Use the appropriate check box to turn orphan or widow control on and off. When the check box is selected, the spinner to its right lets you determine the minimum number of lines that must appear on the page from a given paragraph. The default setting for both is two, meaning one line alone is an orphan or widow, but two lines together are sufficient.

 In Word, widow and orphan control are linked, so you get both or neither. Writer gives you independent control over the two conditions. In addition, in Word, you can't determine what constitutes a widow or an orphan.

In some cases, you want an entire paragraph on the same page, regardless of its length. Select the Do not split paragraph check box to keep the whole paragraph together. This setting is incompatible with widow and orphan control, so you have to turn those off before you can select the check box. (Of course, if the paragraph is longer than a page, it continues on the next page.)

There's one more situation you may want to control. In some cases, you want to ensure a particular paragraph appears on the same page as the paragraph that follows it. For example, you rarely want to leave a heading at the bottom of the page with the material it heads on the next page. Select Keep with next paragraph for the heading paragraph to prevent this kind of orphan.

How do I set tabs?

As in Word, tabs in Writer are associated with a paragraph, but unlike Word, you actually set them in the Paragraph dialog. Use the Tabs tab (shown in **Figure 11**).

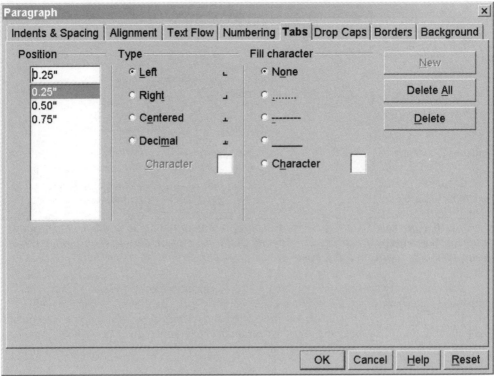

Figure 11. You can set a variety of tabs in the Paragraph dialog.

For each tab, you have three options: position, type, and leader (in Writer, called *fill character*). Position, of course, determines where to place the tab stop.

Type determines what happens when you move to that tab stop. With a left tab, typing proceeds to the right of the tab. With a right tab, the end position for the text is fixed and typed characters move to the left. Use right tabs, for example, to position text at the right margin. With a centered tab, the middle of the text is fixed at the tab stop and characters move to both sides. Finally, a decimal tab is handy for dealing with columns of figures. The decimal point appears at the tab stop, with the integer portion to the left and the decimal portion to the right. For decimal tabs, you can specify the character that serves as the decimal point.

The fill character determines what, if anything, fills the space left empty by the tab. This is useful in such places as a table of contents, or an index, where you want to use dots between the item and the page number. You can choose any of several options provided or specify a character.

Figure 12 shows a document using a variety of tab types and settings. Nonprinting characters have been turned on (View | Nonprinting Characters) to make it easier to see the structure of the document.

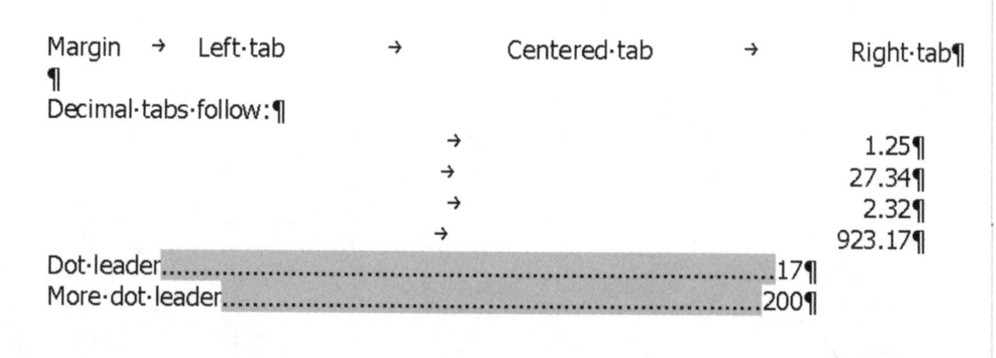

Margin	→	Left·tab	→	Centered·tab	→	Right·tab¶
¶						
Decimal·tabs·follow:¶						
			→			1.25¶
			→			27.34¶
			→			2.32¶
			→			923.17¶
Dot·leader..17¶						
More·dot·leader..200¶						

Figure 12. Writer supports a variety of tab types, as well as the ability to add leaders to a tab stop.

To add a tab using the dialog, specify the position, type, and fill character you want, and then click the New button.

You can also specify tabs by setting them on the Ruler. Use View | Ruler to display the ruler, and then click at the position where you want the tab. By default, this creates a left tab. Right click your new tab to change its type or double-click anywhere on the Ruler to open the Tabs tab of the Paragraph dialog.

How do I right-align text?

You have several choices for putting text at the right margin. The appropriate choice depends on the situation.

To right-align an entire paragraph, use the Align Right button on the Text Object toolbar or choose Right on the Alignment tab of the Paragraph dialog.

If you want to right-align some text on a line where other items appear to the left, as for example in page headings, use a right tab. (See the preceding section "How do I set tabs?")

Finally, if you need to have multiple lines of both left-aligned and right-aligned text with word wrap in each group, use a table with two cells. Set the left cell for left alignment and set the right cell for right alignment. See Chapter 7, "Dressing up Documents," for the details of creating and using tables.

How do I specify the kind of paper I'm using?

Not surprisingly, the size and orientation of paper is considered Page formatting and is part of the Page Style dialog. Paper settings are found on the Page tab of the dialog, shown in **Figure 13**.

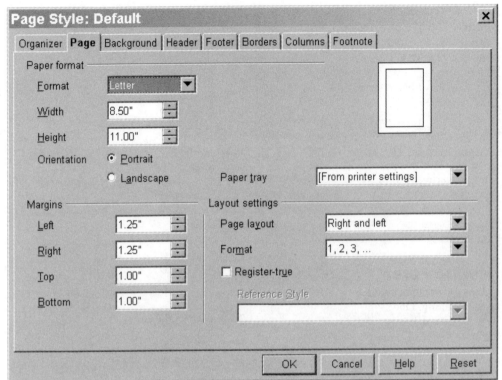

Figure 13. This tab of the Page Style dialog lets you specify the size and orientation of your paper, as well as the margins you're using.

The Format drop-down list includes most of the widely used sizes for both paper and envelopes. When you make a choice from this list, the Width and Height spinners change to reflect your choice and the diagram of the page at the upper right adjusts.

If the paper size you're using isn't in the list, you can set the Width and Height yourself. When you do so, the Format drop-down list shows "User."

Use the Orientation option buttons to indicate whether you're printing across the narrow (portrait) or wide (landscape) edge of the paper. Again, the Width and Height spinners change to reflect your choice, as does the diagram.

How do I set margins?

The Page tab of the Page Style dialog (Format | Page, Figure 13) also controls margins. The Page layout drop-down list in the Layout settings section determines whether the margins you set apply to all pages or only some of them. There are four possibilities, shown in **Table 1**. The choice you make here can change the labels for the margin setting spinners, and modify the diagram of the page.

Table 1. *Your choice for Page layout determines how Writer applies the margins you set.*

Page layout	Meaning
Right and left	These settings apply to all pages.
Mirrored	These settings apply to all pages, but you specify Inner and Outer margins rather than Left and Right. You would probably use this setting for a book.
Only right	These settings apply only to right-hand pages.
Only left	These settings apply only to left-hand pages.

Ordinarily, you specify left, right, top, and bottom margins for a page, but when you choose Mirrored for Page layout, the first two settings instead let you indicate the margin for the inside edge of the page (the right margin of a left-hand page, and the left margin of a right-hand page) and the outside edge of the page. This allows you to leave larger margins on the binding edge.

How do I create bulleted lists?

It's easy to set up a bulleted list. Click the Bullets On/Off button on the Text Object toolbar to begin bulleting. Once you start bulleting, each time you press Enter, the next line is bulleted as well. To stop bulleting, either click the button again to turn bulleting off or press Enter twice at the end of a line.

If you already typed the text you want bulleted, highlight it and click the Bullets On/Off button. If only one paragraph is to be bulleted, just position the cursor anywhere in the paragraph and click the Bullets On/Off button.

Bulleted items you create this way use a small round bullet (the first group in **Figure 14**). You can specify other bullets using the Number/Bullets dialog (**Figure 15**) available on the Format menu. Two different tabs offer bulleting options: the Bullets tab and the Graphics tab. In either case, click the bullet style you want, and then click OK. The second group in Figure 14 uses one of the choices from the Bullets tab.

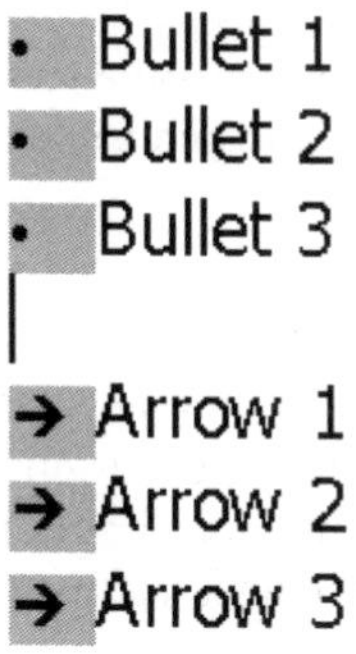

- Bullet 1
- Bullet 2
- Bullet 3

→ Arrow 1
→ Arrow 2
→ Arrow 3

Figure 14. *A variety of bullet styles is available. By default, bulleted items use the small dot shown in the first group.*

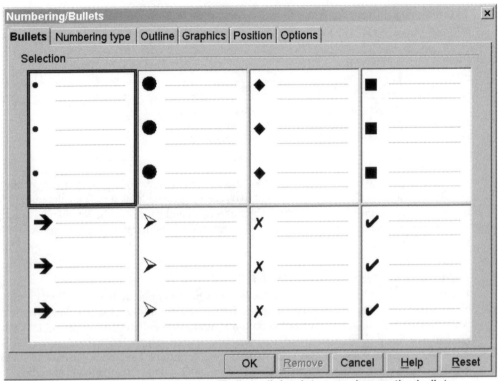

Figure 15. *The Bullets tab of the Number/Bullets dialog lets you choose the bullet style you want.*

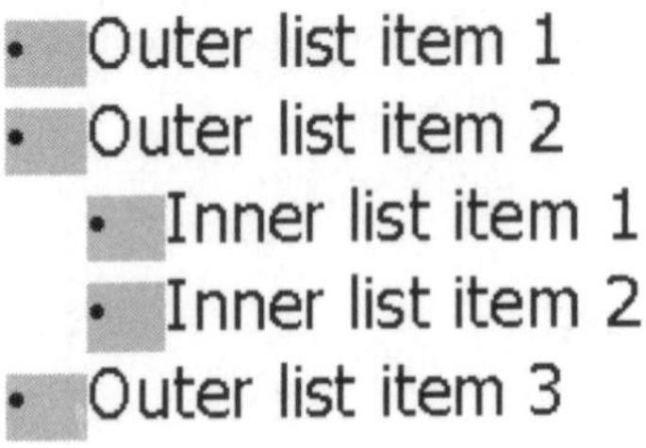

- Outer list item 1
- Outer list item 2
    - Inner list item 1
    - Inner list item 2
- Outer list item 3

Figure 16. *One bulleted list can contain another. Use Tab to move in and Shift-Tab to move out.*

In some situations, you want to put one bulleted list inside another, in a sort of outline format. You can do this in a couple of ways.

To use the same bullet symbol at all levels of the list, start bulleting as usual. When you want to create a sub-list, press Tab to move in one level. **Figure 16** shows an example of such a list. Use Shift-Tab to move back to the main list. Use the Increase Indent and Decrease Indent buttons on the Text Object toolbar to move existing items to a different level of the list.

You can also use a different symbol for each bulleted level. The easiest way to do so is by opening the Outline tab of the Numbering/Bullets dialog. The last option there offers four different bullet styles.

Finally, you can build your own list of bullet symbols, using the Options tab (**Figure 17**) of the Numbering/Bullets dialog. Choose a level from the list on the left, and then use the Numbering drop-down list to indicate whether that level uses bullets, numerals, letters, roman numerals, or another choice. For bullets, click the Character button and choose the bullet symbol you want at that level.

 Unfortunately, there doesn't appear to be a way to save a custom list of bullets once you create it. It applies only to the paragraph in which you're using it.

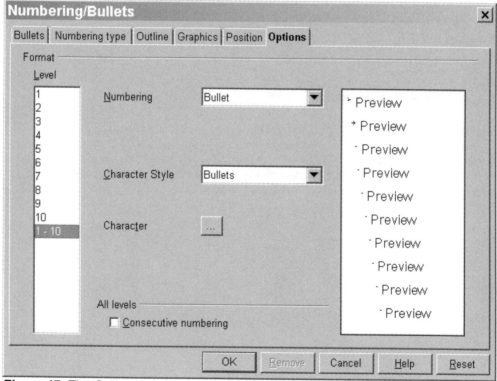

Figure 17. The Options tab lets you build your own list of bullet symbols or numbering formats.

> The gray background for the bullet (and for numbers in a numbered list) is a visual clue that the items were created automatically, not by typing. You can't position your cursor in the gray area. The gray doesn't appear when the document is printed.

How do I create numbered lists?

As with bullets, you have several choices for creating numbered lists. The simplest is to click the Numbering On/Off button on the Text Object toolbar before starting the list. In this case, the list uses arabic numerals with a period after each. **Figure 18** shows an example. As with bulleted lists, click the button again to stop numbering, or press Enter twice.

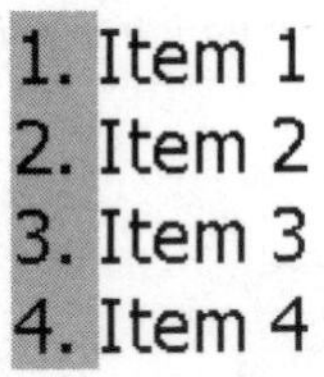

1. Item 1
2. Item 2
3. Item 3
4. Item 4

Figure 18. You can create a simple numbered list by clicking the Numbering On/Off button on the Text Object toolbar.

To number existing paragraphs, highlight them and click the Numbering On/Off button.

For more control over the numbering, use the Numbering type tab (**Figure 19**) of the Numbering/Bullets dialog. This tab lets you choose between arabic numerals, Roman numerals (both upper and lower case), and letters (both upper and lower case); it also provides some choices regarding the punctuation following the "number."

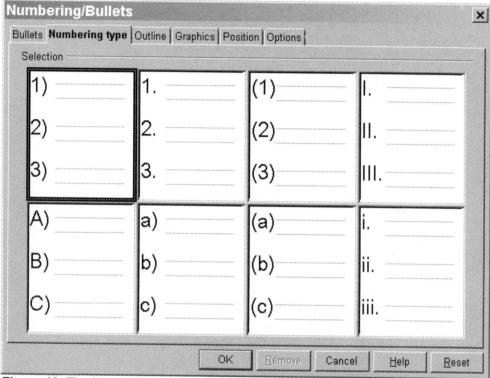

Figure 19. *The Numbering type tab lets you determine the numbering style for lists.*

As with bullets, you can put a numbered list inside another numbered list. When you use the default numbering or choose from the Numbering Type tab, the sub-list uses the same numbering style and begins again with "1" or "A." **Figure 20** shows an example.

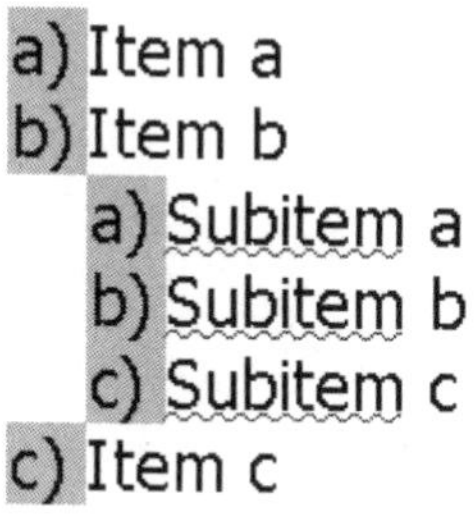

a) Item a
b) Item b
    a) Subitem a
    b) Subitem b
    c) Subitem c
c) Item c

Figure 20. *If you choose from the Numbering type tab, a sub-list uses the same numbering style and starts over from the beginning.*

Usually, when one numbered list is inside another, though, you really want an outline structure. Use the Outline tab (**Figure 21**) of the dialog to choose the outline format.

Unfortunately, none of the formats provided is exactly the normal style used for outlines, and only one offers more than four levels of different formatting.

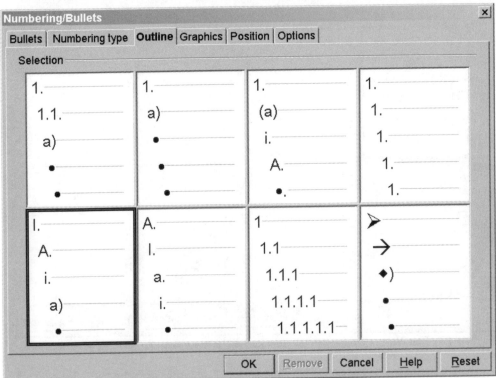

Figure 21. The Outline tab lets you chose the type of outline formatting you use.

As with bullets, you can design your own numbered outline structure; use the Options tab of the dialog. The inability to save your custom outline formats is a serious limitation.

How do I find out how long my document is?

When you're working in the default view, the status bar indicates the number of pages in your document. However, there are other useful statistics about a document, such as the number of words or characters.

Statistical information about a document is available in the Properties dialog (File | Properties from the menu). The General tab of the dialog includes creation and modification dates for the file and the file size. The Statistics tab (**Figure 22**) gives you a whole collection of metrics.

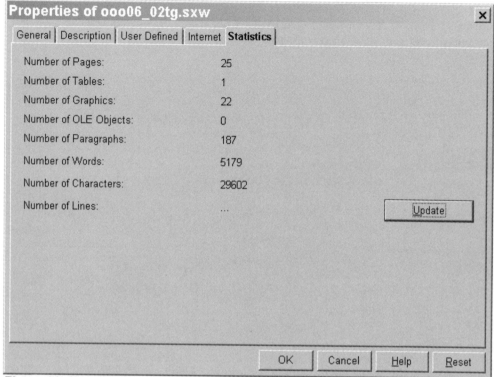

Figure 22. The Statistics tab of the Properties dialog tells you how many "things" your document contains.

At present, there's no way to get the same information for a block of text through the user interface; you can do so with a macro. (See Chapter 18, "Macros and Automation.") As journalists and others have reported to the OOo development community that counting words in a block of text is important to their daily process, it's likely that feature will be added in an upcoming version.

How do I print my document?

Not surprisingly, the easiest way to print a document is to click the Print button on the Function toolbar. That sends the entire document to the default printer or, if it was previously printed on a different printer, to that printer. (The document keeps track of what printer it was printed on.)

If you need different behavior, use File | Print or Ctrl-P to open the Print dialog (**Figure 23**). The dialog lets you choose a printer, specify the pages to print, and indicate how many copies to print.

You can get even more control over what prints by clicking the Options button to open the Printer Options dialog (**Figure 24**). This dialog lets you specify whether all components of the document print or only some of them. For example, you can eliminate graphics or tables.

The dialog also lets you control the pages that get printed based on content. You can print only the left pages or only the right pages, useful if you're printing something like a book, but your printer can't print on both sides of a piece of paper without manual intervention.

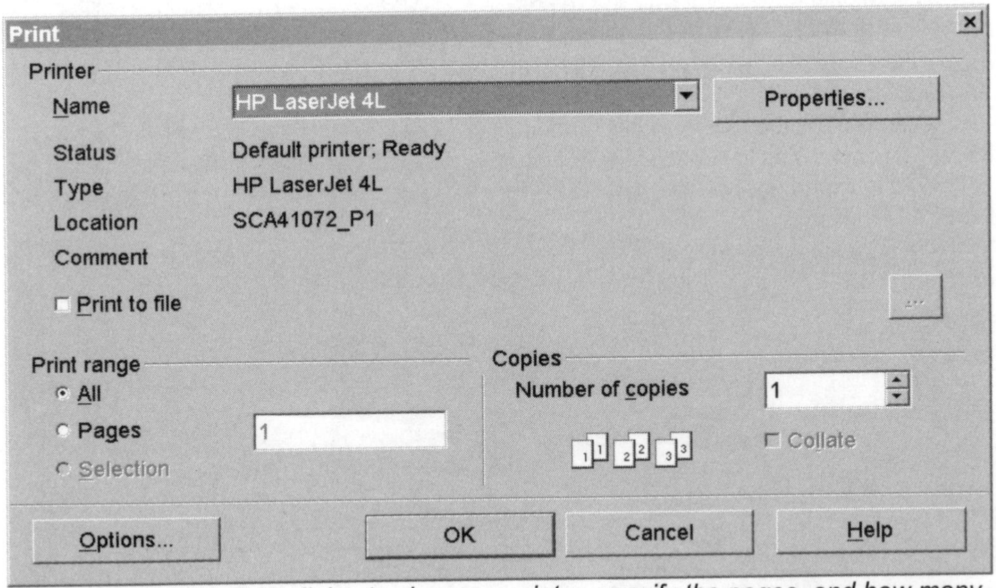

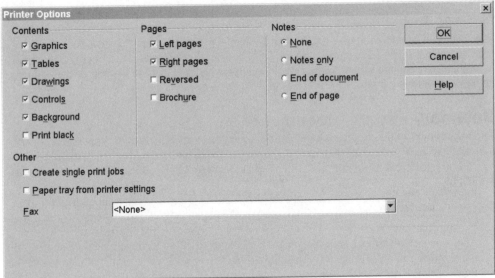

Figure 23. Use the Print dialog to choose a printer, specify the pages, and how many copies to print.

Figure 24. The Printer Options dialog lets you specify the portions of a document to print.

How do I create a PDF from my document?

The Adobe Acrobat PDF format has rapidly become a nearly universal method for exchanging formatted documents. The free, downloadable reader means anyone can view a PDF document.

Beginning with OOo 1.1, creating PDF files from Writer is as easy as can be. Choose File | Export as PDF from the menu or click the Export Directly as PDF button on the Function toolbar. In either case, the Export as PDF dialog appears to let you specify the file name for the resulting PDF file.

When you use the Export as PDF option on the menu, the PDF Options dialog (**Figure 25**) appears next. You have a couple of choices. First you can choose how much of the document to export: the entire document or just a portion of it. (You can specify an individual page or a range of pages, such as "2-5.") Second, you can determine the quality of the output by choosing a compression style. When the resulting file will only be viewed on monitors, lower quality is usually acceptable.

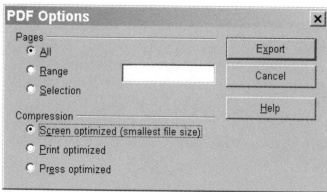

Figure 25. *The PDF Options dialog determines whether you export the entire document or just a section, and the quality of the output.*

When you use the Export Directly as PDF button on the Function toolbar button, the entire document is exported, using the most recent compression choice.

Summary

The information in this chapter should get you started creating documents with Writer. In the next chapter, I look at more advanced features, such as including pictures and tables.

Updates and corrections to this chapter can be found on Hentzenwerke's web site, **www.hentzenwerke.com**. Click "Catalog" and navigate to the page for this book.

Chapter 7
Dressing Up Documents

Once you get basic documents down, you will probably want to use some more complex features of Writer. This chapter shows you how to add page numbers, tables, and graphics to your text documents, plus how to perform a mail merge and more.

How do I put things like date and time into a document?

There are some pieces of data frequently used in documents. Perhaps the most common is the current date, but you might also want to include the author's name, the document's original creation date, and other information.

You add this sort of information by choosing Insert | Field from the menu, and then choosing the appropriate item to insert. A submenu includes the most common items to save time and clicks. If the item you want isn't on that list, choose Other to open the Fields window (**Figure 1**). The window is divided into tabs organized by the type of information presented.

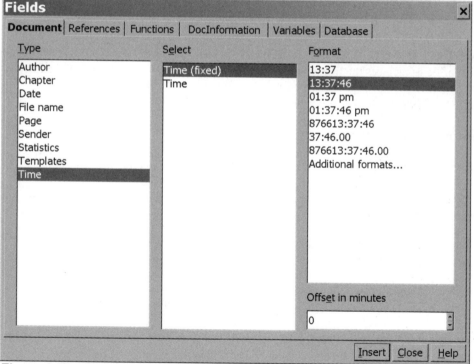

Figure 1. The Fields window lets you insert data items like the current date and time, the author of the document, when it was last printed, and so forth.

You can also insert field data by clicking the Insert Fields button on the Main toolbar. (By default, it's the second from the top). If you click it and release, the Fields dialog opens. If you click and hold (long click), a list of commonly used fields appears (the same list as the submenu for Insert | Fields).

The Fields window is a little different from most Writer dialogs. When you choose Insert (the default action), the dialog doesn't close. However, it does insert the currently highlighted item into the document at the current insertion point. Because this window isn't a dialog, you can click in the document, make changes, and return to the Fields window to insert another field. When you finish inserting fields, choose Close to close the window.

Choosing the field you want to insert is a multi-step process. Once you're on the right page (the Document and DocInformation tabs contain this kind of information), you choose the type of field from the list on the left. (In Figure 1, Time is chosen). The center list offers data items of that type, if there's more than one. Finally, many of the items offer multiple formats. For example, in Figure 1, you have a choice of how the time appears in the document.

The Date and Time types on the Document tab give you a choice between inserting the current date and time, or inserting an updateable date or time. Choose Date (fixed) or Time (fixed) to insert the current date or time. Choose Date or Time to insert a field that updates each time you open the document.

Once you insert some fields into a document, you normally see the current value of the fields. You can see their definition instead by pressing Ctrl-F9 or choosing View | Fields from the menu. Ctrl-F9 or View | Fields again toggles them back to showing their values.

How do I insert the path and filename of the document?

The list of fields includes the filename in several formats. Use the Document tab of the Fields dialog (Insert | Fields | Other from the menu) and click File name in the Type list. In the Format list, choose the format you want—for the path and filename choose Path/File name.

How do I add page numbers?

The list of fields available for a document includes both the current page number and the number of pages in the document. So, you add page numbers in the same way you add date, time, or other items. (See the preceding section.)

If you choose Page Numbers or Page Count from the Insert | Fields submenu, they use arabic numerals. If you prefer another format, open the Fields window (Insert | Fields | Other from the menu), choose the appropriate Type, and then the desired Format. Arabic numerals, Roman numerals, and letters are available.

To have "Page x of y" formatting, click where you want the page numbers to appear (typically in a header or footer—see "How do I get page headers and footers?" later in the chapter), type "Page ", insert the Page Numbers item (Insert | Fields | Page Numbers), type "of ", and finally insert the Page Count item (Insert | Fields | Page Count).

How do I change the page numbers?

Sometimes, you want to do something more complex than just number the pages in a document starting with 1. Most often, you either want to use no numbers on some initial pages (such as a title page), and then start numbering the main body of the document from 1, or you want to have several different groups of numbers in a document, each starting from 1. For example, it's common in books for the front matter (the table of contents, the foreword, and so forth) to be numbered with small roman numerals and for the main part of the book to use arabic numerals starting from 1.

The solution for this problem only works when you explicitly start a new page. (That's usually the case when you want to change page numbers.) At the end of the text before the page with the new numbering, choose Insert | Manual Break from the menu. This opens the Insert Break dialog (**Figure 2**). Choose the Page Break option button, and then choose the page style for the new page. Once you make a style choice, the Change page number check box is enabled. Select it and specify the page number for the new page in the spinner.

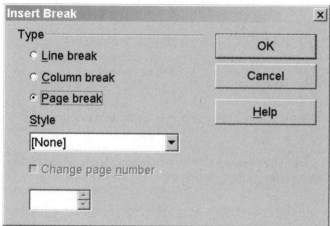

Figure 2. *To change the page number for subsequent pages, insert a manual page break.*

A different approach works when you want to change the number on the first page of a document. (You can use this approach at any time, actually.) Put the cursor in the first paragraph of the page where the numbering should change (or the first page, if you want to start with a number other than 1). Choose Format | Paragraph from the menu to open the Paragraph dialog. Choose the Text Flow tab (shown in Figure 10 of Chapter 6, "Creating Simple Documents"). In the Breaks section of the page, select the Enable check box. Once you do so, a number of controls are enabled. Make sure the Type drop-down list is set to Page and the Position drop-down list is set to Before. Select With Page Style and make sure the drop-down list shows the Page Style currently in use. In the Page Number spinner, specify the number for the page.

How do I get page headers and footers?

Headers and footers are the portions of a page at the top and bottom and contain information that should appear on each page, such as titles, page numbers, and so forth. To add a page header to a document, choose Insert | Header from the menu and make sure Default is selected. To add a footer, choose Insert | Footer and select Default. These choices add a header or footer using the default settings for the page's style.

You can fine tune the settings using the Header (**Figure 3**) and Footer tabs of the Page Style dialog (Format | Page). The dialog lets you specify the position of the header or footer, as well as whether the same header and footer are on even and odd (left and right) pages. In this book, for example, the odd page headers include the chapter name and title, while the even headers hold the book's title.

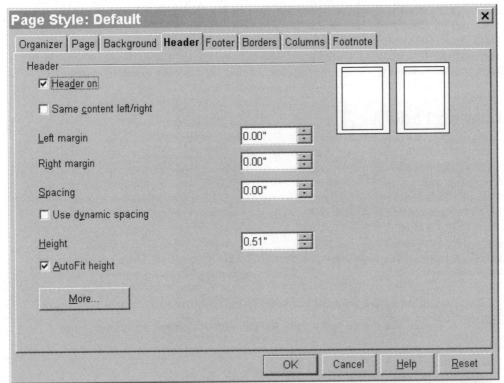

Figure 3. *You adjust the settings for a header using this tab of the Page Style dialog. Use the Footer tab to modify footer settings. The two are independent of each other.*

Writer handles the issue of different headers for a first page differently than Microsoft Word. In Word, you select a check box to indicate that the first page has headers different from the rest of the pages in the chapter. In Writer, you use a separate page style. You can modify the built-in First Page style for this use, or create your own style to use for first pages. (See Chapter 5, "Making Life Easier with Templates and Styles" for details on creating and modifying styles.) In either case, make sure the Next Style setting for your first page style points to the appropriate page style. If you use the same headers on odd and even pages, point to the regular page style (Default or some other). If you use different headers for odd and even pages, you probably want to point to the style for even pages, because in that situation, usually a chapter or section begins on the right (odd) page.

Once you turn headers and/or footers on, putting content in them is easy. Make sure you're not in Online Layout view (View | Online Layout), and then simply click in the header or footer you want to edit. When you're done, click in the main body of the document.

How do I change headers or footers in the middle of a document?

Like so much else in OOo, headers and footers are linked to styles. So, to change the header or footer within a document, you need to use a different page style. That is, once you add a header or footer to a document, that information is part of the page style for the document. When you want to change the header or footer layout, create a new page style and use that style for the pages that need the modified header or footer. See Chapter 5, "Making Life Easier with Styles and Templates" for the details of creating styles.

How do I add pictures to a document?

According to the old saying, a picture is worth a thousand words, and adding pictures to a document can make the difference between clarity and confusion.

You can add pictures to Writer documents in several ways: cut-and-paste, drag-and-drop, through the menu (Insert | Graphics | From File), using the Insert button on the Main toolbar, or from the Gallery. (See "What is the Gallery?" in Chapter 4, "The OpenOffice.org Interface" for an explanation of the Gallery.) When you choose Insert | Graphics | From File from the menu or Insert Graphics from the main toolbar, the Insert Graphics dialog opens. This is a specialized version of the standard File Open dialog that includes a preview panel. When you click a graphic file in the dialog, you can see what it looks like. There's a slight delay before the preview appears, so if you know which file you want, you don't have to wait for it to display.

For a list of the graphic formats Writer supports, check the Files of type drop-down list in the Insert Graphics dialog.

Whichever way you add the picture, by default, it's anchored to the current paragraph, which means it moves with that paragraph. **Table 1** lists the choices for anchoring a picture. You can change the anchoring of a picture by right-clicking it and choosing Anchor, using the Type page of the Graphics dialog (shown in **Figure 4,** use Format | Graphics from the menu or Graphics on the picture's shortcut menu to open it), or on the Graphics toolbar that appears when a graphic object is selected. (You may need to click the left arrow at the end of the toolbar to switch to the right set of buttons.)

Table 1. *You can anchor graphics in a variety of ways. Your anchoring choice determines how the graphic moves as text changes*

Anchoring type	Effect
To Page	Attaches the graphic to the page that contains it and it cannot move to another page. You can indicate where on the page the graphic is positioned.
To Paragraph	Attaches the graphic to the paragraph current when it's added. As that paragraph moves, the graphic moves with it.
To Character	Attaches the graphic to the character current when it's added. As that character position moves, the graphic moves with it.
As Character	Does not attach the graphic to any other object Instead, it is positioned as if it is a character typed at the insertion point.

The type of anchoring determines your choices for positioning the graphic and for the interaction of text with it. Graphics anchored as characters can't have text wrapped around them and have more limited choices for positioning. The other three anchoring choices let you determine whether the graphic is at the top, middle, or bottom of the anchoring object, and whether it anchors at the left, center, or right. Choose Alignment from the graphic's shortcut menu or use the Type tab of the Graphics dialog to make these choices.

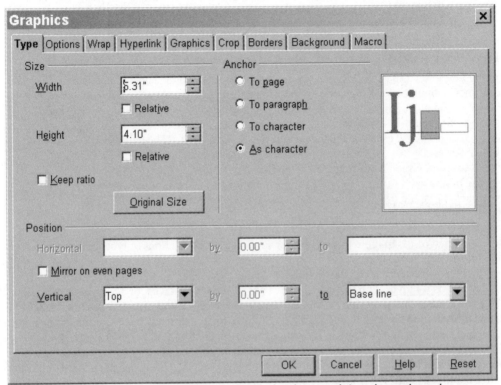

Figure 4. The Graphics dialog lets you determine how a picture is anchored, positioned, and much more.

You can wrap text around graphics, except for those anchored as characters. There are several choices for how text wraps, including running the text right through the graphic (as you might with a watermark or a "Draft" designation). To specify wrapping, choose Wrap from the graphic's shortcut menu or use the Wrap tab of the Graphics dialog.

Be aware that the Graphics dialog offers more options for both positioning and wrapping than the shortcut menu.

By default, all pictures use a style named Graphics, which is a Frame style. (See Chapter 5, "Making Life Easier with Templates and Styles" for a full discussion of styles and style types.) You can modify this style or create additional styles with the settings you want, so you don't have to adjust each picture as you insert it.

How do I put a table in a document?

As with pictures, there are several ways to add a table (something like Table 1 earlier in this chapter or **Figure 10** later in the chapter) to a document. You can use Insert | Table from the menu, Ctrl-F12, or the Insert Table button on the Main toolbar (by default, it's the first button). Whichever technique you use, the Insert Table dialog (**Figure 5**) appears. In the dialog, you can specify the size of the table, as well as how it should behave if it reaches the end of a page. In addition, you can name the table. Tables are listed in the Navigator, so assigning a name makes it easy to identify.

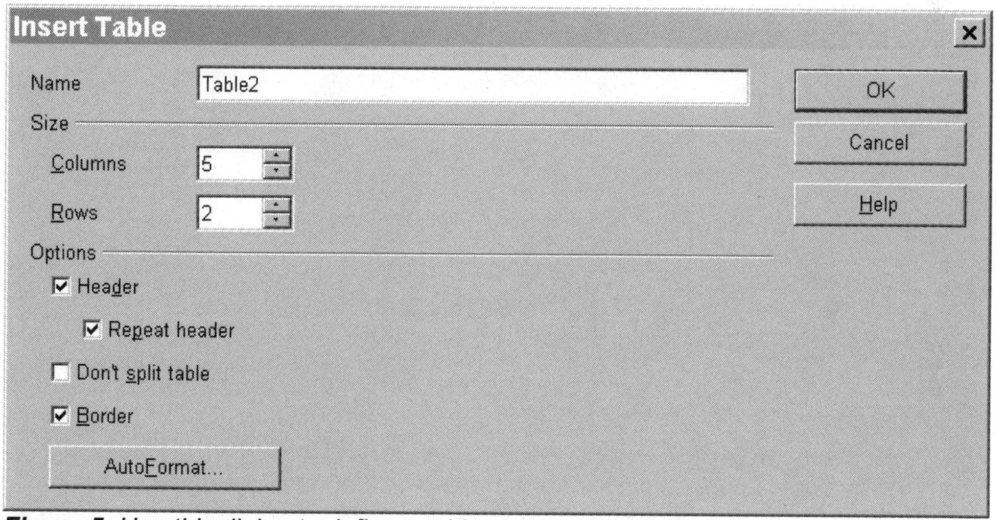

Figure 5. *Use this dialog to define a table. Assigning a table a name makes it easier to identify it in the Navigator.*

As Figure 5 shows, the default size for a table includes two rows. If the Header check box is selected and there are at least two rows, the first row uses the Table Heading Style. All rows after the first use the Table Contents style, as does the first row when Header is cleared or only one row is specified.

> *When the cursor is positioned inside a table, the Edit | Select All (Ctrl-A) functionality changes. The first time you Select All, all text in the current cell is highlighted (if there is any). Choose Select All again and the whole table is selected. A third Select All highlights all text in the document.*

Don't worry about getting things exactly right when you insert the table. Once a table exists, you can change its settings in a variety of ways. To work on the table as a whole, with the cursor positioned in the table, choose Format | Table or choose Format from the table's shortcut menu to open the Table Format dialog (**Figure 6**). In addition, the Cell, Row, and Column items on the Format menu and on the table's shortcut menu offer control over various aspects of a table's appearance and behavior.

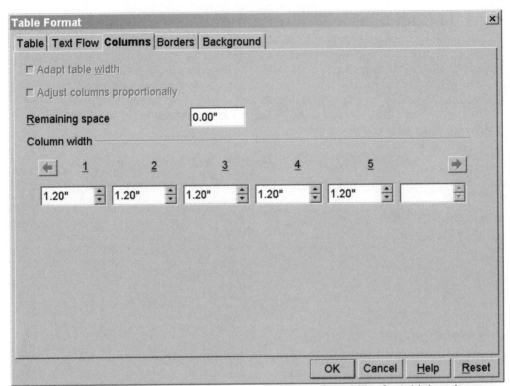

Figure 6. The Table Format dialog lets you determine the width of a table's column, add space above or below the table, as well as determine what happens when a table passes a page break.

> The behavior of the Ctrl-F12 shortcut varies, depending on the situation. When focus is inside a table, Ctrl-F12 opens the Table Format dialog. When focus is not in a table, Ctrl-F12 opens the Insert Table dialog.

How do I set column widths?

If you know how wide you want each column to be as a measurement, use the Columns tab of the Table Format dialog (Format | Table on the menu or Table on the table's shortcut menu) to specify them. Be aware that changing the value for one column affects the column to its right, which gets wider or narrower to keep the total table width the same. (Changing the last column impacts the first.) You can change this behavior by selecting the Adapt table width check box on the same page; when that item is selected, the size of the table changes based on the column widths you specify. (When Alignment is set to Automatic for the table, which is the default, the width of the table is fixed and this check box is disabled. Choose a different alignment on the Table tab of the dialog to allow you to change the table size.)

If you prefer to "eyeball" the column widths, you can use the keyboard. Position the cursor in the column you want to change and use Alt-Left Arrow to shrink the cell or Alt-Right Arrow to enlarge it. The effect of this action on other columns depends on a setting in the Options dialog (Tools | Options on the menu). **Figure 7** shows the Table page of the Text Document section of the Options dialog, where you specify a number of default behaviors. Sizing of rows and columns via the keyboard is affected by the setting for Behavior of rows/columns. When this item is set to Fixed, a change to one column affects the next column. When it's set to Fixed, proportional, a change to one column affects all other columns proportionally. Finally, when it's set to Variable, the table size changes to accommodate changes to a column's widths and other columns keep their sizes.

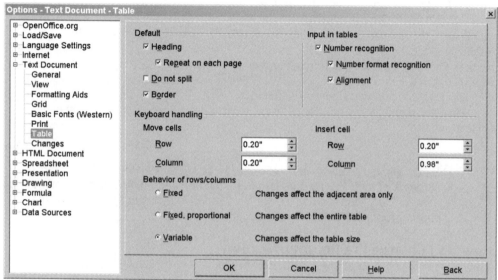

Figure 7. *This page of the Options dialog lets you determine default behaviors for tables, including what happens when resizing columns and rows.*

The Options dialog setting for Behavior of rows/columns affects only resizing with the keyboard, and not other kinds of resizing. This appears to be a bug and may be fixed in later versions of OOo.

You can also resize columns with the mouse. Position the mouse over the divider between columns, click, and drag. (When you get the mouse in the right place, it turns into a resizer icon.)

If you want to change a single column, you can use the Column Width dialog (**Figure 8**), that opens by choosing Format | Column | Width from the menu or Column | Width from the shortcut menu. As with the Table Format dialog, changing the width of one cell changes the width of the adjacent cell.

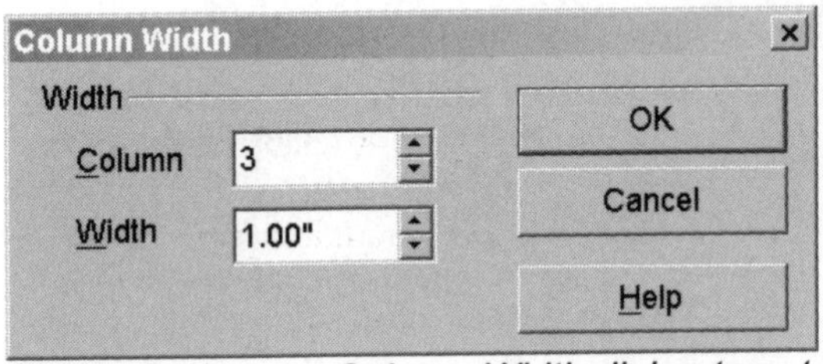

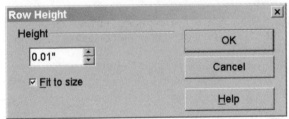

Figure 8. *Use the Column Width dialog to set the width of individual columns.*

Finally, the best choice for resizing cells is often to wait until you fill the table with information, highlight the whole table, and choose Format | Column | Optimal Width from the menu or Column | Optimal Width from the shortcut menu. Writer then figures out the best width for each column based on its contents. If one or more columns or cells within columns are highlighted, only those columns are affected.

When you highlight one or more columns, there's also a Space Equally option on the Column submenu.

> *Be careful not to confuse the Format | Column menu item, which affects columns of a table with the Format | Columns item, which affects columns on a page. See "How do I put multiple columns in a document?" later in the chapter for information on using columns on pages.*

How do I change the height of a row?

As with column widths, there are several ways to change a row's height. You can use Alt-Up Arrow to shrink a row and Alt-Down Arrow to increase it. Here, too, the setting for Behavior of rows/columns in the Options dialog comes into play. When resizing a row with the keyboard, you can never make it too small to hold its contents.

You can also adjust the height of a row by choosing Format | Row | Height from the menu or Row | Height from the shortcut menu. The Row Height dialog (**Figure 9**) appears. When Fit to size is selected, the height you specify is a minimum—the row is the larger of the specified height and the height necessary to contain its contents.

Figure 9. *You can set a row's height to a specific value or tell it to choose a height based on its contents.*

When Fit to size is cleared for a row, the submenu for row height (Format | Row | Height on the menu, Row | Height on the shortcut menu) also includes an Optimal Height item. Choosing that item is the same as selecting Fit to size in the dialog.

How do I control the behavior of a table at a page break?

You have several options regarding tables and page breaks. You can require the table to appear on a single page (assuming it fits on one page) or not. If you allow a table to be split across pages, you can specify whether the table header repeats on pages after the first.

If you know you want to prevent a table from being placed across multiple pages when you create it, check Don't split table in the Insert Table dialog. If you already created a table and want to change this setting, use the Do not split table check box on the Text Flow tab of the Table Format dialog (Format | Table).

When a table splits across multiple pages, you may or may not have headings that should appear on each page. Again, you can make this choice either when you create the table or later. In the Insert Table dialog, select the Repeat Header check box; in the Table Format dialog, select the Repeat heading check box on the Text Flow tab.

How do I make an irregular table?

By default, every row of a table has the same number of columns and every column has the same number of rows. However, there are situations where you might want some other arrangement. One typical case is putting one heading across several columns. Figure 10 shows an example of such a table.

Name		Address			
First	Last	Street	City	State	Zip
John	Smith	1234 N. Main	Phila.	PA	19101
Roberta	Jones	17 E. Street Rd.	Phila.	PA	19111

Figure 10. You can merge and split cells in a table to create irregular arrangements.

To consolidate several cells into a single cell, highlight the cells you want to combine, and then choose Format | Cell | Merge from the menu or Cell | Merge from the shortcut menu. The highlighted cells combine into a single result cell.

You can also divide a cell into multiple cells. Make sure focus is in the cell or cells you want to split and choose Format | Cell | Split from the menu or Cell | Split from the shortcut menu. The Split Cells dialog (**Figure 11**) displays. Specify the number of cells you want to create from the single cell, and then choose the direction. Choosing horizontal puts the new cells in a single column, but in different rows. Choosing vertical does the reverse, resulting in several cells in the same row, but in different columns.

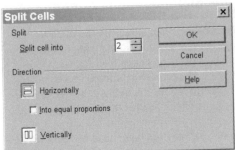

Figure 11. You can split a cell into multiple rows or multiple columns, but not both.

Be aware that the behavior of irregularly shaped tables can be confusing. Cells that are merged or split don't necessarily resize with the rest of their row or column, so you can have multiple cells in what seems to be the same row that are all different heights.

How do I have more than one heading row?

For most tables, it's sufficient to repeat a single row on each new page on which the table appears. However, in some cases, you want to have several rows of headings before the actual data (as in Figure 10). Writer's solution to this problem is a little strange.

Highlight the existing header row. Use Format | Cell | Split to turn it into multiple rows. All the newly created rows are treated as header rows, along with the original.

Unfortunately, this means header rows are particularly prone to the problem discussed in the last paragraph of "How do I make an irregular table?" To get the appearance you want, you may have to assign explicit row heights to all the cells involved.

How do I control the lines around and within a table?

The Borders tab (shown in **Figure 12**) of the Table Format dialog (Format | Table on the menu) controls the lines around and within a table. The Line Arrangement option buttons offer five common set-ups, including no lines at all, and lines both around the entire table and between all cells. To create a more complex arrangement, choose the line style you want from the Style list, and then click in the diagram where you want that line to appear. Be aware that even with all borders turned off, you will see faint lines around the tables cells while editing. However, those lines do not print.

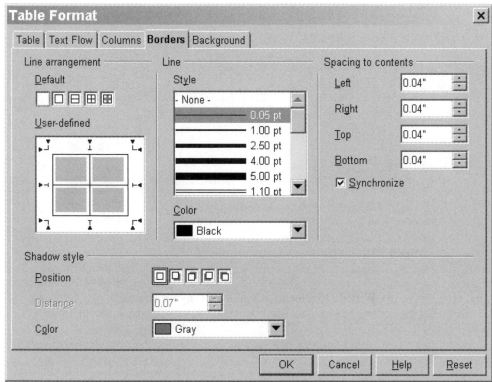

Figure 12. The Borders tab of the Table Format dialog controls the lines around and within a table. You can choose a standard arrangement by clicking one of the line arrangement option buttons, or you can set the individual border and grid lines by choosing the type of line you want and clicking in the diagram.

How do I put multiple columns in a document?

Columns in a document can work in two ways. One type is often called "newspaper-style columns" or "snaking columns," where text goes to the bottom of one column and then continues at the top of the next (as in **Figure 15** later in this chapter). As the name implies, this kind of column is used in newspapers, magazines, and newsletters. The other kind of column, sometimes called "parallel columns," allows information in different columns to be adjacent to each other, as in a telephone book.

The best way to create parallel columns is using a table. Depending on the data, a one-row table may be sufficient or you may need multiple rows. The secret to giving the appearance of columns is to turn all borders off for the table, as described in "How do I control the lines around and within a table?" earlier in this chapter.

There are two ways to create snaking columns in Writer. If you want an entire page to have the same number of columns, use the Columns tab (**Figure 13**) of the Page Format dialog (Format | Page on the menu). You can choose one of several common arrangements or set up as many columns as you want, with each having its own width. You can also control the presence or absence of lines between columns.

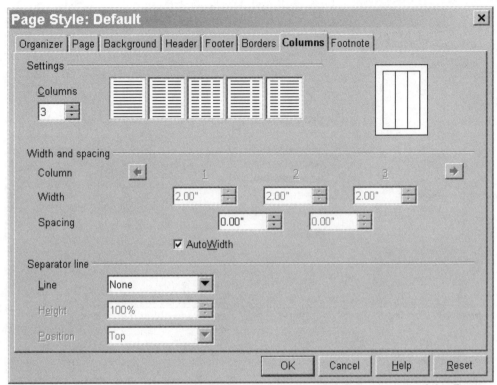

Figure 13. *To set up an entire page with columns, use the Columns tab of the Page Style dialog.*

If you need only part of a page to have columns, use sections. Writer's sections are quite different from Word's. In Word, inserting a section break creates a new portion of the document with its own settings for paper size and type, page layout, headers and footers, and so forth. Writer's sections are simply insertions in the document that can have a different number of columns and a different background color.

To switch from one arrangement of columns to another on a page, use Insert | Section from the menu, which opens the Insert Section dialog (**Figure 14**). You can name the new section, making it easier to identify in the Navigator. The Columns page of the dialog is identical to the Columns tab of the Page Format dialog and allows you to specify the number of columns in this section.

Insert Section
Section
Columns
Background
Footnotes/Endnotes
New section
Section1
Link
Link
DDE
File name
Section
Write protection
Protect
With password
Hide
Hide
With condition
Insert
Cancel
Help
Reset

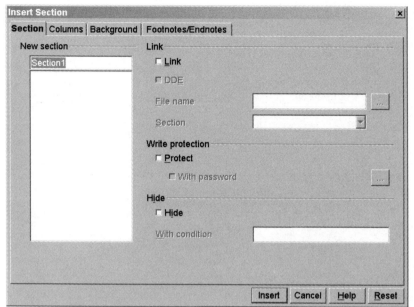

***Figure 14**. The Insert Section dialog lets you insert multi-column sections into a document. Use it when you want only part of a page to have multiple columns.*

When you choose Insert from the Insert Section dialog, the new section is added to the document at the cursor location. Visually, it looks like a table with one row and the specified number of columns. However, unlike a table, text snakes from one column to the next. Figure 15 shows an example with three columns; spacing between columns is set to 0.2”.

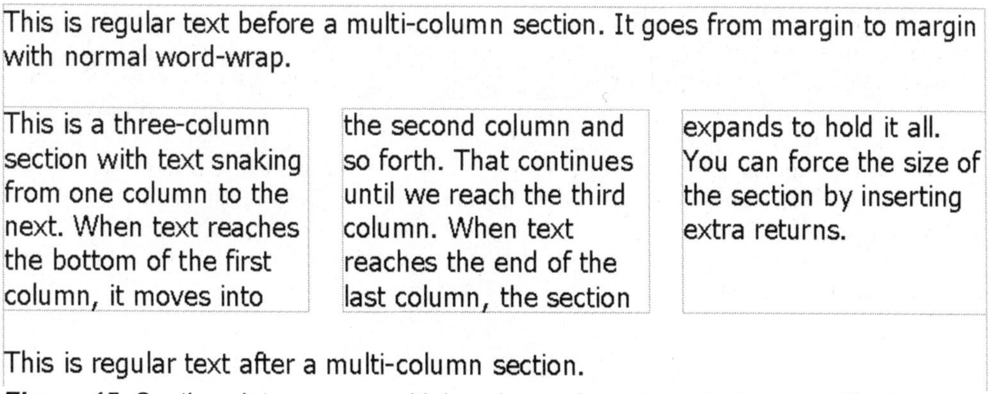

This is regular text before a multi-column section. It goes from margin to margin with normal word-wrap.
This is a three-column section with text snaking from one column to the next. When text reaches the bottom of the first column, it moves into
the second column and so forth. That continues until we reach the third column. When text reaches the end of the last column, the section
expands to hold it all. You can force the size of the section by inserting extra returns.
This is regular text after a multi-column section.

***Figure 15**. Sections let you use multiple columns for only part of a page. The borders around each column do not print.*

To change the structure of a section, choose Format | Sections from the menu to open the Edit Sections dialog (**Figure 16**). Choose the section you want to change. To change the number of columns or the background color, click the Options button.

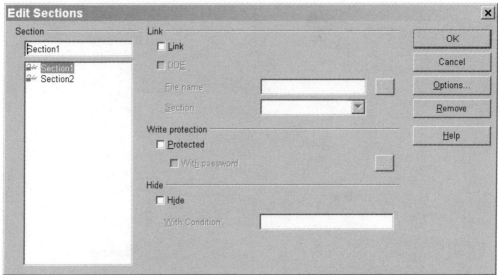

Figure 16. *You can modify a section after you add it by choosing Format | Section from the menu. Click the Options button to see the column arrangement and other details for the current section.*

How do I get my headings to show up in the Navigator?

One of the most useful features of the Navigator is its ability to show you the overall structure of a document. When you expand the headings section, you see the outline of your document.

However, to do so, you have to tell Writer what are the headings in your document. By default, you indicate headings by using the built-in styles Heading 1, Heading 2, and so forth. Any paragraphs using those styles appear in the Navigator.

In some documents, however, you may want to use custom styles for headings. You can tell Writer which styles constitute headings using the Outline Numbering dialog (**Figure 17**), available by choosing Tools | Outline Numbering from the menu.

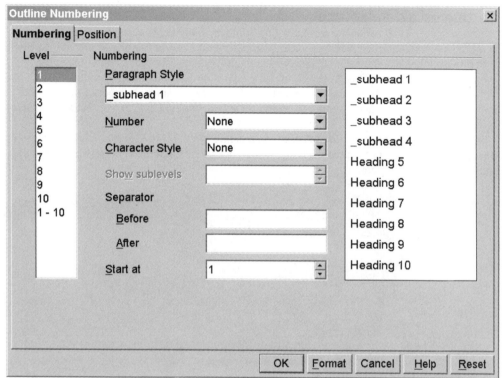

Figure 17. *To specify your own styles as headings, choose the level from the Level list, and then choose the appropriate style from the Paragraph Style drop-down list.*

For each heading style you use, pick the outline level it applies to in the Level list, and choose the style in the Paragraph Style drop-down list.

 Unfortunately, your settings for headings are saved only if you actually use the heading styles you specify in the document or template. Since you rarely want to actually put one of each type of heading in a template, that makes setting this up once and forgetting it difficult.

How do I do a mail merge?

Mail merge is the killer use of word processors, the task that put them on desks in millions of offices around the world. Not surprisingly, Writer can combine a form letter with data to produce personalized results.

Writer's approach to mail merge is quite different from Microsoft Word's and there's no tool like the Mail Merge Helper to walk you through the process. Nonetheless, it does involve the same three steps: setting up a data source, creating a document that includes data from a data source, and performing the actual merge.

Setting up a data source

A data source in OOo can come from any of a number of places. The first time you run OOo, it prompts you to set up an Addresses data source, and allows you to point to the address book that provides the data. You can set up additional data sources using the Data Source Administration dialog. OOo can use a number of types of data, including a spreadsheet, a delimited text file, an ODBC data source, dBase format tables, and a number of others. The details of defining and manipulating data sources are covered in Chapter 17, "Managing Data with OpenOffice.org."

For mail merge, the best way to access data is through the Data Sources window (**Figure 18**); choose View | Data Sources from the menu, click the Data Sources button on the Main toolbar or press F4 to open it.

	Identifier	Type	Address	Annote	Author	Booktitle	Chapter	Edition	Edit
⊞ Addresses	▶ BOR02a	1			Borges, Malte; Schumacher, Jörg				
⊟ Bibliography	BOR02b	1			Borges, Malte; Schumacher, Jörg				
⊞ Links	BUS00	1			Busch, David D.; Olsen, J.W.				
⊞ Queries	DAN00	1			Dandenell, Malin; Ek, Jesper				
⊟ Tables	FAC01	1			Facundo Arena, Hector				
biblio	GAE02	1			Gäbler, Rene				
	HAB00	1			Habraken, Joe				
	JON00	1			Jones, Floyd; Haugland, Solveig				
	MOL02	1			Molla, Ricard				
	RAP00	1			Rapion, Anne				
	RIN01	1			Rinne, Karin				
Record 1	of	13							

Figure 18. The Data Sources window allows you to drag data into documents and to specify the fields to use in a mail merge.

Once you define a data source, you can use it for many different mail merge documents.

 Writer can't use another Writer document as the data source for a merge.

Creating the mail merge document

The second step in performing a mail merge is to create the document to be merged. (In Microsoft Word, this is the "main document.") A mail merge document contains all the text that's to be the same in each case, as well as placeholders for the data to be inserted.

To create a mail merge document, start with a new text document (or open an existing document you want to turn into a mail merge document). Open the Data Sources view window (View | Data Sources or the Data Sources button on the Main toolbar). At each point where you want to insert data, click the name of the field to be inserted in the Data Sources view window, drag the field name to the insertion point, and then drop it. The name of the field surrounded by angle brackets is inserted into the document. **Figure 19** shows an example.

Dear <Author> ‚

Figure 19. When you drag a field name from the Data Sources view window into a document, it appears with angle brackets to indicate that it will be replaced with actual data.

Be careful to drag the field name, not the field data. You can drag actual data from the Data Source view window into a document, but that puts the data values themselves into the document rather than creating a mail merge document. You know you did it right when the entire column is highlighted in the Data Sources view window and the field name appears in angle brackets with a gray background.

Once you create the mail merge document, it's a good idea to save it before performing the actual merge.

Doing the merge

To perform the merge, choose Tools | Mail Merge from the menu. A dialog asks whether you want to create (that is, merge) from the current document or a template. If the main document is already open, choose "From this document." Next, the Form Letter dialog (**Figure 20**) opens. In this dialog, you choose which records to merge and what to do with the results. The easiest way to include a record in the merge is to click the gray button next to it in the Form Letter dialog. To select more than one record, use Shift-Click or Ctrl-Click. (Shift-Click selects everything from the record you last clicked to the one you're now clicking on; Ctrl-Click lets you select individual records while leaving previously selected rows chosen. In Figure 20, Shift-Click was just used at the cursor position to leave three records selected.)

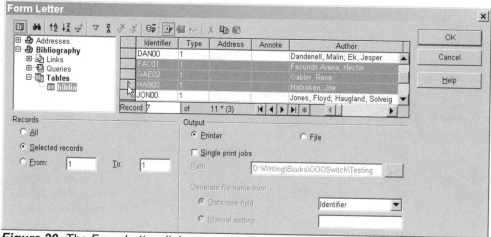

Figure 20. The Form Letter dialog sets things up for the actual mail merge. Choose the records to merge and the output destination.

Another way to choose the records to include in the merge is to select them in the Data Sources window, and then click the Mail Merge button in that window. A smaller version of the Form Letter dialog appears, omitting the data sources section at the top.

The Output section of the Form Letter dialog determines where to send the results. By default, the form letters created by the merge go to the printer. You can instead send them to files; a file is created for each record merged.

When you choose the File option button, the Path and Generate file name from sections of the dialog are enabled, allowing you to specify the folder in which to store the results, and the mechanism for naming the resulting files. The documents can be named based on the data in one of the fields, or you can specify a stem that is combined with a sequential number to create the file name.

 There's no way to send mail merge results to a new document, perhaps the most common choice in Word.

Limiting records in a mail merge

As noted in the preceding section, you can manually choose which records to merge. However, often you may want to filter the records to be merged based on their content. You can handle simple conditions using the Form Letter dialog or the Data Sources window. To create a filter, click the Default Filter button in the dialog (it looks like a funnel). The Filter dialog (**Figure 21**) opens and you can specify up to three conditions to apply to the data. For each condition, you specify a field, the operator to apply (such as "=" or "<"), and the value to match. In Figure 21, data is limited to those records where the Year field is equal to 2000.

Criteria				
Operator	Field name	Condition	Value	OK
	Year	=	2000	Cancel
AND	- none -			Help
AND	- none -			

Figure 21. The Filter dialog lets you apply simple conditions to the data source before merging.

When you click OK in the Filter dialog, the condition(s) you specify are applied to the data source and only the matching records display. More importantly, if you perform the merge at this point, it only merges the records displayed.

To remove this sort of filter, but leave it defined (that is, to see all records), click the Apply Filter button in the Form Letter dialog or Data Sources window. This button is a toggle that lets you turn the filter on and off. To clear the Filter dialog, click the Remove Filter/Sort button.

You can handle more complex filtering requirements by defining queries based on the data. You create a query from the Form Letter dialog, the Data Sources window, or the Data Source Administration dialog. See "Can I define subsets of my data?" in Chapter 17, "Managing Data with OpenOffice.org" for instructions on creating queries.

You can use a query rather than the original table in the Form Letter dialog or Data Sources window. Expand the Queries section for your data source, choose the query that includes the appropriate records and fields for your merge, and then perform your merge as usual.

Sorting merge results

In addition to filtering data to include only some records, you can also determine the order of the results. When merging to files, the order doesn't really matter, but when merging to the printer, you may want your results in a particular order. For example, in some cases, you want letters in zip code order to facilitate bulk rate mailing.

You specify the sort order by modifying the order of the records in the Form Letters dialog or Data Sources window. To sort based on a particular field, click the field name to select it, and then click the Sort Ascending or Sort Descending button.

You can also specify more complex sorting criteria by clicking on the Sort Order... button. That opens the Sort Order dialog (**Figure 22**). Choose the field to sort on and the sort order (ascending or descending) for each of three fields. The fields you choose apply in order, so in Figure 22, records sort first on Author. If any records have the same author, they then sort on Booktitle.

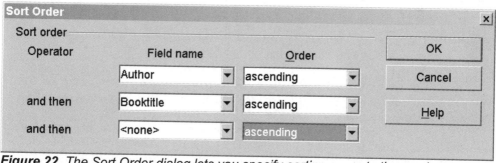

Figure 22. The Sort Order dialog lets you specify sorting on up to three columns.

How do I create envelopes?

Creating envelopes with Writer isn't difficult, but it can be tricky to get them just right. The process also isn't quite as automated as in Microsoft Word.

Choose Insert | Envelope from the menu, which opens the Envelope dialog (**Figure 23**). The first tab of the dialog defines the envelope contents. By default, Writer inserts the User Data from the Options dialog (Tools | Options, the User Data page in the OpenOffice.org section) as the sender information. Unlike Word, however, addressee information isn't inserted automatically. You can cut and paste it from the document. However, be sure to copy the address from the document onto the clipboard before you open the Envelope dialog. (You can also build a mail merge envelope using fields from any registered data source.)

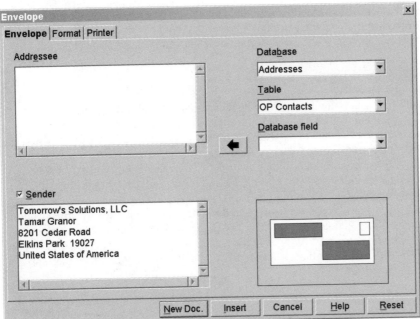

Figure 23. The Envelope dialog lets you specify the sender and addressee, as well as the type of envelope and the way the printer handles it.

Much of the work you need to do with envelopes has to do with printer interaction. The Format tab of the dialog lets you specify the type of envelope and where to print on it. The Printer tab specifies the interaction of the envelope with the printer.

The Format drop-down list of the Format tab (**Figure 24**) lists a number of standard paper sizes (including envelopes such as #10 business size). When you choose one of those, the other controls reflect the settings for that type, but you can adjust them if you like. The diagram on this tab shows you the layout of the envelope.

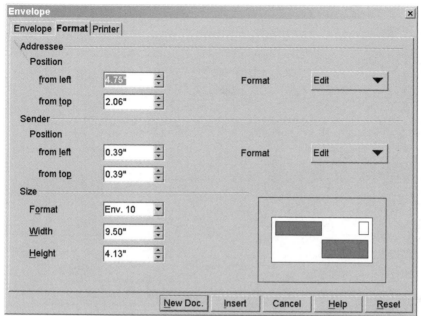

Figure 24. *Use the Format tab of the Envelope dialog to specify the size and layout of your envelope. A number of standard envelope types are predefined.*

The Printer tab (**Figure 25**) of the dialog lets you specify how envelopes feed into the printer. It also gives you access to the Printer Setup dialog where you specify, for example, manual feed for the envelope rather than a paper tray. Click the Properties button to make changes to the printer setup.

 *At present, specifying an envelope type in the Envelope dialog doesn't change the paper type for the printer. This results in envelopes printing poorly (with addresses not in the right places). To solve the problem, use the Properties button on the Printer Setup dialog. When the Document Properties dialog opens, choose the Layout page. Click the Advanced button to open the Advanced Options page (**Figure 26**). On that page, change the Paper Size setting to match your envelope type.*

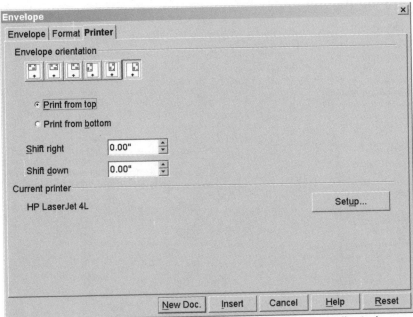

Figure 25. *Use the Printer tab of the Envelope dialog to indicate how envelopes feed into your printer.*

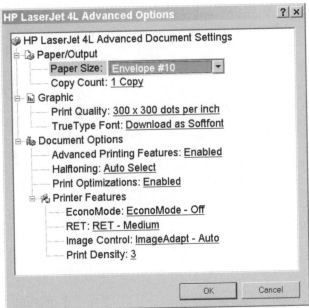

Figure 26. *Be sure to change the Paper Size in the printer's Advanced Options dialog to ensure your envelope prints correctly.*

Once you set up the envelope and printer correctly, you have two choices in the Envelope dialog. Choose New Doc. to create the envelope as a new, separate, document. Choose Insert to add the envelope to the same document.

Summary

While there are still more features in Writer, the information in this chapter and the preceding chapter should let you create just about all of the documents you need on a daily basis. If you need more advanced Writer features, the experience you gained, along with the Help file, should enable you to tackle those as well.

Updates and corrections to this chapter can be found on Hentzenwerke's web site, **www.hentzenwerke.com**. Click "Catalog" and navigate to the page for this book.

Section III
Number Crunching with Calc

Chapter 8
Creating Simple Spreadsheets

Spreadsheet software was the breakthrough application for personal computers, the one that led to their widespread acceptance in the business world. OpenOffice.org's spreadsheet application, Calc, provides the features you'd expect: the ability to enter numbers and formulas, have calculations update as the numbers change, format the results for attractive reporting, and more.

As with text documents, most people need to do only a few things with a spreadsheet. This chapter looks at the basic operations of Calc, including creating workbooks, putting data into them, and printing them.

How do I start Calc?

You can open Calc in a number of different ways. If QuickStarter is running, right-click it and choose Spreadsheet to open Calc with a new blank spreadsheet. Choose Open File from QuickStarter and pick an existing Calc or Excel workbook to open Calc with that workbook loaded. A third choice with QuickStarter is to choose From Template, and then choose a Calc template; that opens Calc with a new workbook based on the chosen template.

> *Calc uses the term "spreadsheet" to refer to the type of document it creates. Microsoft Excel prefers "workbook." The two terms are used interchangeably here.*

If you have another OpenOffice.org application open, choose File | New | Spreadsheet from the menu or long click the New button on the Function toolbar and choose Spreadsheet to open Calc with a blank spreadsheet. Choose File | Open or the Open button to open Calc with an existing workbook.

Finally, depending on your operating system, you may be able to open Calc from a menu. In Windows, choose Start | Programs | OpenOffice.org <version> | OpenOffice.org Calc.

What do I see when I first open Calc?

The first time you open Calc, the Stylist and Navigator will probably be open. (See Chapter 5, "Making Life Easier with Templates and Styles," for details on the Stylist and Chapter 4, "The OpenOffice.org Interface," for information about the Navigator.) The workbook is zoomed to fit the entire width of your screen.

Figure 1 shows the initial layout of Calc.

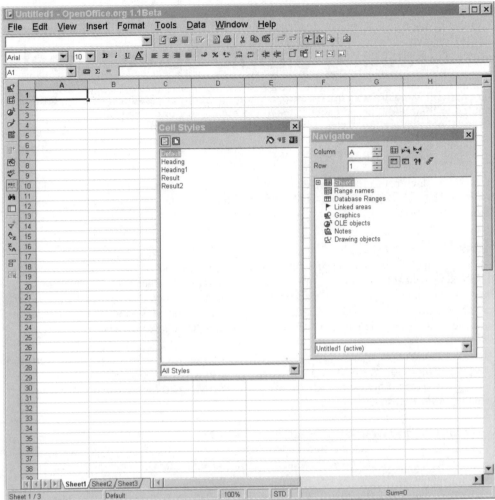

Figure 1. *By default, Calc opens with both the Stylist and Navigator displayed and four toolbars docked, three at the top and one at the left.*

Four toolbars are docked by default. The Function toolbar is beneath the menu and includes common operations such as New, Open, Save, and Print, as well as Cut, Copy, Paste, and others. Docked beneath the Function toolbar is the Spreadsheet Object Bar. It has controls for font attributes (including font name, font size, bold, italic, and so forth), alignment, formatting of numbers, and more.

The third toolbar docked at the top is the Formula Bar. This one is different from the others in a couple of ways. First, it can't be undocked. You can hide it using View | Toolbars | Formula Bar, but you can't undock it and put it elsewhere. Second, the textbox that makes up the largest portion of the Formula Bar changes size as the width of the Calc window changes. The Formula Bar contains controls used in entering values and formulas.

Finally, the Main toolbar is docked at the left. It contains controls for adding other kinds of objects to a spreadsheet, to check spelling, for managing data stored in a spreadsheet, and more. (The Main, Function, and Object toolbars can be hidden. See Chapter 4, "The OpenOffice.org User Interface," for details.)

Beneath the Formula Bar are column letters. Click a column letter to highlight the entire column. Right-click a column letter to see a shortcut menu of column operations.

Similarly, to the right of the Main toolbar are row numbers. Click a row number to highlight the entire row. Right-click a row number to see a shortcut menu of row operations.

At the bottom of the Calc window, there are tabs for the individual worksheets in the workbook. Click a tab to switch to that worksheet. A set of "VCR buttons," to the left of the tabs, controls the tabs you see, though they don't actually switch sheets.

How do I create new spreadsheets?

As described in "How do I start Calc?" earlier in this chapter, you can create a new workbook in several ways when you open Calc. The same techniques work to create another new workbook once you're working in Calc.

How do I enter data?

As in other spreadsheet applications, you put data into a cell by setting focus to that cell (either by clicking into it or by navigating to the cell with the keyboard) and typing in the data.

Calc examines what you enter and formats it appropriately. The formatting chosen is based both on the content and on the language settings. For example, with US English, entering 1.24 results in a number, but with German, it interprets 1.24 as a date and converts it to 01.01.2024.

You can format cells (see "How do I format my data?" later in this chapter) to clarify the meaning of a particular value.

How do I edit data?

As you enter data, it displays both in the cell itself and in the input line section of the Formula Bar. To edit a value, you need to set focus to the input line and edit the value shown there.

While you type or edit, the buttons next to the input line change to include a red "X" for cancel, and a green check mark to accept the entry (shown in **Figure 2**). You can also accept an entry by pressing Enter or navigating to another cell.

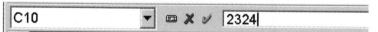

Figure 2. *While you're entering or editing a value, the Formula bar includes buttons to accept or reject the entry. The Sheet Area drop-down list on the left indicates which cell you're working on.*

How do I enter a series of numbers quickly?

It's common when creating a worksheet to enter a series of values in a row or column, or to put the same value in a series of cells in a row or column. For example, you might want to label a series of rows with the names of the months. Calc makes tasks like this a breeze.

Enter the first value in the appropriate cell, and then click the cell. The cell is highlighted and in the lower right corner, there's an extra handle (**Figure 3**.). Grab the handle and drag down the column or across the row where you want the series of values. As you drag, a tooltip shows you the value to be inserted in the last cell of the range. When you release, the values are inserted. This technique works with numbers, dates, month names, days of the week, and even strings that begin or end with a number like "1st quarter" or "Area 1." For other kinds of values where Calc can't figure out how to increment, the same technique copies the original value to each cell in the range. There may be times where you want to copy numbers or dates to each cell in a range rather than incrementing. You can still drag, but in that case, hold down the Ctrl key while dragging.

Figure 3. Grab the square handle at the bottom right of the highlighted cell and drag to autofill a row or column.

In other cases, you may need more control than simply adding 1 to the value. Highlight the range of cells, including the initial value. Choose Edit | Fill | Series from the menu to open the Fill Series dialog (**Figure 4**). In the dialog, you indicate how to compute the successive values. Choose Linear to add a fixed amount (specified by Increment) or Growth to multiply the value by the increment. When you choose Date, the Time unit option buttons become available and you can choose to increment by days, weekdays, months, or years.

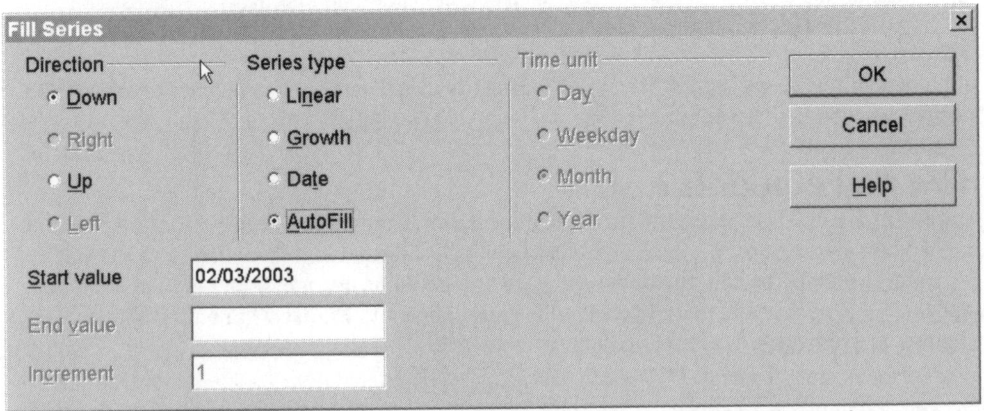

Fill Series			✕
Direction	**Series type**	**Time unit**	OK
● Down	○ Linear	○ Day	Cancel
○ Right	○ Growth	○ Weekday	Help
○ Up	○ Date	● Month	
○ Left	● AutoFill	○ Year	
Start value	02/03/2003		
End value			
Increment	1		

Figure 4. The Fill Series dialog lets you determine how to modify values when copyiing to each cell in a range.

How do I enter formulas?

What makes spreadsheet applications so useful is the ability to enter formulas that are evaluated regularly. To enter a formula, you need to tell Calc what you're doing. The easiest way to do so is to begin with an equal sign. You can either type the equal sign or click the "=" button on the Formula Bar (**Figure 5**).

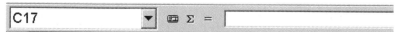

Figure 5. *When you're not editing, the formula bar includes an equal sign to begin a formula, and a sum button to simplify entering formulas for totals.*

Once you have the equal sign, you can type the actual formula or create it by pointing and clicking. As in other spreadsheets, the formula can refer to other cells. To enter a formula with the keyboard, use the arrow keys to navigate to the appropriate cell. Next, type the operator to follow that cell reference, and then navigate to the next cell in the formula. When the formula is complete, press Enter or click the check mark in the Formula Bar.

By default, when you refer to other cells by pointing with the mouse or the keyboard, you get a *relative reference*. Relative references are adjusted when a formula is copied or moved. Suppose cell C2 contains the formula =A2+B2. If you copy the formula to cell C3, it becomes =A3+B3.

In some situations, you want to refer to the same cell, even if a formula is copied or moved. Such a reference is called an *absolute reference*. You specify an absolute reference by putting a "$" before each component of the cell address. For example, an absolute reference to cell A3 is written $A$3.

It's also possible to mix relative and absolute references, making the column relative and the row absolute or vice versa. In that case, only the relative portion of the address changes when the formula is copied or moved. For example, $A3 refers absolutely to column A, but has a relative reference to row 3. If the formula containing this reference is in cell D3, and is copied to D4, the reference changes to $A4. However, copying the formula to cell E3 leaves the reference to $A3 unchanged.

You can change the type of a reference without typing the dollar signs. Position the cursor in the input line anywhere within a reference (including right after it) and press Shift-F4 to cycle through the choices. For example, if the reference is initially A3, pressing Shift-F4 once changes it to $A$3. The second Shift-F4 changes it to A$4, a third makes it $A4, and a fourth Shift-F4 returns to the original A4.

Using functions in formulas

Calc includes many functions that perform a variety of calculations. You can simply type in the function name and its arguments, but there are easier ways to make sure you get it right.

The easiest function to include is SUM(), which totals all the cells provided to it. To put a total into a cell, click the Sum button (the sigma symbol) on the Formula bar. Calc inserts a formula, totaling the column containing the formula. It includes all cells from the first one in the column that contains a number down to the cell immediately above the formula. For example, in **Figure 6**, the Sum button was clicked with focus in cell B8. The formula inserted was =SUM(B4:B7).

	A	B
1		
2	Type	Value
3		
4		23
5		8273
6		
7		
8		8296

Figure 6. The Sum button on the Formula Bar makes it easy to set up formulas for totaling.

You're not restricted to the specified range when you use the Sum button. Once the formula appears, you can change the range just as you would with any other function. (See the next section "Specifying ranges and multiple values for functions.")

For other functions, you can use the Functions AutoPilot. To start it, click the AutoPilot:Functions button in the Formula Bar (immediately to the left of the Sum button). The AutoPilot (**Figure 7**) shows all available functions along with information about the selected function. Choose the function you want. Use the Category drop-down list to make it easier to find the right function.

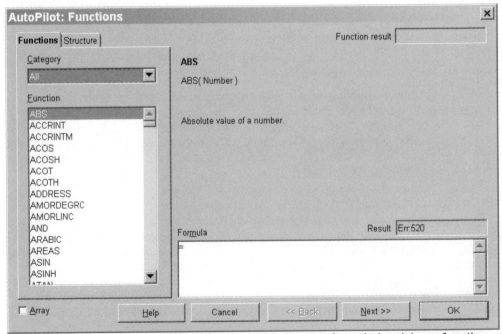

Figure 7. The Functions AutoPilot helps you construct a formula involving a function. First, choose the function you want to use.

Once you have the right function, press Next to move to the arguments page (**Figure 8**) of the AutoPilot. On this page, you specify the values the function should use in the calculation.

The appearance of the page depends on the function chosen. In Figure 8, you can specify up to 30 arguments for the Average function.

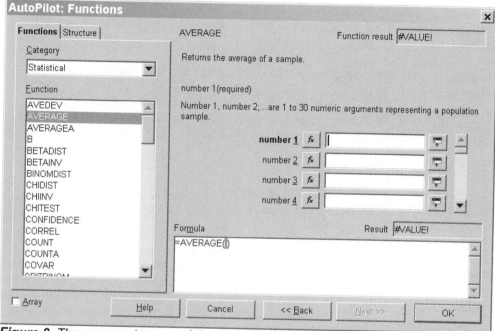

Figure 8. *The arguments page of the Functions AutoPilot lets you specify what values the function uses in its calculations.*

Once you move to the arguments page, the Category drop-down list automatically changes to the category containing the specified function.

There are four ways of specifying each argument. First, you can simply type it into the appropriate position in the Formula text box. Alternatively, you can type it in the text box for that argument. In either case, what you type can be actual values or cell references. However, you can also specify cell references by pointing. If you can't see the cells you want, click the Shrink button to the right of the text box for the argument to reduce the AutoPilot to toolbar size (**Figure 9**), and then point to the cell or range using the mouse or keyboard. When you complete the range, click the same button (now labeled "Maximize") to restore the AutoPilot.

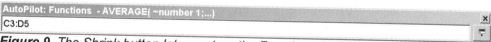

Figure 9. *The Shrink button lets you turn the Functions AutoPilot into a toolbar so you can specify cells by pointing.*

The final option for any argument is to use another function to specify it. To do so, click the function button (labelled "*fx*") to the left of the argument's text box. This returns you to the first page of the AutoPilot, but whatever you choose becomes an argument to the function you already chose. In this way, you can nest function calls as needed.

As you work in the AutoPilot, you can see the formula being constructed and the current value for that formula. When the formula for the function call is complete, click OK to close the AutoPilot and insert the new formula in the cell that had focus when you opened the AutoPilot.

Specifying ranges and multiple values for functions

Many functions operate on multiple values or groups of values. When a function requires several values to perform its calculation, separate the arguments with semi-colons. For example, the CONCATENATE() function lets you combine up to 30 text values into a single string. A call to CONCATENATE() might look like this:

```
=CONCATENATE(A4;" and ";A5)
```

Other functions like SUM() and AVERAGE() operate on ranges (groups of cells). You indicate a range by specifying opposite corners separated by a colon. A range can include cells from just one row, just one column, or multiple rows and columns. However, a range is always rectangular. For example, B3:D14 specifies the rectangle bounded by B3, D3, B14, and D14.

You can specify a range by pointing to it with the mouse or keyboard. With the mouse, click into one corner, and then Shift-Click the opposite corner. With the keyboard, navigate to one corner, and then hold down the Shift key while you navigate to the opposite corner.

> *The order in which you specify the corners of a range doesn't matter, nor does it matter whether you specify upper left and lower right, or upper right and lower left. Calc always adjusts the range to the form "upper left:lower right" before inserting it into a formula.*

In some cases, a function can work with multiple ranges. (For example, the formula SUM(A1:B10; A20:B50) adds the values in the two ranges of cells while ignoring the cells in between the two ranges.) To specify multiple ranges with the mouse, choose one as above and use Ctrl-Click to begin the next range. Calc automatically inserts the semi-colon needed to separate the ranges. With the keyboard, you have to type the semi-colon yourself.

Naming ranges

If you're going to use a particular range repeatedly, you can make things easier by giving the range a name that you can then use in formulas. To do so, highlight the range and choose Insert | Names | Define from the menu. The Define Names dialog (**Figure 10**) opens. The highlighted range shows in the Range textbox. Type the name for the range and click Add to define the range.

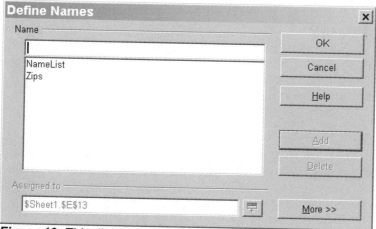

Figure 10. This dialog lets you assign a name to a range, so you can refer to it by name and don't have to keep selecting it.

You don't actually have to highlight the range you want before opening the dialog. Once you enter a name for a range, you can click back into the workbook and select the range to be named. When you do so, the dialog shrinks to toolbar size. You can force it to shrink by clicking the Shrink button next to the range textbox. When you select the right range, click the same button to expand the dialog.

Once you define a range, it's listed in the Range Names section of the Navigator. You can highlight a range by double-clicking its name in the Navigator. You can also drag-and-drop the name of a range into a formula.

If you use a named range in a formula and later change the range assigned to that name (that is, point the name to a different range), the formula refers to the new range. Similarly, if you insert or delete a row or column within the named range, the range adjusts itself.

Referring to other worksheets

A formula can refer to cells in other worksheets of the workbook. You set this up by pointing to the appropriate cells or by typing in the references. The format for referring to a cell or range in another worksheet is:

```
SheetName.Cell
```

or

```
SheetName.Range
```

For example, a formula on Sheet1 of a workbook would refer to the range B2:C7 of Sheet2 of the workbook as Sheet2.B2:C7.

How do I format data?

As in Writer, it's a good idea to use styles to format data rather than formatting it directly. Styles make it easier to make across-the-board changes. Unlike Writer, however, Calc includes only a few built-in styles. See Chapter 5, "Making Life Easier with Templates and Styles," for instructions on defining new styles and modifying existing styles. Here I look at some of the things you're likely to want to change, whether in a style or directly.

Setting cell formats

If you don't specify otherwise, Calc examines the data you type in and chooses a format based on the data itself. For example, when you type something Calc recognizes as a number, it uses a numeric format. If you precede a number with a dollar sign (using US settings), Calc recognizes currency and formats the cell as such. When you type something Calc identifies as a date, it uses a date format for that cell, and so forth.

However, sometimes you want something different from the default, whether it's to format a particular value differently than Calc assumes, or to make a different choice of numeric, currency, or date format. To change the format of a cell or range of cells, choose Format | Cells from the menu or from the shortcut menu. The Cell Attributes dialog opens—use the Numbers tab (**Figure 11**) to choose the overall formatting for a cell or range.

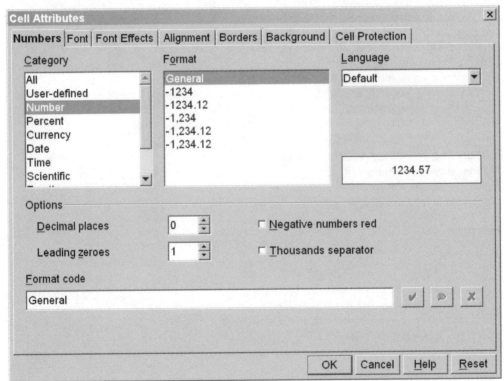

Figure 11. The Numbers tab of the Cell Attributes dialog lets you indicate the type of value in a cell or range of cells and specify the formatting to use.

> *Dates are stored as numeric values (with 31-Dec-1899 as day 1). If you format a cell containing a date using one of the Numeric formats, you see a number rather than a date.*

A large number of formats are predefined and available on the Numbers tab. However, if what you need isn't included, you can define your own format. The easiest way to define your own format is to start with one similar to what you want and edit the format code to get exactly what you want.

Format codes use special characters to indicate the various components of the value. For example, "#" indicates a digit with leading and trailing zeroes suppressed, while "YYYY" indicates a four-digit year. The Help topic, "Number Format Codes," includes a complete list of format codes.

Calc lists format codes you define in the User-defined category, as well as in the category they best fit in. (For example, those that include date components land in the Date category.)

You can make life easier by adding a comment to your custom format codes, explaining their purpose or use. To do so, click the Edit Comment button (the yellow speech balloon) next to the Format code text box. The description beneath the Format code text box becomes editable, as in **Figure 12**. When you finish editing, click the Add (check mark) button or click OK to close the dialog.

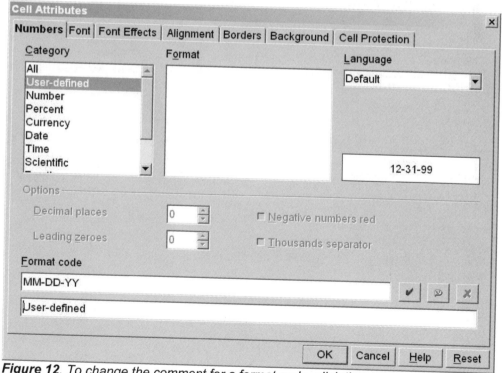

Figure 12. To change the comment for a format code, click the yellow speech balloon.

You set the format for an entire column or row by clicking the column or row label before choosing Format | Cells.

Setting text orientation

Calc lets you orient text vertically as well as rotate the contents of a cell. Use the Alignment tab (**Figure 13**) of the Cell Attributes dialog. For vertical text, click the large vertical button that says "ABCD" vertically. **Figure 14** shows an example.

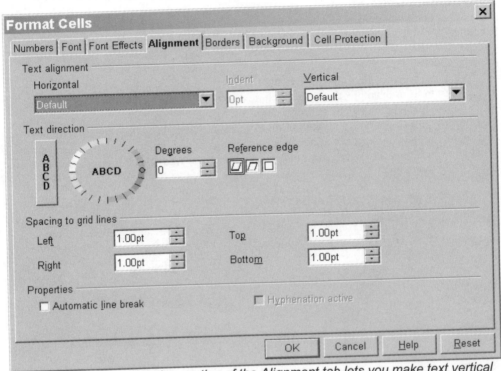

Figure 13. The Text direction section of the Alignment tab lets you make text vertical or rotate it as you wish.

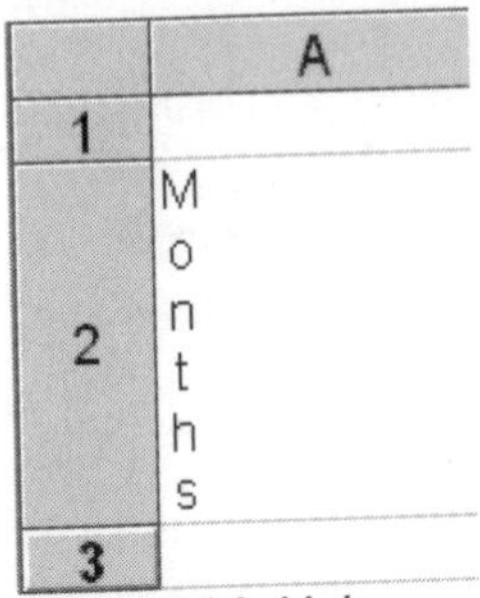

Figure 14. Using vertical text is as easy as clicking the Vertical Text button on the Alignment tab.

To rotate an item, you need to specify two things, the amount of rotation and where to start. You can specify the angle of rotation in one of two ways, either by typing it into the Degrees text box or by clicking in the circle. Whichever you choose, the sample text ("ABCD") inside the circle displays with that rotation.

The Reference edge option buttons let you determine where the rotated item appears. By default, the text is anchored to the bottom edge of the cell and rotates outward from there. The middle button rotates the text from the top edge of the cell, while the right button rotates only within the cell. With the first two settings, rotated text can extend beyond its cell. **Figure 15** shows the same value rotated 45 degrees using each of the Reference edge settings.

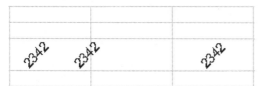

Figure 15. The Reference edge setting for rotated text determines where it's anchored. Here, the left cell uses the bottom edge, the middle cell uses the top edge, and the right cell keeps rotated text in the cell.

Conditional formatting

In some situations, you want to display data differently depending on its value. The most common case is showing negative numbers in red. To do this, use the Format Cells dialog; on the Numbers tab, select the Negative numbers red check box. Some people prefer to use parentheses around negative numbers. There are some built-in formats to provide this style (look in the Currency category). You can also create a custom format using a format code like this:

```
0;(-0)
```

The first 0 indicates formatting for positive numbers, while the second shows how to format negative numbers.

In other situations, the decision about how to format values is more complex than just positive or negative. For example, you might want to make all numbers above a certain value or all dates in a certain range stand out. To do this kind of formatting, you must first create a style with the formatting characteristics you want to use to make those values stand out. (See Chapter 5, "Making Life Easier with Templates and Styles.") Next, choose Format | Conditional Formatting from the menu. The Conditional Formatting dialog (**Figure 16**) opens. You can specify up to three distinct conditions for the highlighted range. In Figure 16, cells with a value of 180 or more display bold.

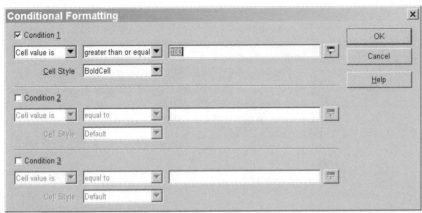

Figure 16. The Conditional Formatting dialog lets you match data values to styles, so different values use different formatting.

You can specify another cell (either by typing or by pointing to it) rather than a particular value to trigger the condition. You can also put a formula in the value text box, so you can compare to the result of a calculation.

If you apply conditional formatting to a range of cells, remember to make cell ranges in the value relative or partially relative if you want to refer to a different cell for each cell in the range being formatted. For example, **Figure 17** shows some population data for the United States. The current population in column D has conditional formatting that makes it red if less than half the population is female. **Figure 18** shows the condition set up for that.

	A	B	C	D	E	F	G
1	GEONAME	GEONAME	TOTPOPHS	TOTPOPCUR	TOTPOPPR(	FEMPOPHS	FEMPOPCU
2	Alabama	4040587	4221932	4455517	2104727	2194735	2313044
3	Alaska	550043	610350	679683	260230	289206	323009
4	Arizona	3665228	4000398	4452859	1854696	2020893	2246862
5	Arkansas	2350725	2441646	2566937	1217920	1262166	1324423
6	California	29760022	31546602	33575312	14863538	15749642	16767433
7	Colorado	3294394	3630585	4079905	1663315	1829591	2053524
8	Connecticut	3287116	3275195	3261723	1694467	1685708	1677174
9	Delaware	666168	707864	757702	343224	364186	389614
10	District Of C‣	606900	571592	530751	324005	304640	282896
11	Florida	12937926	13849741	14933526	6676516	7134287	7682227
12	Georgia	6478216	7020384	7713623	3334160	3606091	3957412
13	Hawaii	1108229	1186692	1278719	544330	585344	633386

Figure 17. The total population of states where less than half the population is female display in red. The condition needed is shown in Figure 18.

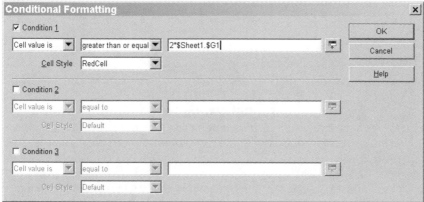

Figure 18. The condition applied to column D of Figure 17 uses the RedCell style for any cell whose value is more than half of the corresponding cell in column G.

How do I set column width?

A spreadsheet usually looks better with columns sized to fit their contents. The easiest way to resize a column is to position the mouse on the space between that column and the one to its right, so the pointer changes into a sizer, and then double click, which sets the column to the width necessary for its contents. If you highlight multiple columns when doing this, they all resize to fit their contents. **Figure 19** shows the mouse positioned to resize column F.

Figure 19. Put the mouse between columns to resize the column to the left. If you double-click, the column is set to fit its contents.

You can also resize columns by dragging. Again, position the mouse between columns, and then click and drag to the desired size. A tooltip appears telling you the column width as you go.

A third approach is to click the column header to select the entire column, and then choose Format | Column | Width or Format | Column | Optimal Width from the menu or Column Width or Column Optimal Width from the shortcut menu. When you choose Format | Column | Width or Column Width, the Column Width dialog (**Figure 20**) appears. Specify the desired width. To return to the default size, select the Default Value check box.

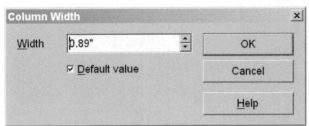

Figure 20. As soon as you change the width value in the Column Width dialog, the Default value check box is cleared. Select it to put the default width back into the text box.

When you choose Format | Column | Optimal Column Width or Optimal Column Width, the Optimal Column Width dialog (**Figure 21**) appears. In this dialog, you specify how much space to add to the width of the widest cell in the column to determine the total column width. Again, the Default value check box lets you restore the default setting.

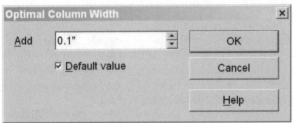

Figure 21. The Optimal Column Width dialog specifies how much space to add to the widest cell to get the column width.

Be careful. If you right-click a column header and set the width without clicking the column first, the new width applies to the column (or columns) containing the currently selected cell (or cells), which is not necessarily the one on which you right-clicked.

How do I center a heading above a bunch of columns?

Many spreadsheets use one or more rows at the top as headings for the entire document. It's useful to be able to center those headings across all the columns in use. While you can do this, more or less, by trial and error, Calc offers an easy way to get it right.

In the row where a heading appears, select the cells above all the relevant columns (those above which the header should be centered). Choose Format | Merge Cells | Define from the menu. This merges those cells into a single cell. Choose Align Center Horizontally from the Spreadsheet Object Bar or choose Center alignment on the Alignment tab of the Cell Attributes dialog (Format | Cells from the menu). **Figure 22** shows an example of this technique.

	A	B	C	D	E
1			Sales by Quarter		
2					
3	Q1	Q2	Q3	Q4	Total
4					

Figure 22. *To center a heading over a group of columns, merge the cells, and then choose Center alignment.*

How do I move or copy cell contents using the mouse?

When you want to move or copy the contents of a group of cells in Calc, it's easy. Highlight all the cells in the group and drag (to move) or Ctrl-drag (to copy) them to the new location. However, moving or copying a single cell is a little tricky.

If the cell to be moved or copied holds a number or text, you can triple-click in the cell and drag (to copy) or Shift-drag (to move) that value. When a formula is involved, however, that approach prevents the formula's relative references from adapting to the move. Instead, click in the cell and, holding the left mouse button down, drag to the right until both that cell and the next cell are highlighted. Next, move the mouse back to the left until only the desired cell is highlighted. Now you can drag (to move) or Ctrl-drag (to copy) as with a range of cells.

How do I copy the value of a cell rather than the formula?

By default, when you copy a cell containing a formula to another cell, the formula is pasted into the new cell (adjusted appropriately if it uses relative references). There are times, though, when you want to copy the result of the calculation, not the calculation itself.

Calc gives you tremendous control over what is pasted, if you ask. When you use Edit | Paste, the Paste button on the Function toolbar, or the Paste item on the shortcut menu, Calc pastes the formula. However, if you choose Edit | Paste Special or Paste Special from the shortcut menu, the Paste Special dialog (**Figure 23**) appears. Clear the Paste All check box (if it's selected) and clear Formulas. Make sure Numbers is selected, and then click OK.

To duplicate exactly the Values choice in Microsoft Excel's Paste Special dialog, clear everything except Numbers.

How do I switch rows and columns?

Sometimes, you find after you lay out the information in a spreadsheet that you prefer to have what's in columns become rows and what's in rows become columns. For example, you might start tracking employee information by using one column for each employee, and having rows for things like name, social security number. and the like. After the number of employees grows a little, it may become clear that it would be better to use one row per employee with one column for each piece of information.

This kind of change is called a *transposition* and you use the Paste Special dialog (Figure 23) to perform it. To transpose data in place, highlight the data, cut it (Ctrl-X, Edit | Cut from the menu, or Cut on the Function toolbar or shortcut menu). Next, choose Edit | Paste Special from the menu or Paste Special on the shortcut menu, and select the Transpose check box. Click OK to paste the transposed data.

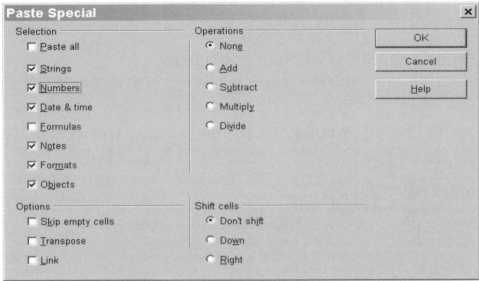

Figure 23. The Paste Special dialog lets you decide what is pasted. Clear the Formulas check box to copy the result of a formula rather than the formula itself.

How do I change the number of worksheets in a workbook?

By default, new spreadsheets are created with three worksheets. If you need additional sheets in a workbook, you can add them by choosing Insert | Sheet from the menu or by choosing Insert Sheet from the shortcut menu for the sheet tabs. In either case, the Insert Sheet dialog (**Figure 24**) opens. Specify the number of sheets to add and whether the new sheets go before or after the current worksheet.

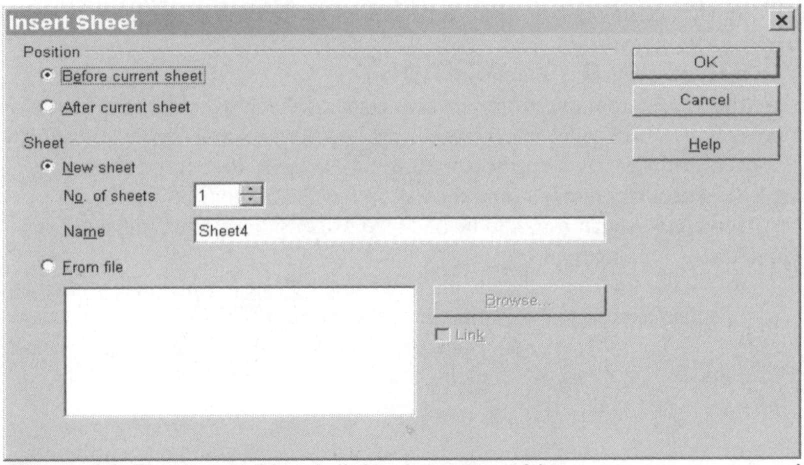

Figure 24. The Insert Sheet dialog lets you add one or more new worksheets to a workbook. They can come from another workbook.

To remove a worksheet, click its tab, and then choose Edit | Sheet | Delete from the menu or Delete Sheet from the tab's shortcut menu. In either case, a confirmation message displays.

How do I change a worksheet's name?

When you create a new workbook, Calc names the worksheets Sheet1, Sheet2 and so forth. To give them meaningful names, choose Format | Sheet | Rename from the menu or Rename Sheet from the shortcut menu for the sheet's tab. In the Rename Sheet dialog that appears, type the new name.

How do I move a worksheet within a workbook?

Sometimes, you find the order of sheets within a workbook is wrong. To change the order of worksheets, click the tab for the sheet you want to move, and then choose Edit | Sheet | Move/Copy from the menu or Move/Copy Sheet from the shortcut menu for the tab. The Move/Copy Sheet dialog (**Figure 25**) appears. In the Insert before list, choose the new position for the sheet.

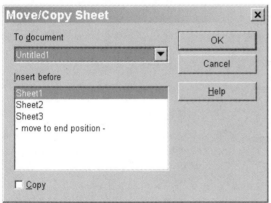

Figure 25. Use this dialog to move a worksheet within a workbook or to make a copy of a worksheet in another workbook.

You can also use this dialog to make a copy of a worksheet. Choose another workbook or "- new document -" from the To document drop-down list, and then choose the position for the worksheet in that workbook. For a new document, the only choice is "- move to end position -".

How do I print my spreadsheet?

Similar to Writer documents, the easiest way to print a spreadsheet is clicking the Print button on the Function toolbar. Doing so prints to the default printer (or if you previously printed this spreadsheet to another printer, it goes to that printer). Only the used area of the spreadsheet prints.

For more control, choose File | Print and the Print dialog appears. You can choose a printer, as well as indicate whether to print the whole spreadsheet, selected pages, or the currently selected portion.

The Format menu offers a couple of ways to gain additional control over printing. Choose Format | Page to open the Page Style dialog. The Sheet tab (**Figure 26**) includes several options for printing. Select Grid to include gridlines in your output; clear Zero values to replace zeroes with white space in your output. If you want to print out the formulas behind a spreadsheet rather than the results, select Formulas (but realize that many of your columns may not be wide enough to show the formulas they contain).

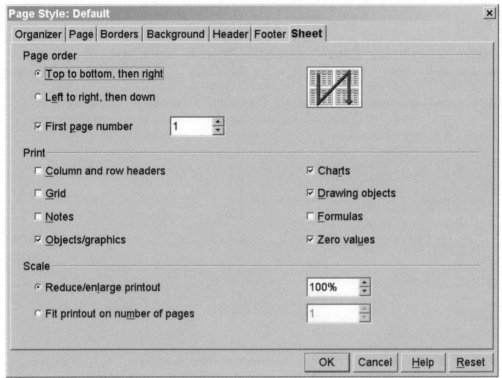

Figure 26.The Sheet tab of the Page Style dialog lets you specify printing options.

The Header and Footer tabs of the Page Style dialog let you specify page headers and footers to appear on each page of your output. In the dialog itself, you indicate the position on the page for the header or footer. Click the Edit button to specify the content. **Figure 27** shows the Header dialog set to include "Page x of y" information at the top left of each page, as well as the sheet name (which is centered in the header by default).

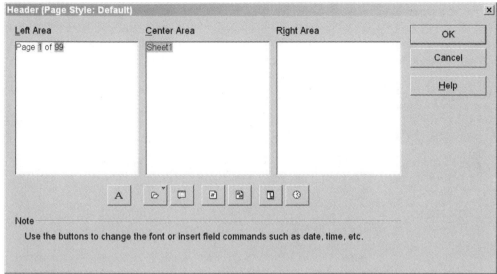

Figure 27. The Header and Footer dialogs let you put information at the top or bottom of each page.

Once you print or preview (see "How do I preview what will get printed?" in the next section) a spreadsheet, subtle page dividers appear. The dividers are grid lines darker than the default light gray. In **Figure 28**, the page break occurs between columns G and H. You can turn this feature off on the View page of the Spreadsheet section of the Options dialog (Tools | Options)--clear the Page breaks check box. Alternatively, you can change the color of the regular grid lines on the same page; when you do so, the page breaks are still dark gray.

F	G	H	I
May	Jun	Jul	Aug

Figure 28. Once you print a workbook, page dividers appear as slightly darker grid lines. Here, the page break falls between columns G and H.

How do I decide what gets printed?

You can determine what prints rather than letting Calc do it automatically. Highlight the range or ranges you want to print and choose Format | Print Ranges | Define from the menu. You can choose all the relevant ranges before choosing the menu item, or do them one at a time. In the latter case, use Format | Print Ranges | Define for the first range, and then use Format | Print Ranges | Add for subsequent ranges.

Regardless of how you specify the ranges, when you print the spreadsheet, only the specified ranges print. Note that the individual ranges print in their normal positions—they're not put closer together to fill the page.

To restore normal printing, choose Format | Print Ranges | Remove.

How do I preview what will print?

You can save a lot of paper by previewing your output before actually printing it. Choose File | Page Preview from the menu and Calc switches to preview mode. The first page of output displays and the Page View Object Bar (**Figure 29**) appears.

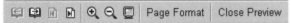

***Figure 29**. When you choose Page Preview from the menu, the Page View Object Bar lets you navigate within your preview.*

The leftmost group of buttons is for navigating pages. You can move one page at a time or to the first or last page. The magnifying glass buttons zoom in and out.

Summary

Creating a basic spreadsheet that performs simple calculations isn't too hard. In the next chapter, I look at using Calc as a simple database.

Updates and corrections to this chapter can be found on Hentzenwerke's web site, **www.hentzenwerke.com**. Click "Catalog" and navigate to the page for this book.

Chapter 9
Database Manipulation with Calc

Calc has the ability to treat its data like a database, reading data from disparate sources and performing various operations. This chapter looks at Calc's database functionality.

While it's not a full-fledged database program, the row and column nature of a spreadsheet, along with the ability to have calculated values always up-to-date, makes it useful to do some database tasks in a spreadsheet. In Calc, you can work with both data stored only in the spreadsheet and with data from other sources. OpenOffice.org also provides more powerful database manipulation tools—see Chapter 17, "Managing Data with OpenOffice.org."

A little terminology is in order before jumping into this topic. In the database world, the term *database* refers to an entire set of related data, such as the accounts receivable records for a company. A database is composed of *tables*, with each table containing information about one kind of entity. For example, in an accounts receivable database, there might be a table of customers, a table of orders received, a table of products the company sells, and quite a few others. Finally, each piece of information within a table is a *field*. In the accounts receivable example, fields include the customer's zip code, the date of an order, and the unit price of a product.

Calc lets you put one or more tables into a spreadsheet and manipulate them in various ways.

How do I create a database table in a spreadsheet?

To put data into a spreadsheet, typically, you use one column for each field you want to store, putting the name of the field as a heading. **Figure 1** shows a portion of a spreadsheet containing names and addresses. The first row of the range holds the field names while the rest of the rows hold the actual data.

First Name	Last Name	Address	City	State	Zip
John	Smith	1234 N. Front St.	Phila.	PA	19122
Mary	Jones	17 S. 10th St.	Phila.	PA	19103
Robert	Rodgers	47 Church Road	Elkins Park	PA	19027
Elizabeth	Martin	1776 Patriots Drive	Boston	MA	02120
Howard	Bailey	94 Ocean Drive	Venice	CA	92403

Figure 1. You put database-type information into a spreadsheet by simply arranging it into columns with the field names at the top.

How do I import data into a spreadsheet?

Often, you have data stored in a database of some sort (or even in a text file) and you want to manipulate some of that data in a spreadsheet. You can import the data and even maintain a connection to the original data so changes are reflected.

There are a number of ways to bring outside data into a spreadsheet. You need to choose the one that fits the situation, based on where your data is currently stored and whether you need changes to the original data to affect the spreadsheet.

Importing from a database

The first possibility is to use the Data Sources bar (**Figure 2**), accessed via View | Data Sources, the Data Sources button on the Main toolbar, or the F4 key. The window shows the various data sources defined in OOo. You can drag a table or query from the window into a spreadsheet. Data you add this way remains linked to the original, so the spreadsheet reflects changes to the data source. (See Chapter 17, "Managing Data with OpenOffice.org," for the details on getting data listed in Data Sources.)

Figure 2. *The Data Sources bar lists any defined data sources. Use drag-and-drop from the left pane to put updateable data into a spreadsheet.*

Importing from a spreadsheet or web page

The second technique also creates a link to the original data. It's designed for grabbing data from another spreadsheet or a web page. Choose Insert | External Data from the menu, and the External Data dialog (**Figure 3**) appears. Point to the URL or file containing the data and the Available tables/ranges list fills in with the sections of the web page or file you can insert. Choose one and click OK to insert the data.

Importing text or dBase data

Another way to bring data into a spreadsheet is to import a text file or a dBase file. In this case, you don't add the data to an existing spreadsheet, but create a new workbook containing the data. Data imported in this way isn't linked to the original.

A common format for import is CSV (comma-separated value), but you may also have dBase format files (with an extension of ".DBF"), which you can read in the same way. (A dBase file is typically one table in a database.) Many applications have the ability to export their data in these two formats.

To create a spreadsheet from a CSV or DBF file, use File | Open and choose the appropriate type in the Files of type drop-down list. Navigate to the file and click Open. For a CSV file, the Text Import dialog (**Figure 4**) opens to let you indicate how to parse the text. Select the Comma check box in the Separated by section—that indicates the fields have commas between them. Click OK to import the data. For a dBase file, depending on the way the file was originally created, you may see the Import dBase Files dialog (**Figure 5**). The dialog lets you specify the *code page* for the data; the code page indicates the character set used for the data. Choose the one appropriate to the file; in the United States and other English-speaking countries, you most likely want "Western Europe (ASCII/US)."

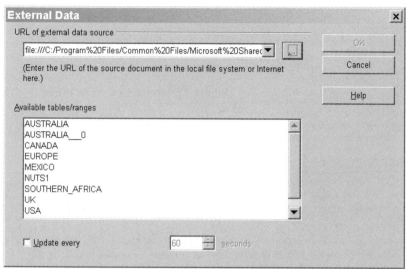

Figure 3. *The External Data dialog lets you point to a file and see the various data ranges available.*

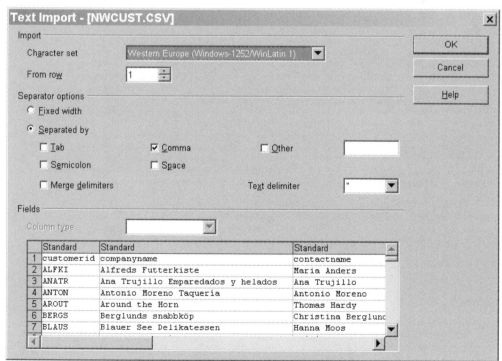

Figure 4. *The Text Import dialog lets you guide OOo's parsing of a text file into data.*

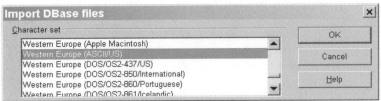

Figure 5. When you import dBase files, you may need to specify the character set used to create them, so accented characters are properly represented.

How do I sort the data?

To sort data in a spreadsheet, put focus anywhere in the data (by clicking or using the keyboard). Choose Data | Sort from the menu. Calc is smart enough to figure out what range you want to sort, and highlights the entire table, including the headings. The Sort dialog (**Figure 6**) displays. On the Sort criteria tab, choose the field on which you want to sort. You can choose up to three fields so, for example, you can sort on zip code, and then by last name within zip code, and then by first name within last name and zip code. For each field, you specify ascending (A to Z) or descending (Z to A) order.

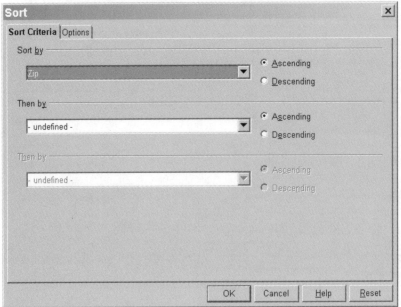

Figure 6. You can sort data in a spreadsheet on up to three fields.

The Options tab (**Figure 7**) of the dialog lets you fine tune the sort. The most important item on this tab is the Range contains column labels check box. When selected, Calc understands the range to be sorted has the field names at the top and should leave them there.

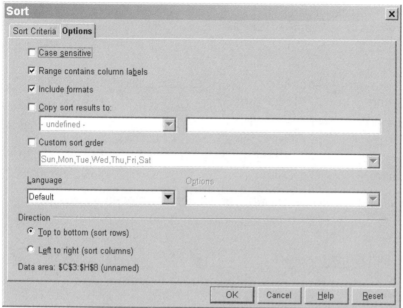

Figure 7. The Options tab of the Sort dialog lets you prevent field names from being included in the sort, put sort results elsewhere in the workbook, and even sort columns rather than rows.

The Copy sort results to check box lets you sort data while leaving the original alone. Select the check box and either choose a defined range from the drop-down list (see Chapter 8, "Creating Simple Spreadsheets," for instructions on defining ranges) or specify the cell where the sort results should be placed. (The cell you specify becomes the upper left corner of the result range.)

There may be situations where you have data running across the page, with one column per record and one field per row. To sort data in this format, choose the Left to right option button in the Direction section. Once you do so, the drop-down lists on the Sort Criteria tab contain the field names from the first column in the range.

 While Excel can also handle sorting columns rather than rows, when you do so, there's no way to indicate that the first column contains field names rather than actual data. In Calc, once you specify Left to right sorting, the appropriate check box updates to say "Range contains row labels."

How do I limit the data displayed?

Another option with data is to limit which records display by filtering based on the data. The easiest way to do this is to choose Data | Filter | AutoFilter. When you do so, each column header (field name) turns into a drop-down list that includes each unique value for that field, as well as "- all -" and "- Top 10 -." You can open any of the lists and choose an item to restrict the display to records that match your choice in each field. When you make a choice from one of the drop-down lists, the drop arrow turns blue, so you know you filtered on that column. **Figure 8** shows the data from Figure 1 set up for this type of filtering, while **Figure 9** shows the same portion of the spreadsheet after choosing "PA" from the State drop-down and "Phila." from the City drop-down.

First Name	Last Name	Address	City	State	Zip
John	Smith	1234 N. Front St.	Phila.	PA	19122
Mary	Jones	17 S. 10th St.	Phila.	PA	19103
Robert	Rodgers	47 Church Road	Elkins Park	PA	19027
Elizabeth	Martin	1776 Patriots Drive	Boston	MA	02120
Howard	Bailey	94 Ocean Drive	Venice	CA	92403

Figure 8. The AutoFilter option lets you turn field names into drop-down lists for filtering on that column.

First Name	Last Name	Address	City	State	Zip
John	Smith	1234 N. Front St.	Phila.	PA	19122
Mary	Jones	17 S. 10th St.	Phila.	PA	19103

Figure 9. After filtering on the City and State columns, only two rows of the data area display. The other rows are hidden from view.

You can make the drop-down arrows disappear by choosing Data | Filter | AutoFilter again or by choosing Data | Filter | Hide AutoFilter from the menu. When you do so, any hidden records remain hidden, so you may want to reset the filtered columns beforehand (by selecting "- all -" from the drop-down list).

You can also filter data using more complex conditions much as you do in the Data Sources dialog. Choose Data | Filter | Standard Filter or choose "- Standard -" from any of the AutoFilter drop-down lists to open the Standard Filter dialog (**Figure 10**). The dialog lets you specify three conditions, each based on a single field, and combine them with AND or OR.

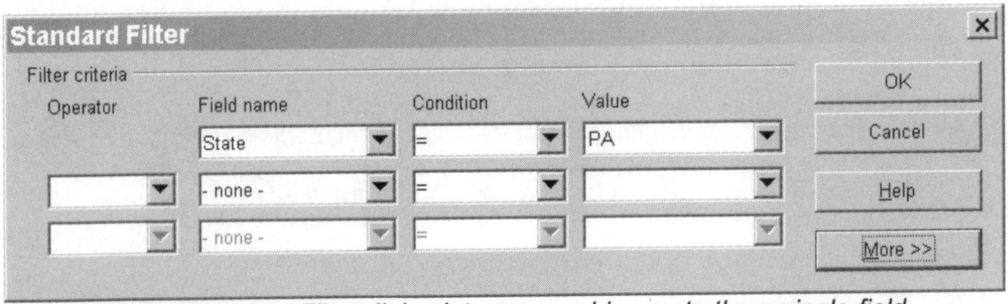

Figure 10. The Standard Filter dialog lets you combine up to three single-field conditions with AND or OR.

Each condition contains a field name, an operator, and a value. The operators include the usual tests for equality, greater than, less than, greater than or equal, and less than or equal, as well as finding the smallest n, the largest n, the smallest n%, or the largest n%. The four smallest and largest operators work only with numbers and dates, not with text values. The Value drop-down list includes all the values in the specified field, as well as the special values "- empty -" and "- not empty -."

Figure 11 shows another simple data set, this one including people's name, birth date, height, and weight. In **Figure 12**, a filter is set to find the oldest member of the group (the one with the smallest birth date). **Figure 13** shows the results.

Name	BirthDate	Height	Weight
Smith	03/27/60	65	185
Jones	09/29/70	68	175
Martin	12/01/58	66	150
Jackson	08/23/34	65	172
Brown	07/17/68	70	180
Roberts	01/22/54	64	152
Olson	02/29/64	67	160

Figure 11. Data in a spreadsheet shows people's birth date, height, and weight.

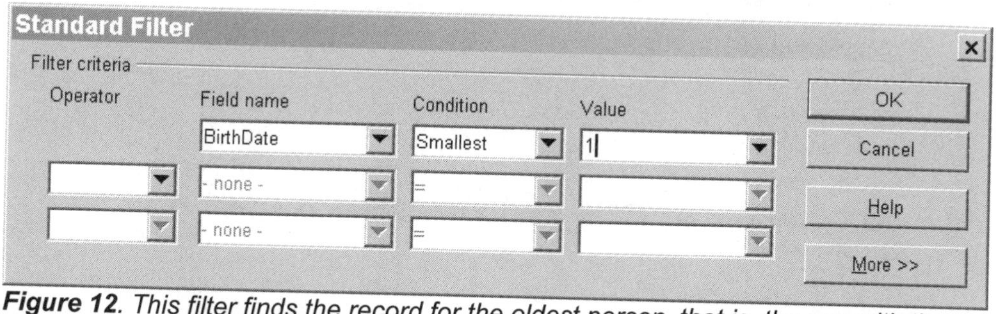

Figure 12. This filter finds the record for the oldest person, that is, the one with the smallest (earliest) birth date.

Name	BirthDate	Height	Weight
Jackson	08/23/34	65	172

Figure 13. After applying the filter in Figure 12, only one record appears.

The Value drop-down list uses auto-completion, jumping to the first value that matches what you typed so far. When entering the number for a smallest or largest filter or the percent for a smallest % or largest % filter, you may have to delete unwanted characters. For example, in Figure 12, when I typed 1, the value "12/01/1968" appeared. It was necessary to delete everything after the "1" to get the right result.

The More button on the Standard Filter dialog expands the dialog (**Figure 14**) to include additional options, including case-sensitivity. As with the Sort dialog, you can specify whether the range to be filtered includes the field names and you can put the filter results elsewhere, leaving the original data untouched. (The copy is independent of the original data, so changes to the original don't change the copy.)

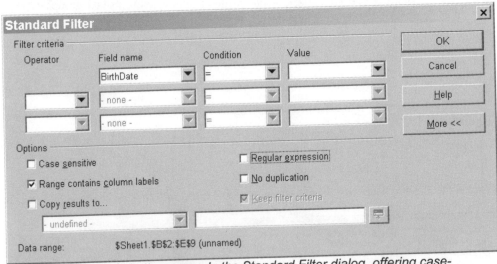

Figure 14. The More button expands the Standard Filter dialog, offering case-sensitivity, recognition of field names, and more.

How do I compute totals and subtotals for groups of records?

Data can often be broken into subgroups, for example, all records from a particular state or all records from a particular year. Once you have such subgroups, it can be useful to compute aggregate results for those groups, including subtotals, averages, and so forth. To group and compute aggregates for data in Calc, make sure focus is in the data area, and choose Data | Subtotals. The Subtotals dialog (**Figure 15**) appears.

You can specify up to three levels of grouping. At each level, you indicate which field to group on using the Group by drop-down list. Next, you can specify what kind of aggregation to do for each field. (The dialog calls this a "subtotal" whether you're computing the sum, average, count, or something more complex.) To specify a "subtotal," select a field, and then choose the function to apply to that field. In Figure 15, records are grouped by State and the count for each state is computed. **Figure 16** shows the results, including the ability to expand and contract each group or the data as a whole.

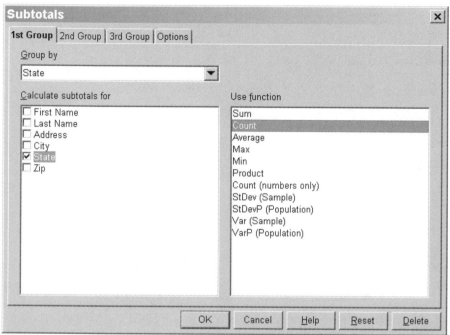

Figure 15. Use the Subtotals dialog to break data into groups and provide aggregate data for each group.

	First Name	Last Name	Address	City	State	Zip
	Howard	Bailey	94 Ocean Drive	Venice	CA	92403
						1
	Elizabeth	Martin	1776 Patriots Drive	Boston	MA	02120
						1
	John	Smith	1234 N. Front St.	Phila.	PA	19122
	Robert	Rodgers	47 Church Road	Elkins Park	PA	19027
	Mary	Jones	17 S. 10th St.	Phila.	PA	19103
						3
						5

Figure 16. When you compute subtotals, controls appear in the margin to let you expand and contract the groups. Click a "-" to contract a group; click a "+" to expand it. The underlined number after each group is the count for that group.

How do I restrict data to valid values?

Often, the acceptable values for a particular field are limited in some way. You can set up your spreadsheet data to impose those restrictions and even help users enter data that follows the rules. To do this, highlight the cells to restrict and choose Data | Validity from the menu. The Validity dialog opens. Use the Criteria tab (**Figure 17**) to specify the restrictions for that field. In the Allow drop-down, you indicate the type of data permitted, such as whole numbers or dates. Use the other controls on the tab to limit the data further. For example, you might restrict a field to dates between January 1, 2003 and December 31, 2003. The Allow blanks check box determines whether cells in the specified range may be empty or not.

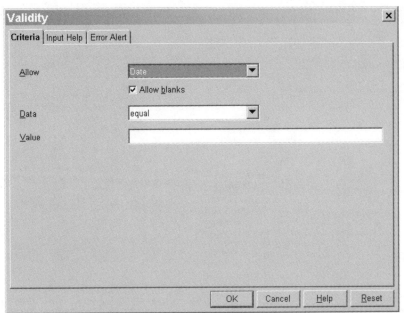

Figure 17. On the Criteria tab of the Validity dialog, you indicate acceptable values.

Once you specify some criteria, you must set up error reporting to actually have your criteria applied. Use the Error Alert tab (**Figure 18**) of the dialog. At a minimum, you need to select the Show error message when invalid values are entered check box. You can also specify what the error message will say by entering a title and message. If you leave those items blank, the error message simply says "Invalid value"; you probably want to help the user out by providing more information. **Figure 19** shows the error message defined in Figure 18, which displays when something other than a date is entered in the specified cells. After dismissing the dialog, the newly entered value is removed.

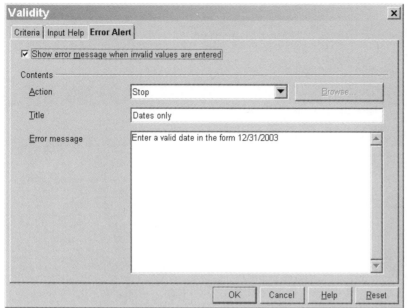

Figure 18. *The Error Alert tab lets you customize the error message displayed when a user enters a value that doesn't meet the criteria specified.*

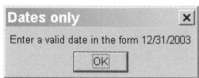

Figure 19. *This custom error message, defined in Figure 18, displays when a value other than a date is entered in the restricted range.*

The middle tab of the dialog, Input Help (**Figure 20**), lets you guide yourself (or those using the spreadsheet you create) so you can avoid error messages. Select the check box, and then specify a title and message to appear when focus lands on any of the cells in the range. **Figure 21** shows the tip defined in Figure 20.

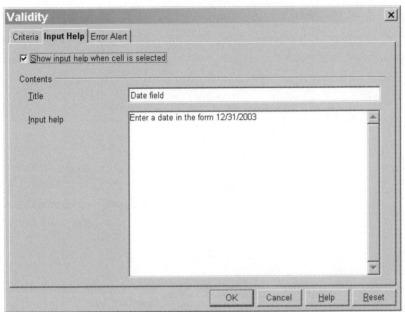

Figure 20. The Input Help tab lets you guide users so they can avoid error messages.

Figure 21. You can guide yourself or others in using a spreadsheet you create by specifying input help for restricted fields.

Turning off restrictions on data is harder than it should be. You need to change the Allow drop-down on the Criteria tab to "All," as well as clear the check boxes on the Input Help and Error Alert tabs.

How do I create a pivot table?

A pivot table lets you reorganize and summarize data to look at it in different ways. To create a pivot table in Calc, you use the DataPilot. To get started, choose Data | DataPilot | Start from the menu. A dialog (**Figure 22**) appears asking where to find the data. Choose Current Selection to use data from the spreadsheet; choose Data source registered in OpenOffice.org to use external data without putting it into the workbook. The third option on this dialog ("External source/interface") is unavailable at this time.

Figure 22. *This dialog appears for you to identify the data source when you start the DataPilot.*

If you choose to use a registered data source, the Select Data Source dialog (**Figure 23**) appears. Choose the data source, and then choose the table within the data source that contains the data you want to slice and dice.

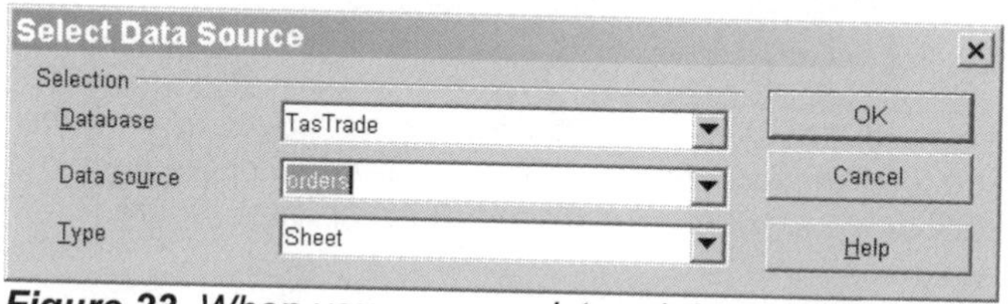

Figure 23. *When you use a registered data source, you need to specify the database and table.*

Once you specify the data to use, the DataPilot (**Figure 24**) opens, and you can set up the pivot table. Drag the fields to the positions where they should be placed. If you put a field in the row or column area, you get one row or column for each distinct value of that field. When you drop a field into the data area, by default, you get the total for that field for the specified values of the row and column data. **Figure 25** shows the set-up for a simple pivot table that shows total sales for each product by employee.

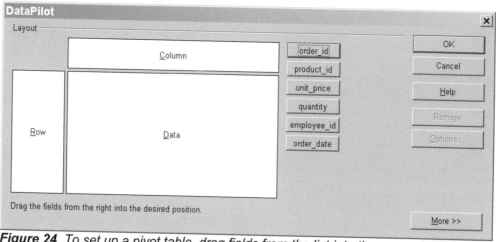

Figure 24. *To set up a pivot table, drag fields from the list into the row, column, and data areas. By default, fields dropped in the data area are totaled.*

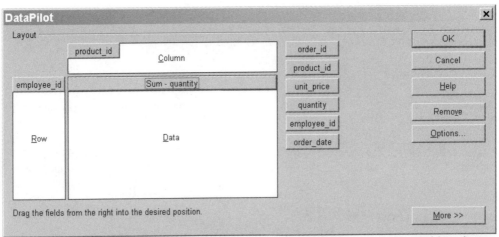

Figure 25. In this example, the pivot table has one row for each employee id and one column for each product id. The intersection of a row with a column indicates how many units of the specified product were sold by the specified employee. Figure 26 shows the results for this set-up.

Once the Pivot Table is set up as desired, click OK and the pivot table is inserted into the workbook. When working with data already in the sheet, Calc places the pivot table directly below the data range. With external data, it places the pivot table with the upper left corner at the cell with focus when the DataPilot started. **Figure 26** shows a portion of the pivot table created by the set-up shown in Figure 25.

	Filter							
2824	Filter							
2825								
2826	Sum - quantity	product_id						
2827	employee_id	1	2	3	4	5	6	7
2828	1	3	100000					10
2829	2	83	99		106	24	76	3
2830	3	455	343	110	79	120		104
2831	4	18	39	9	26	12	1	76
2832	5	117	92	30	85	115	48	180
2833	6	75	176	30	87			60
2834	7	75	140	14	21			22
2835	8	20		20	25			
2836	9	286	413	160	154	105	47	228
2837	10	80	30	20	10		82	20
2838	13				50		70	93
2839	14	25						5
2840	15	52	55	28				34
2841	Total Result	1289	101387	421	643	376	324	835

Figure 26. This pivot table, set up as shown in Figure 25, indicates how many of each product each employee sold. Both rows and columns are totaled.

You can create much more complex pivot tables than the simple cross-tabulation shown in Figure 26. For example, you can include more than one field in the row or column area. When you do so, you get all combinations of the fields listed. For example, if you include both employee_id and order_date in the row area, the resulting pivot table has one row for each combination of employee and date, showing the orders for each product taken by that employee on that date. **Figure 27** shows a partial result in this case—note that with the example data in use, most of the cells in the result are empty.

> *The ways you can combine fields in the row and column area is limited by the size of a spreadsheet. Because you get one row or column in the result for each combination of values specified, the number of rows or columns you need can grow very fast. This is a particular problem for columns as Calc is limited to 256 columns. The row limit is 32,000, so you have more flexibility in that direction.*

Filter						
Sum - quantity		product_id				
employee_id	order_date	1	2	3	4	5
1	07/11/92					
	08/29/92					
	10/24/92					
	12/17/92					
	12/26/92					
	01/14/93					
	03/05/93					
	04/01/93					
	06/25/93					
	08/07/93					
	08/14/93					
	09/08/93					
	09/18/93					
	10/02/93					
	10/26/93					
	11/10/93					
	12/25/93					
	01/04/94					

Figure 27. A pivot table can include multiple fields in either the row or column area (or both). In this example, you see the sales of each product by each employee on a daily basis.

You can also include more than one field in the data area. When you do so, the resulting pivot table has one row for each of those fields for each combination otherwise specified by the rows.

The data fields aren't restricted to totaling, either. Once you put a field in the data area, you can click Options to bring up a list of functions (**Figure 28**) you can apply to the field. **Figure 29** shows the set-up for a pivot table that shows both the number of units sold and the average unit price for those sales; **Figure 30** shows part of the resulting pivot table.

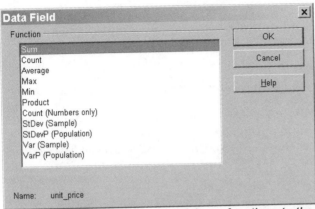

Figure 28. You can apply any of these functions to the fields placed in the data area.

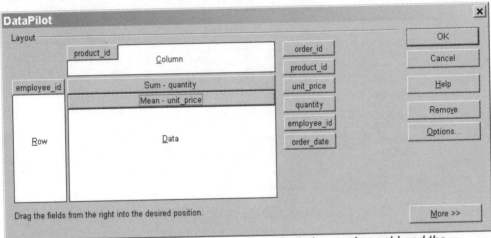

Figure 29. The pivot table specified here shows both the number sold and the average unit price for each combination of employee and product. Although the dialog says "Mean – unit price," the Average function was chosen in the Data Field dialog.

Filter							
		product_id					
employee_id	Data	1	2	3	4	5	6
1	Sum - quanti▶	3	100000				
	Average - uni▶	$18.00	$19.00				
2	Sum - quanti▶	83	99		106	24	76
	Average - uni▶	$16.80	$18.37		$19.72	$19.18	$25.00
3	Sum - quanti▶	455	343	110	79	120	
	Average - uni▶	$15.47	$16.69	$7.67	$16.40	$19.20	
4	Sum - quanti▶	18	39	9	26	12	1
	Average - uni▶	$14.40	$19.00	$10.00	$22.00	$17.00	$25.00
5	Sum - quanti▶	117	92	30	85	115	48
	Average - uni▶	$16.10	$17.10	$8.00	$19.00	$19.51	$18.50
6	Sum - quanti▶	75	176	30	87		
	Average - uni▶	$14.80	$16.83	$10.00	$19.80		
7	Sum - quanti▶	75	140	14	21		
	Average - uni▶	$14.20	$14.32	$10.00	$22.00		
8	Sum - quanti▶	20		20	25		
	Average - uni▶	$18.00		$7.00	$22.00		
9	Sum - quanti▶	286	413	160	154	105	47
	Average - uni▶	$15.60	$17.35	$10.00	$18.33	$16.30	$21.88
10	Sum - quanti▶	80	30	20	10		82
	Average - uni▶	$18.00	$13.30	$10.00	$17.60		$25.00
13	Sum - quantity					50	70
	Average - unit_price					$22.00	$25.00
14	Sum - quanti▶	25					
	Average - uni▶	$18.00					
15	Sum - quanti▶	52	55	28			
	Average - uni▶	$13.50	$17.00	$7.00			
Total Sum - quantity		1289	101387	421	643	376	324
Total Average - unit_price		$15.85	$16.97	$9.06	$19.27	$18.45	$23.18

Figure 30. *This is the pivot table defined in Figure 29. It shows both total number and average unit price sold for each item.*

Click the More button in the dialog for additional control over the result. You can specify where to put the pivot table, including an entirely new sheet, whether to total rows and columns, and more.

Manipulating a pivot table

Once you create a pivot table, you're not done. You can modify the results in several ways. First, you can rearrange the rows and columns. To do so, drag the button with the field name to a different position and drop it. The pivot table reorganizes the results. For example, Figure 27 shows rows grouped first by employee_id, and then by order_date. You can drag the order_date button to the left of the employee_id button to get the results shown in **Figure 31**. You can change a column into a row or a row into a column by dragging its button to the appropriate location.

Filter							
Sum - quantity		product_id					
order_date	employee_id	1	2	3	4	5	6
05/09/92	5						
05/12/92	10						
05/13/92	6						
05/14/92	7						
05/15/92	7						
05/19/92	8						
05/20/92	5						
05/21/92	9						
05/22/92	3						
05/23/92	5						
05/27/92	7						
05/28/92	2						
05/29/92	3						
05/30/92	6						
06/02/92	3						
06/04/92	9						
06/05/92	13						
06/06/92	14						
06/09/92	4						
06/10/92	5						
06/12/92	14						
06/13/92	9	60					
06/16/92	15						

Figure 31. You can rearrange the rows or columns of a pivot table. Using the version in Figure 27, this arrangement was created by dragging the order_date button to the left.

You can also cut down the data a pivot table displays. Click the Filter button at the top of the pivot table to open the Filter dialog **(Figure 32),** where you can specify up to three conditions combined with AND and OR to apply to the pivot table.

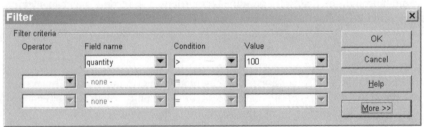

Figure 32. Use the Filter dialog to cut down the data in a pivot table.

Figure 33 shows the result when the filter "quantity>100" is applied to the pivot table in Figure 26. Note that the filter applies to the original data, not to the sum shown in the pivot table.

In Microsoft Excel, the row and column labels open drop-down lists showing the values for that item. You can choose a value on which to filter. Calc doesn't offer this feature.

Filter								
Sum - quanti▶	product_id							
employee_id	2	24	27	29	39	40	41	
1	100000							
3				110			120	
9		110	120		130			
10						998		
Total Result	100000	110	120	110	130	998	120	

Figure 33. You can cut down the data in a pivot table by filtering.

Summary

While it can't do everything a database application can do, Calc offers a lot of power for manipulating tabular data. It lets you connect to external data sources, sort, filter and subtotal data, limit input to ensure correct data, and create pivot tables to "slice and dice" your data.

In the next chapter, you will see why a picture is worth 1000 words, as I examine Calc's graphing abilities.

> Updates and corrections to this chapter can be found on Hentzenwerke's web site, **www.hentzenwerke.com**. Click "Catalog" and navigate to the page for this book.

Chapter 10
Working with Graphs and Charts

Most people understand information better when presented as a graph or chart than when they look at the raw data. Calc has the ability to graph data in a variety of ways and offers a wizard-type interface to guide you.

For some reason, spreadsheet programs tend to use the term "chart" for what most people call a "graph," a pictorial representation of data. This chapter uses the two terms interchangeably.

How do I create a graph?

There are a couple of ways to start the process of adding a graph to a spreadsheet. You can choose Insert | Chart from the menu. When you do so, the AutoFormat Chart dialog (**Figure 1**) appears. You can click the Insert Object button on the Main toolbar. (If it's not currently set for adding a chart, you need to long click and choose Insert Chart from the toolbar that appears.) In that case, the mouse pointer changes (as shown in **Figure 2**) and you need to click the location in the spreadsheet where the graph should go. After that, the AutoFormat Chart dialog opens.

AutoFormat Chart		✕

Selection

Range |$Sheet1.$A$1:$AI$52

☑ First row as label

☑ First column as label

Chart results in worksheet

Sheet1 ▼

If the selected cells do not contain the desired data, select the data range now.

Include the cells containing column and row labels if you want them to be included in your chart.

Help	Cancel	<< Back	Next >>	Create

Figure 1. The AutoFormat Chart dialog guides you through the initial creation of a graph.

Figure 2. When you use the Insert Chart item from the Main toolbar, the mouse pointer changes to indicate you need to click the position for the graph.

If data is highlighted when you begin graphing, Calc assumes that's the data to graph (the *data range*). If no cells are selected when you begin graphing, Calc makes an intelligent guess as to what constitutes the data to be graphed. You can override Calc's assumption in either case by typing a range into the dialog, or by pointing to the right range. (As in other dialogs, use the Shrink button to get the dialog out of the way.) By default, each selected column constitutes a data series in the graph.

The two check boxes in Figure 1 indicate whether the first row and first column of the data being graphed contain labels for use in the graph and the legend. Again, Calc makes a pretty good guess based on what it finds.

The drop-down list lets you specify the destination for the graph. You can put it on any existing sheet of the workbook, or create a new sheet. The graph is placed at the cursor position on the specified sheet. A graph is a free-floating object, so you can move it on the worksheet once it's created.

Once the settings for data, labels, and destination are correct, click Next to go to the next page (**Figure 3**), where you specify the type of graph to create. See "What kinds of graphs can I create?" later in this chapter for specifics. On this page and all subsequent pages of this dialog, you can indicate whether the data you want to graph is in columns or rows.

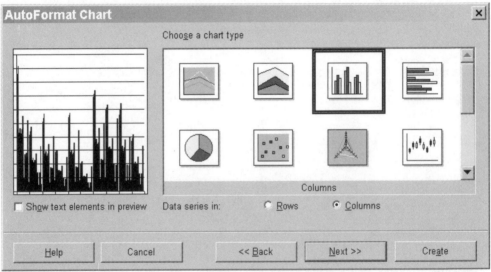

Figure 3. *The second page of the AutoFormat Chart dialog lets you choose the type of graph to create.*

The diagram on the left shows a preview of the graph. As you change the type of graph, the diagram changes. Select the check box to include legends and labels in the preview. Note that when you do so, the preview won't necessarily show all data items. For performance reasons, the number of data items shown is limited.

When you're happy with your choices on this page, click Next to move to the third page (**Figure 4**) where you choose from among variants for the chosen graph type. Depending on the type of graph chosen, you may also be able to indicate whether to include grid lines for the X, Y, and/or Z axis.

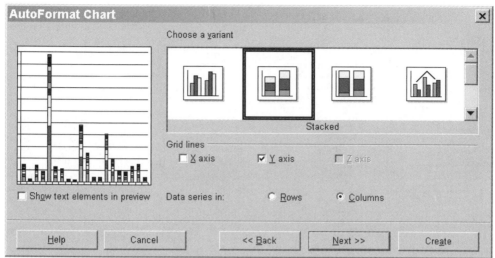

Figure 4. Once you select a graph type, you can specify details for the type of graph.

Again, click Next when you have the choices you want on this page.

The final page of the dialog (**Figure 5**) lets you specify various titles and indicate whether the graph has a legend, an area that maps colors to the information they represent. You get one last chance to switch between columns and rows for your data, as well.

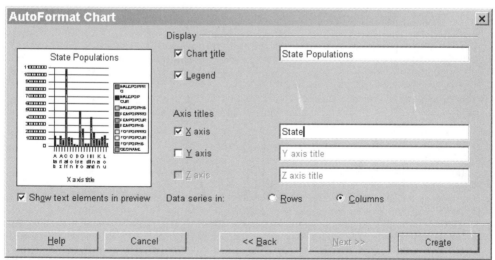

Figure 5. The fourth page of the dialog deals principally with the textual components of the graph, titles and legends.

When all the settings are as you want them, click Create to generate the graph. **Figure 6** shows some of the data being graphed, while **Figure 7** shows the graph created in the previous figures. As you can see, this graph needs some work before it's really usable. (Actually, the choice of stacked bars for this particular data makes the graph fairly meaningless.)

	A	B	C	D	E	F	G	H	I
1	GEONAME	GEONAME	TOTPOPHI	TOTPOPCU	TOTPOPPR	FEMPOPHI	FEMPOPCU	FEMPOPPR	MALEPOPH
2	Alabama	4040587	4221932	4455517	2104727	2194735	2313044	1935860	2027197
3	Alaska	550043	610350	679683	260230	289206	323009	289813	321144
4	Arizona	3665228	4000398	4452859	1854696	2020893	2246862	1810532	1979505
5	Arkansas	2350725	2441646	2566937	1217920	1262166	1324423	1132805	1179480
6	California	29760022	31546602	33575312	14863538	15749642	16767433	14896483	15796959
7	Colorado	3294394	3630585	4079905	1663315	1829591	2053524	1631079	1800994
8	Connecticut	3287116	3275195	3261723	1694467	1685708	1677174	1592649	1589487
9	Delaware	666168	707864	757702	343224	364186	389614	322944	343678
10	District Of O	606900	571592	530751	324005	304640	282896	282895	266952
11	Florida	12937926	13849741	14933526	6676616	7134287	7682227	6261410	6715454
12	Georgia	6478216	7020384	7713623	3334160	3606091	3957412	3144056	3414293
13	Hawaii	1108229	1186692	1278719	544330	585344	633386	563899	601348
14	Idaho	1006749	1120679	1270278	505853	562163	636315	500896	558516
15	Illinois	11430602	11760900	12177648	5879080	6037679	6242901	5551522	5723221
16	Indiana	5544159	5752928	6017915	2856315	2957899	3089520	2687844	2795029
17	Iowa	2776755	2823048	2880078	1432397	1453192	1480271	1344358	1369856
18	Kansas	2477574	2543745	2625638	1263216	1294143	1333637	1214358	1249602
19	Kentucky	3685296	3814122	3981255	1900357	1963079	2045975	1784939	1851043
20	Louisiana	4219973	4313195	4419968	2188796	2232628	2285361	2031177	2080567
21	Maine	1227928	1241451	1256627	630181	635781	642393	597747	605670
22	Maryland	4781468	5008060	5278406	2463018	2575802	2712835	2318450	2432258
23	Massachuse⤴	6016425	6012972	6041000	3128254	3120601	3130873	2888171	2892371
24	Michigan	9295297	9521288	9784220	4783173	4889877	5017593	4512124	4631411

Figure 6. When this data is graphed in a stacked bar chart (which isn't really meaningful in this case), the state names in column A become labels on the X axis and the titles in Row 1 are used in the legend.

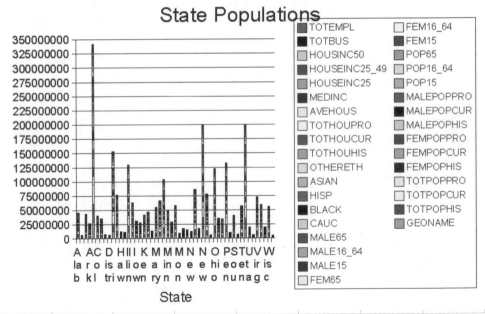

Figure 7. The first attempt at a graph may need some tweaking.

Fortunately, you're not stuck with the graph as you originally build it. You have considerable flexibility in modifying a graph to get just what you want. See "How do I change a graph?" later in this chapter for details.

What kinds of graphs can I make?

Although Calc offers fewer types of graphs than Microsoft Excel, there's still quite a variety. The list contains both two-dimensional and three-dimensional options. Almost every type of chart has several variants. **Table 1** lists the chart types and their variants.

Table 1. Calc's graphing engine includes a wide variety of graph types.

Graph type	Description	Variants
Lines	Uses a different-colored line or curve for each data series.	Normal, Stacked, Percent, Symbols, Stacked with symbols, Percent with symbols, Cubic Spline. Cubic Spline with symbols, B-Spline, B-Spline with symbols
Areas	Uses an independent line for each data series, filling the area under the line with color.	Normal, Stacked, Percent
Columns	Creates a vertical bar chart using a different-colored set of bars for each data series.	Normal, Stacked, Percent, Lines and columns, Lines and stacked columns
Bars	Creates a horizontal bar chart using a different-colored set of bars for each data series.	Normal, Stacked, Percent
Pies	Creates a pie chart. Most variants can only use one data series.	Normal, Rings, Offset (two variations)
XY chart	Plots one data series against another.	Symbols only, Lines with symbols, Lines only, Cubic Spline, Cubic Spline with symbols, B-Spline, B-Spline with symbols
Net	Circular graph with a separate Y axis for each item on the X axis. Points within a data series are connected to form a polygon.	Normal, Stacked, Percent, Symbols, Stacked with symbols, Percent with symbols
Stock chart	Shows change from one data series to the next for each X value.	Four variations using different graphical representations of the change.
3D Lines	Shows each data series as a different-colored 3D surface.	Deep
3D Areas	Shows each data series as a different-colored solid	Stacked, Percent, Deep
3D Bars	Creates a 3D horizontal bar chart with different-colored bars for each data series.	Normal, Stacked, Percent, Deep, Tubes, Tubes stacked, Tubes percent, Tubes deep, Horizontal pyramids, Horizontal pyramids stacked, Horizontal pyramids percent, Horizontal pyramids deep, Horizontal cones, Horizontal cones stacked, Horizontal cones percent, Horizontal cones deep
3D columns	Creates a 3D vertical bar chart with different-colored bars for each data series.	Normal, Stacked, Percent, Deep, Tubes, Tubes stacked, Tubes percent, Tubes deep, Horizontal pyramids, Horizontal pyramids stacked, Horizontal pyramids percent, Horizontal pyramids deep, Horizontal cones, Horizontal cones stacked, Horizontal cones percent, Horizontal cones deep

The best way to get a handle on what the various types of graphs do is to take a simple data set with a couple of data series and run through the options.

How do I change a graph?

Once you create a graph, you can change almost anything about it from its position on the spreadsheet to its type to the data it's based on. In many cases, the hardest part is getting access to what you want to change.

When you click a graph, the entire graph is selected as an object. Green sizing handles appear at the four corners and in the middle of each side. The shortcut menu for the selected graph contains items related to the size and position of the graph. With one exception (discussed later in this chapter), none of the shortcut menu items reflect the content of the graph. The Drawing Object toolbar replaces the Spreadsheet Object toolbar. The remainder of this chapter refers to this single click action as "selecting the graph."

Double-click a graph to get "inside" so you can work with the content. When you double-click, a gray border appears (as in **Figure** 7) to indicate you're editing the graph. The shortcut menu includes a variety of items for changing the content of the graph, such as the labels on the axes and the legend. The Main toolbar changes to include a variety of options for editing the graph. The rest of this chapter refers to this double-click action as "editing the graph."

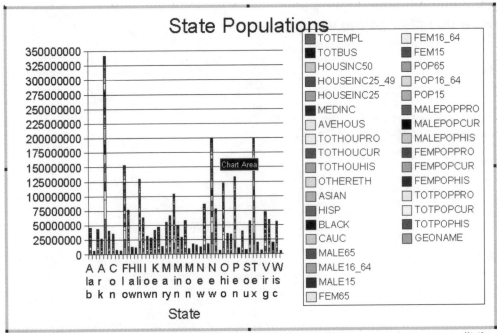

Figure 7. When you double-click a graph, a gray border appears and you can edit the components of the graph.

Once the gray border displays, you can click various components of the graph, such as the legend, the axes, or the actual graphed data (the "chart wall") to select that component. The shortcut menu includes items for modifying that component. This action is called "selecting the <component>" in the following discussion, where "<component>" refers to a particular component of the graph.

You can also double-click textual components (such as titles) once you're editing the graph. This enables direct editing of the contents rather than the appearance of the component. The following discussion refers to this action as "editing the <component>."

Once you select or edit a component of the graph, you can't return directly to editing the graph as a whole. When you click elsewhere within the graph, the graph as a whole is selected (although the gray border persists indicating editing mode). You need to click outside the graph area and double-click the graph again to return to editing the graph.

To stop editing a graph or its components, click outside the graph area in the spreadsheet.

The following sections describe the various techniques for changing the components of a graph.

How do I move a graph?

To move a graph within the worksheet, select it and drag it to the new location. You can also move a graph by selecting it, cutting it, and then pasting it at the new location. Finally, you can move a graph by selecting it and choosing Position and Size from the shortcut menu or Format | Position and Size from the menu. On the Position tab, specify the X and Y coordinates where the upper left corner of the graph is placed.

How do I change the size of a graph?

To resize a graph, select it and put the mouse over one of the green sizing handles. Click and drag to the new size. Alternatively, the Position tab of the Position and Size dialog (Format | Position and Size from the menu or Position and Size from the shortcut menu), lets you specify the exact size you want.

How do I change the type of graph?

Double-click to edit the graph. Next, choose Format | Chart Type from the menu, Chart Type from the shortcut menu, or Edit Chart Type from the Main toolbar. The Chart Type dialog (**Figure 8**) opens, showing the current type. Choose the chart type and variant you want and click OK.

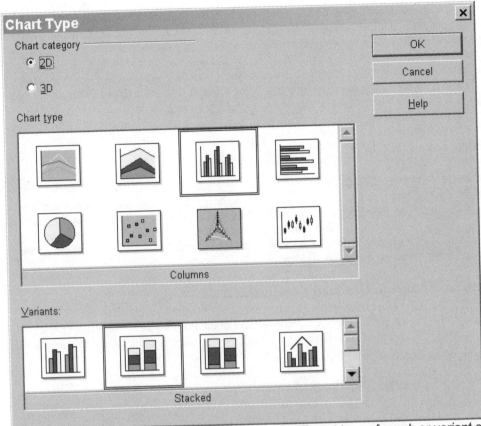

Figure 8. Use the Chart Type dialog to choose a different type of graph or variant of the type you originally chose.

How do I change the data in a graph?

The data for the graph is the one content item changed by selecting the graph rather than editing the graph. The shortcut menu when you select the graph includes Modify Data Range. When you choose it, the Modify chart data range window appears. It's the first page of the AutoFormat Chart dialog with the destination drop-down list disabled. You can type in or point to the desired range. When you press the Create button, the chart updates.

How do I change a graph's main title?

The main title appears centered at the top of the graph. To change the text of the title, edit the title by double-clicking first on the graph, and then on the title. The title takes on a special border (**Figure 9**) to show that it's editable. Edit the text to provide the new title.

Figure 9. When you double-click a title, the border indicates the text is editable.

To modify the appearance of the main title, select the title and choose Object Properties from the shortcut menu or Format | Object Properties from the menu. The Title dialog (**Figure 10**) appears. You can add a border to the title, change the font, font size, font style, and much more.

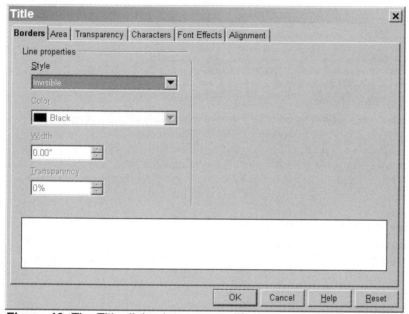

Figure 10. The Title dialog lets you modify the appearance of the title, including changing the font and style, adding a background color, border, or rotating the title.

When the title is selected, you can move it around within the graph by dragging it or with the keyboard arrows. For example, you might move the title to the left side of the graph and switch to vertical text.

How do I change the axis titles?

Changing the title that appears for the X, Y, or Z axis is the same as editing the main title. To modify the title text, double-click the graph, double-click the title to edit, and edit the text. To modify the appearance, select the title and open the title dialog from the menu or shortcut menu.

Is there an easier way to change the text for multiple titles?

If you need to change the text of more than one title, double-clicking each and editing can get tedious. Instead, you can choose edit the graph and choose Insert | Title from the menu to open the Titles dialog (**Figure 11**). For each title you want to include, select the appropriate check box and type the text you want.

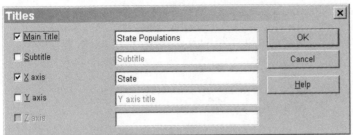

Figure 11. The titles dialog lets you change the text of all titles in one shot.

How do I turn off all titles?

The Titles dialog (shown in Figure 11) offers one way to turn off all titles—just clear each check box. However, you can also turn off titles using the Main toolbar. When you edit the graph, the toolbar includes a Titles On/Off button and an Axes Title On/Off button. Be aware that turning on titles using the toolbar is equivalent to selecting all of the relevant check boxes in the Titles dialog. For example, in the graph in Figure 7, if you click the Titles On/Off button twice, when the main title reappears, so does a subtitle with the text "subtitle."

How do I change the legend?

The legend of a graph tells what the various colors and/or symbols stand for. The text of the legend is automatically generated (based on the row or column labels and the type of graph) and can't be changed. (Neither can the symbols used for each data range.) However, the appearance and position of the legend can.

To change the appearance of the legend, select the legend and choose Object Properties from the shortcut menu or Format | Object Properties from the menu. The Legend dialog appears; it's similar to the Title dialog shown in Figure 10. However, the last tab of the Legend dialog (**Figure 12**) specifies the position of the legend in the graph. By default, Calc places legends to the right of the graphed data.

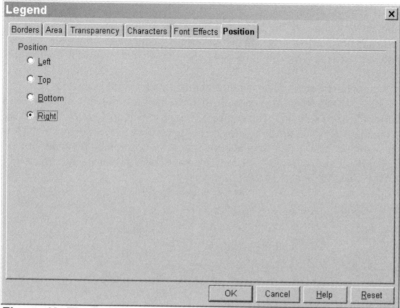

Figure 12. *The Position tab of the Legend dialog lets you specify the location of the legend within the graph area.*

You can also specify the position of the legend, as well as whether or not it should appear, by choosing Insert | Legend from the menu when editing the graph. A cut-down version of the Legend dialog (**Figure 13**) appears. The Display check box determines whether the legend is shown. The Position option buttons determine its position.

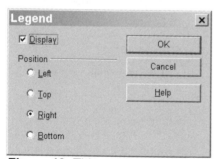

Figure 13. *This version of the Legend dialog appears when you choose Insert | Legend from the menu.*

When the legend is selected, you position it by dragging or with the keyboard. Also, when you edit the graph, the Main toolbar includes a Legend On/Off button. Note that turning the legend off does not resize or reposition the chart itself. The area previously occupied by the legend is left empty.

How do I change the axes?

You can control a number of features of the X, Y, and Z axes, including whether or not they are displayed, the style and color of the line, whether descriptive labels are shown, and the scale used for the axis. As with the other graph features, there are different ways to control the various aspects of the axes.

While editing the graph, the Format menu and the shortcut menu contain an Axis item with a submenu listing the various axes and a special All Axes item. Choose any of these items to open the Axis dialog (**Figure 14**), where you control the appearance of the axes themselves, and the labels along the axes. The title for this dialog varies according to the menu choice used to access it. (You can also open this dialog for a particular axis by positioning the mouse over the axis and double-clicking. Use the tooltip to determine when the mouse is positioned correctly.)

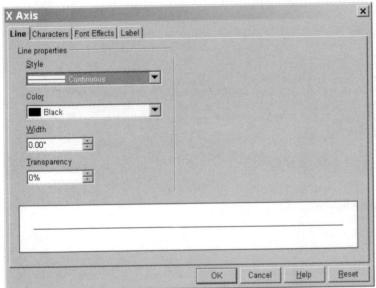

Figure 14. The Axis dialog controls both the appearance of the axis line, and the appearance of the labels on that axis.

Change Style to Invisible on the Line tab to prevent a line from being drawn for the axis.

The tabs available in the Axis dialog vary depending on the axis. If the axis is numeric, it includes Scale and Numbers tabs. The Numbers tab controls the format used for the numeric labels and is based on the Numbers tab of the Format Cells dialog (discussed in Chapter 8, "Creating Simple Spreadsheets"). The Scale tab (**Figure 15**) lets you control the starting and ending values on the axis, the interval between points shown, and more. Generally, Calc does a pretty good job of setting these based on the data, but there are times when you need more control. You can also use this tab to change an axis to use a logarithmic scale for those situations where the data warrants it.

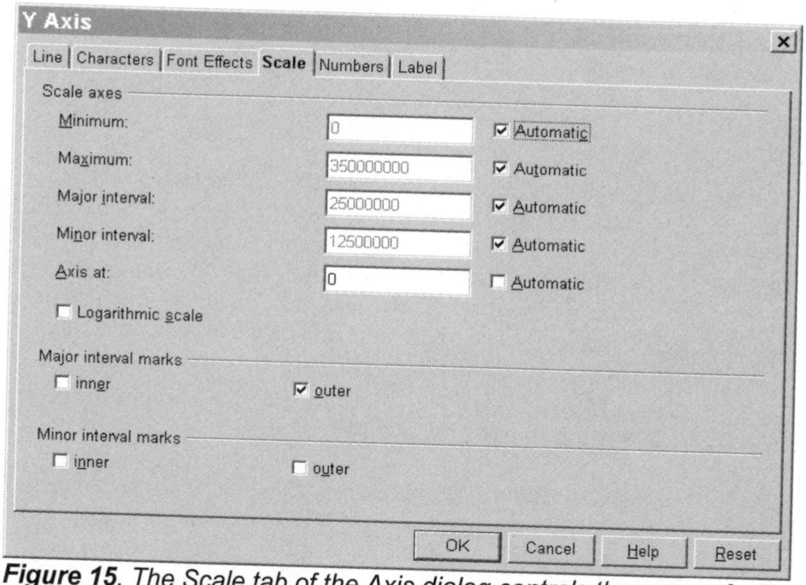

Figure 15. *The Scale tab of the Axis dialog controls the range of values and the size of intervals along the axis.*

The Characters, Font Effects, and Label tabs (**Figure 16**) of the Axis dialog affect the labels that appear next to or below the axis line. On the Label tab, you can turn labels off, or you can modify the way they appear, for example, staggering them to make them fit better. Another thing to try if axis labels don't fit is rotating them, also available on the Label tab.

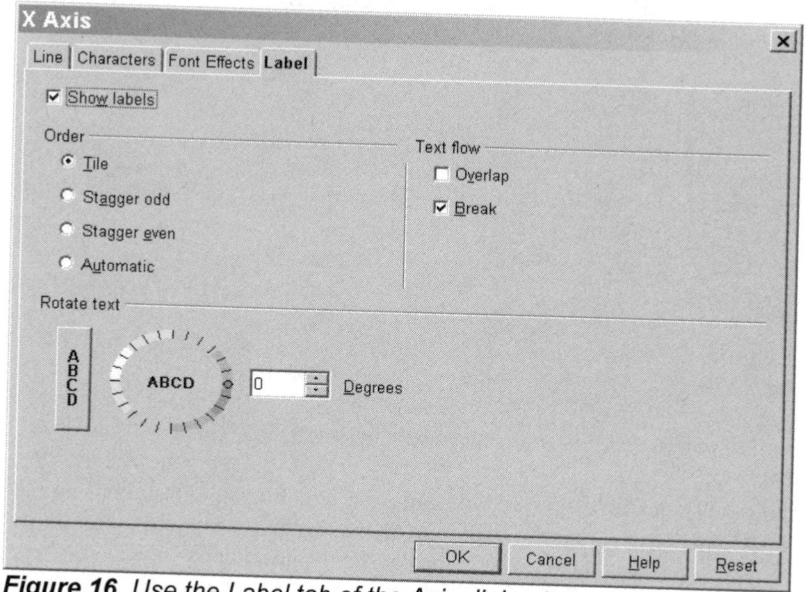

Figure 16. *Use the Label tab of the Axis dialog to turn axis labels on and off, to rotate them, or to reposition labels to fit better.*

Choose Insert | Axes from the menu to open the Axes dialog (**Figure 17**) that lets you determine which axes display at any time.

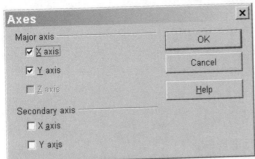

Figure 17. The Axes dialog lets you turn axes on and off.

The Show/Hide Axis Description(s) button available on the Main toolbar when editing the graph turns axis labels on and off. As with the other buttons in this section, this is all or nothing rather than affecting a single axis.

How do I control grid lines in my graph?

When you create a graph, Calc adds the grid lines it thinks make sense. For example, a column chart (vertical bar chart) has horizontal grid lines while a bar chart (horizontal bar chart) has vertical grid lines. You can control both whether grid lines show and what those grid lines look like.

When editing the graph, the Main toolbar contains toggle buttons for both horizontal and vertical grid lines. You can also choose Insert | Grids to open the Grids dialog (**Figure 18**) to choose which grid lines display.

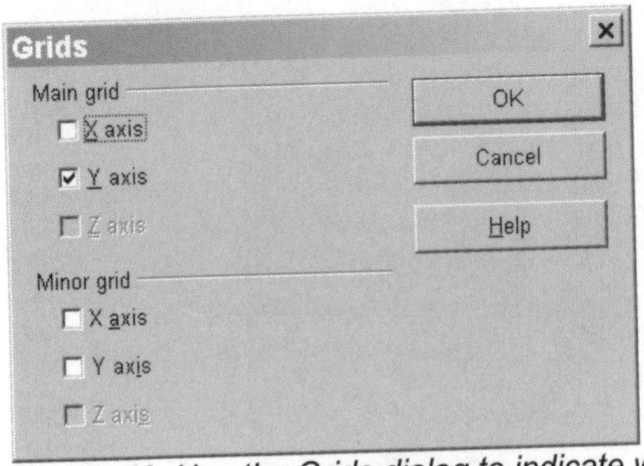

Figure 18. Use the Grids dialog to indicate what grid lines display.

Once the grid lines you want are displayed, you can control their color and style using the Grid dialog (**Figure 19**). To access it, use the Grid item on the shortcut menu or the Format menu. Choosing this item opens a submenu where you choose the grid lines you want to modify or choose All Axis Grids to modify all grid lines at once. You can also open this dialog by double-clicking in the chart when the tooltip indicates you're over grid lines.

Choosing All Axis Grids affects only those grid lines currently turned on. It doesn't turn on any grid lines.

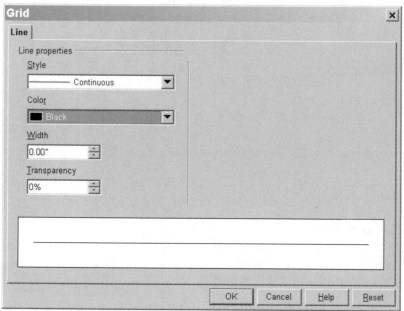

Figure 19. Use the Grid dialog to set the color and style of grid lines.

How do I give a graph a colored background?

There are actually three different backgrounds involved in a single graph. The term "chart area" refers to the whole graph, including the graphed data, the legend, the axis labels, and so forth. The term "chart wall" refers to the area behind the graphed data. For 3D graphs, the "chart floor" is the area at the bottom of the graph. You can set the background for any or all of these.

To modify the chart area, edit the graph and choose Format | Chart Wall from the menu or Chart Wall from the shortcut menu, or double-click the background. In all three cases, the Chart Area dialog opens. Use the Area tab (**Figure 20**) to set the background color.

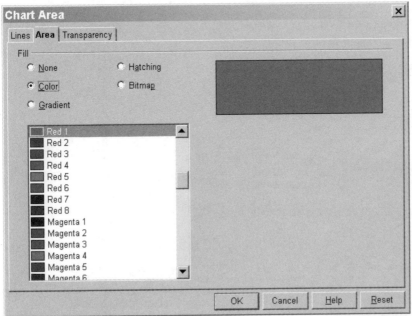

Figure 20*. Use the Chart Area dialog to set the background color for the graph as a whole, including the legends, labels, titles, and so on.*

To change the color of the Chart Wall, choose Format | Chart Wall from the menu or Chart Wall from the shortcut menu, or double-click in the graph when the tooltip says "Chart Wall." The Chart Wall dialog opens; it's identical to the Chart Area dialog, but the choices you make here affect only the area behind the graph.

Editing the Chart Floor is analogous to editing the Chart Wall. Choose Format | Chart Floor from the menu or Chart Floor from the shortcut menu, or double-click the Chart Floor to open the Chart Floor dialog, which looks the same as the Chart Area and Chart Wall dialogs. The Chart Floor item appears only when you work on a 3D graph.

How do I change the colors used to represent data?

To modify the appearance of a data series, select the data series by clicking it while editing the graph. The exact approach needed varies with the type of graph, but typically a single click when the tooltip indicates you're at a data point does the trick.

Once you select the data series, choose Format | Object Properties from the menu or Object Properties from the shortcut menu to open the Data Series dialog (**Figure 21**). Use the Area tab to control the color for the data series.

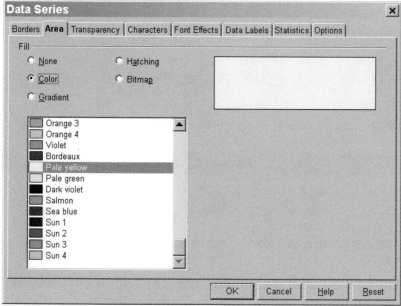

Figure 21. *The Area tab of the Data Series dialog controls the color for a particular data series.*

You can also control individual data points. To select a data point, click it while the data series containing it is selected. Next, choose Format | Object Properties or Object Properties from the shortcut menu to open the Data Point dialog, which is similar to the Data Series dialog. To change the color of the data point, use the Area tab.

How do I display the value for a data item?

In some graphs, it's useful to show the data not just as a point or bar, but to display the actual value that point or bar represents, using what's called a *data label*. Data labels are controlled at the data series and data point level. To turn on data labels for a data series or data point, select the series or point (as described in the preceding section) and use the Data Labels tab (**Figure 22**) of the corresponding dialog.

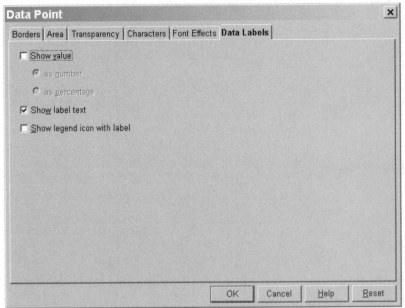

Figure 22. Use the Data Labels tab of the Data Series or Data Point dialog to determine whether the data value displays along with the graphical representation.

You can show the actual data value or the label for the value. For example, in a bar chart, you're likely to show the data value, but in an XY graph, you're more likely to use the data label, which doesn't appear anywhere else in the graph.

The Characters and Font Effects tabs of the Data Series and Data Point dialogs affect whatever data labels you turn on.

Can I look at 3D graphs from another angle?

When you use the 3D graph types, you can rotate the graph so you can see it differently. To do this, double-click the graph and select the graphed data by clicking it. The mouse pointer changes to a horseshoe shape, and you click and drag to rotate the graph.

When you click, the outline of a cube appears showing you the object you're rotating. **Figure 23** shows a graph ready to be rotated. **Figure 24** shows the same graph after dragging down and to the right.

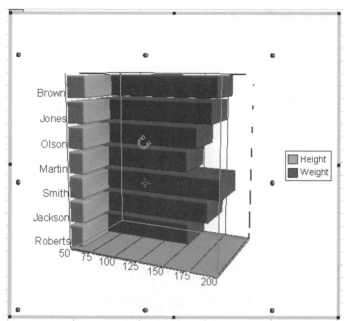

Figure 23*. You can rotate a 3D graph. The horseshoe cursor and the outline of a cube indicate the graph is ready to be rotated.*

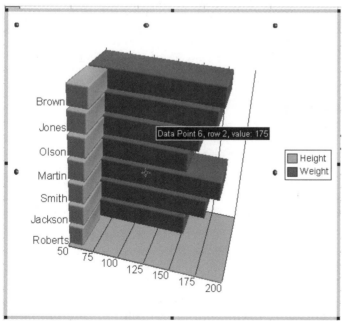

Figure 24*. After rotating down and to the right, you're seeing this graph from above.*

You can also control rotation by choosing Format | Position and Size from the menu or Position and Size from the shortcut menu when the graph data is selected. The Rotation tab (**Figure 25**) of the Position and Size dialog lets you specify the center of rotation and the angle. The default center of rotation appears in Figures 23 and 24 as a circle with compass points.

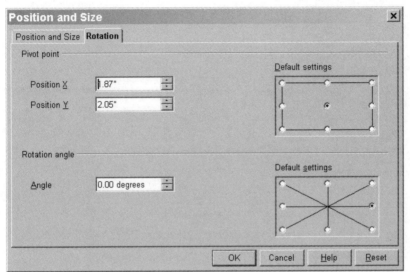

***Figure 25**. The Rotation tab of the Position and Size dialog lets you specify the center of rotation and the amount of rotation.*

There's one more way to control rotation. Choose Format | 3D View from the menu to open the 3D View dialog. You can set rotation about each axis independently.

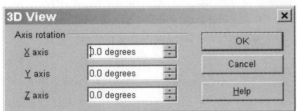

***Figure 26**. The 3D View dialog lets you rotate a graph around any axis or all three.*

Summary

Calc gives you tremendous control over the appearance of graphs. This chapter explores many of the options, but the best way to understand them is to spend some time experimenting.

Updates and corrections to this chapter can be found on Hentzenwerke's web site, **www.hentzenwerke.com**. Click "Catalog" and navigate to the page for this book.

Section IV
Impressing with Impress

Chapter 11
Creating Simple Presentations

Presentations are a very different sort of thing compared to documents or spreadsheets, but learning to create simple presentations isn't hard. This chapter examines the basics of Impress.

Presentations seem to be everywhere these days. The business world has used them for a long time, but now students create them for school projects and elected officials use them in public meetings, too. Impress lets you create slide shows for all kinds of uses.

How do I start Impress?

There are several ways to open Impress. If QuickStarter is running, right-click it and choose Presentation to open Impress with a new blank presentation. Choose Open File from QuickStarter and pick an existing Impress or PowerPoint presentation to open Impress with that presentation loaded. A third choice with QuickStarter is to choose From Template, and then choose an Impress template; that opens Impress with a new presentation based on the chosen template.

If you have another OpenOffice.org application open, choose File | New | Presentation from the menu or long click the New button on the Function toolbar and choose Presentation to open Impress with a blank presentation. Choose File | Open or the Open button to open Impress with an existing presentation.

Finally, depending on your operating system, you may be able to open Impress from a menu. In Windows, choose Start | Programs | OpenOffice.org <version> | OpenOffice.org Impress.

What will I see when I first open Impress?

By default, Impress is configured to run the Presentation AutoPilot (**Figure 1**) when you start a new presentation or simply open Impress. In that case, you can choose to open an existing presentation, to create a new presentation based on a template, or to create a new presentation based on the default (empty) template. You can turn this behavior off on the General page of the Presentation section of the Options dialog or by selecting Do not show this dialog again on the AutoPilot.

If you choose to create a new presentation, based either on the default template or from an existing template, you walk through a series of steps to define the new presentation. Once you click Create, the presentation is created based on your choices. At that point, the Modify Slide dialog (discussed later in this chapter) appears for you to select the layout of the first slide.

If you choose to open an existing presentation, the dialog adds a list of recently used presentations. You can choose one of those or double-click "<Other position>" to open a standard File-Open dialog.

Once you finish creating a new presentation or opening an existing file, you finally enter the Impress environment. As with the other OOo applications, the Stylist and Navigator are likely to be open. **Figure 2** shows a typical arrangement for Impress.

Figure 1. *The Presentation AutoPilot opens when you create a new presentation.*

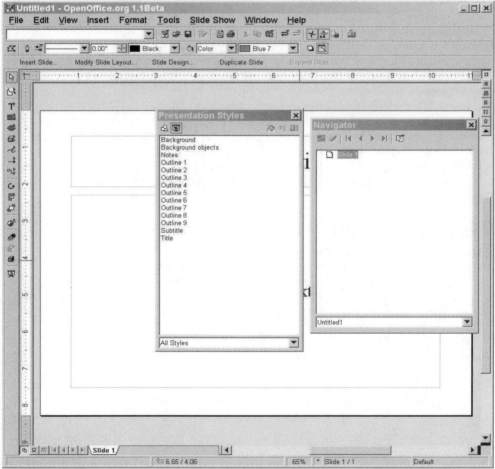

Figure 2. *When you first open Impress, you see one slide. The Navigator and Stylist may be open, and several toolbars are docked at the top and left side.*

By default, several toolbars are docked. As in the other OOo applications, the Function toolbar is docked beneath the menu and includes standard items such as New, Open, Save, Cut, Copy, Paste, and more. The Draw Object bar is docked beneath the Function bar. It includes controls for manipulating drawing objects, including line style, arrow style, colors, and more. The Presentation toolbar is docked below the Draw Object bar. It includes buttons to add a slide, change the slide layout, and more. Finally, the Main toolbar is docked on the left. When you're in Drawing View or Handout View (see "How do I see more than one slide at a time?" later in this chapter for an explanation of the views available), it contains controls for adding text and various kinds of shapes. In Outline View, it offers buttons for managing your outline. (See Chapter 4, "The OpenOffice.org User Interface," to learn how to dock, undock, and move toolbars.)

The Impress environment includes both horizontal and vertical rulers. They're controlled together by the View | Rulers menu item. Change the unit of measure on the General page of the Presentation section of the Options dialog.

At the left end of the horizontal scroll bar are seven buttons in three groups. The first two buttons determine whether the slide itself displays or the master slide. (See Chapter 12, "Presentations with Pizzazz," for an explanation of master slides.) The third button determines how objects contained in different drawing layers appear. The last four buttons form a set of what are often called "VCR controls." They work with the tabs for the individual slides in the presentation immediately to their right; you can use them to jump directly to a particular slide. The VCR controls determine which tabs display there. Be aware that the VCR controls scroll the tabs without actually changing the slide displayed.

The top of the vertical scroll bar also includes a set of buttons. These determine the current view of the presentation. The various views are discussed later in this chapter.

How do I create a new presentation?

As described in "How do I start Impress?" earlier in this chapter, you can create a new presentation in several ways when you open Impress. The same techniques work to create another new presentation once you're working in Impress.

How do I put stuff on a slide?

Every slide in Impress has a layout. A layout is a default structure for the slide. Impress provides a number of default layouts. Except for one, all of the layouts include places to insert text, graphics, or other items. In each case, before you add anything, that section of the slide includes an instruction for how to add content. For text, typically you click in that section and start typing. Other types of content are discussed in Chapter 12, "Presentations with Pizzazz."

Once you add text to a slide, you can format it. Although Impress supports styles, (see Chapter 5, "Making Life Easier with Styles and Templates"), they're less useful than in the other OOo applications. Impress uses only Presentation and Graphics styles, and allows you to define only Graphics styles (although you can modify both types). You can apply your new styles to objects you add to a slide, but objects that are part of the slide design can't have their style changed.

When you work on text, the Text Object bar replaces the Draw Object bar, providing quick access to formatting features like bold, italics, alignment, and so forth.

How do I add slides to my presentation?

The easiest way to add a slide is to click Insert Slide on the Presentation toolbar. You can also choose Insert | Slide from the menu or Slide | Insert Slide from the shortcut menu. In all cases, the Insert Slide dialog (**Figure 3**) opens for you to choose the layout of the new slide. The dialog also lets you name the slide. The name you specify appears on the tab for the slide and in the Navigator, so providing a name is a good idea.

Slide names are not preserved when you save to PowerPoint format.

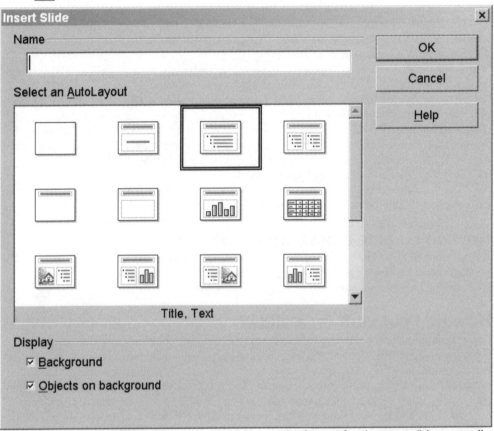

Figure 3. The Insert Slide dialog lets you choose the layout for the new slide, as well as specify a name for it.

How do I change the template for a presentation?

It's not unusual to create a slide show and then find you want to use it in another situation that requires a different template. (I often give the same presentation at several conferences, each of which supplies its own template.) However, Impress doesn't provide a direct route to changing the template for a presentation.

Fortunately, there is a solution. Create a new presentation based on the desired template. Next, open the existing presentation and switch to Slide View. (See "How do I see more than one slide at a time?" later in this chapter.) Select all the slides (using Edit | Select All or Ctrl-A) and choose copy (Edit | Copy or Ctrl-C). Switch back to the new presentation and change it to Slide View. Paste (Edit | Paste or Ctrl-V) the copied slides into the new presentation.

In some cases, the pasted slides may not take on the background characteristics of the new template. This appears to be related to the template used to create the slides originally. In such cases, you may have to cut and paste the contents of the original slides into new slides created with the new template.

If the two templates have some elements positioned differently in the same slide layout (for example, one may have the bullet points near the center while the other puts them off to the left), the copied slides retain their old positioning. However, this is easy to correct, though you have to visit each slide to do so. Return to Drawing View in the new presentation. On each slide that needs adjustment, choose Modify Slide Layout from the Presentation toolbar, Format | Modify Layout from the menu, or Slide | Modify Slide from the shortcut menu. When the Modify Slide dialog (identical to the Insert Slide dialog except for the title) appears, press Enter or click OK to accept the original layout. Doing so forces the formatting to change to match the new template.

How do I see more than one slide at a time?

Impress offers several ways to look at your presentation. By default, presentations are shown in what's called Drawing View, with one slide filling the available space. (Actually, you can control how much of the space is filled, using View | Zoom.)

Slide View corresponds to PowerPoint's Slide Sorter View. Slides are shown four across, using as many rows as necessary. To switch to Slide View, either click the Slide View button in the button set above the vertical scroll bar, choose View | Workspace | Slides View from the menu, or choose Slides View from the shortcut menu. In this view, you can select one or more slides on which to operate. **Figure 4** shows a short presentation in Slide View.

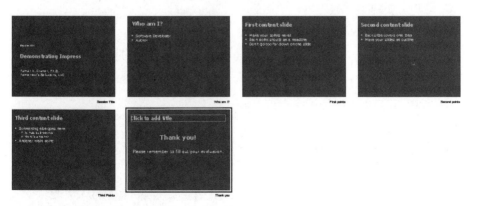

Figure 4. In Slide View, you can see a whole set of slides and work with one or more.

Slide View is useful for rearranging the slides in a presentation. Click a slide to select it (or use Ctrl-Click to select multiple slides), and then use drag-and-drop to move the slide(s) to the new location. As described in "How do I change the template for a presentation?" earlier in the chapter, you can also use Slide View to pick up slides and copy them into other presentations.

While Slide View is good for overall organization, Outline View is useful for reviewing content. To switch to Outline View, use the Outline View button in the button set above the vertical scroll bar, choose View | Workspace | Outline View from the menu, or choose Outline View from the shortcut menu.

In Outline View, which corresponds to the Normal View in PowerPoint 2000 and later, the screen is divided. The left portion shows an outline of the contents of all the slides. The right side shows one slide, the one where the cursor is positioned on the left. You can adjust the relative sizes of the two sections by dragging the divider between them. **Figure 5** shows the same presentation as in Figure 4, but in Outline View.

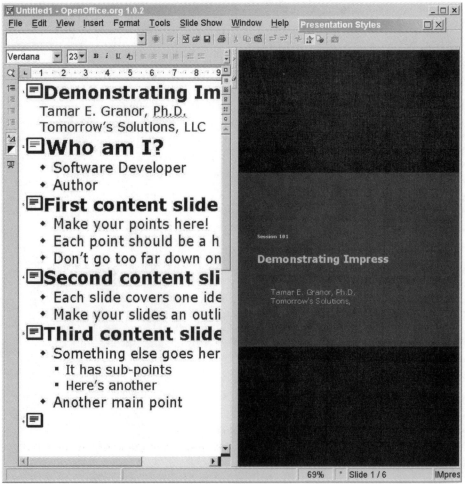

Figure 5. Outline View lets you examine the contents of your presentation. You can edit the contents as well as move slides around.

As in Slide View, Outline View lets you rearrange slides. Click the slide icon next to a slide in the outline and drag it to its new position. Be aware that if you drop a slide into the middle of another slide, the dropped slide moves into that position and any portions of the target slide that follow the drop position are added to the dropped slide. In **Figure 6**, the slide titled "Second content slide" has been dragged in between the bullet points of the "Who am I?" slide. **Figure 7** shows the result of dropping it there.

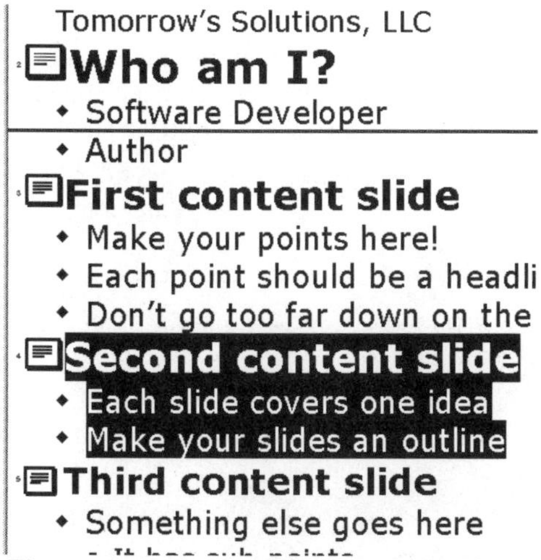

Tomorrow's Solutions, LLC
Who am I?
  ◆ Software Developer
  ◆ Author
First content slide
  ◆ Make your points here!
  ◆ Each point should be a headli
  ◆ Don't go too far down on the
Second content slide
  ◆ Each slide covers one idea
  ◆ Make your slides an outline
Third content slide
  ◆ Something else goes here

Figure 6. In Outline View, you can drag a slide and drop it in the middle of an existing slide. The horizontal bar shows the drop position.

Tomorrow's Solutions, LLC
Who am I?
  ◆ Software Developer
Second content slide
  ◆ Each slide covers one idea
  ◆ Make your slides an outline
  ◆ Author
First content slide
  ◆ Make your points here!
  ◆ Each point should be a headline
  ◆ Don't go too far down on the slide
Third content slide
  ◆ Something else goes here

Figure 7. When you drop one slide in the middle of another, some of the bullet points get moved onto the dropped slide.

Outline View also lets you modify the content of the individual slides. You can edit and format text, and you can move text from one slide to another using the standard approaches.

While in Outline View, the Main toolbar includes buttons that make it easier to work with the outline. You can collapse to show slide titles only for all slides or for the current slide. There are also toggles for showing the slide text as formatted (or all in the same font and style), and showing the slide text in black or white (or its actual colors).

How do I add notes to my presentation?

Like PowerPoint, Impress provides the ability to add notes to each slide that do not display in a presentation. You can use the notes as a guide when actually presenting the material. (To do so, print out the Notes pages.)

To add notes, you need to be in Notes view. Click the Notes View button in the button set above the vertical scroll bar or choose View | Workspace | Notes View from the menu.

Once in Notes view, you can click in the Notes section of the page to enter reminders to yourself. You can format the text you enter in the usual ways. The slide contents are not editable in this view. **Figure 8** shows a slide in Notes View.

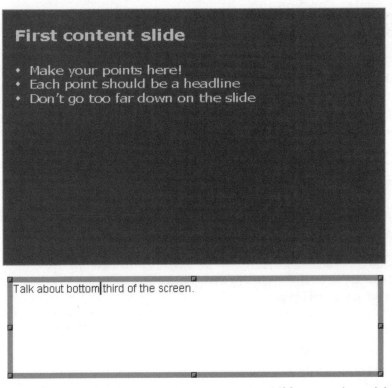

Figure 8. *Notes View lets you add notes to yourself for use when giving the presentation.*

How do I run my presentation?

Starting a slide show in Impress is easy. Both the set of buttons above the vertical scroll bar and the Main toolbar contain a Slide Show button. Click it to run your slide show. You can also choose Slide Show | Slide Show from the menu, choose Slide Show from the shortcut menu, or press F9.

Once a slide show is running, a mouse click, PageDown, or Enter moves to the next slide. Right-click or PageUp moves to the previous slide. The Escape key ends the slide show.

By default, a slide show runs full screen and shows all slides in order. You can make a variety of changes using the Slide Show dialog (**Figure 9**), which you open by choosing Slide Show | Slide Show Settings from the menu. To start with a slide other than the first, choose the From option button and choose the start slide from the drop-down list.

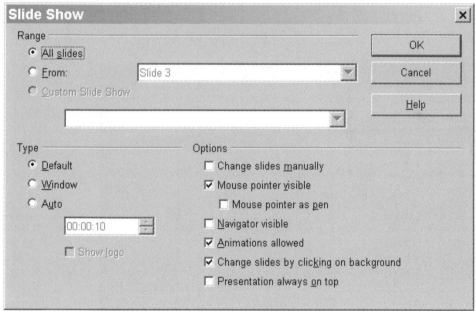

Figure 9. The Slide Show dialog lets you determine which slides display, whether they're full screen or windowed, and a variety of other items.

Unlike PowerPoint, there's no shortcut menu while running the slide show. However, you can have the Navigator available by selecting the appropriate check box. That allows you to jump directly to any slide. You can also change slides by typing in the number of the slide you want to jump to and pressing Enter.

Select Mouse pointer as pen to make it possible to "draw" on your slides as you display them. This lets you circle or underline items as you discuss them and so forth. Your scribbles disappear when you change slides. (Note that you must select Mouse pointer visible to enable Mouse point as pen.)

Additional options for controlling the order of a slide show are discussed in Chapter 12, "Presentations with Pizzazz."

How do I print my presentation?

Impress offers a variety of options regarding printing. You can print the slides themselves, notes pages, handouts that include multiple pages, or the outline. You can include or exclude various items in your output, such as the date and time.

When you click the Print button on the Function toolbar, the current configuration prints without any intervention. For presentations, that's not usually what you want. Instead, choose File | Print to open the Print dialog (**Figure 10**). The item you're most likely to set in this dialog is the Print range. Be aware that the Pages setting uses the slide numbers, not the actual page numbers. This means when printing handouts, for example, you need to specify which slides to include on the handout pages, not which handout pages to print.

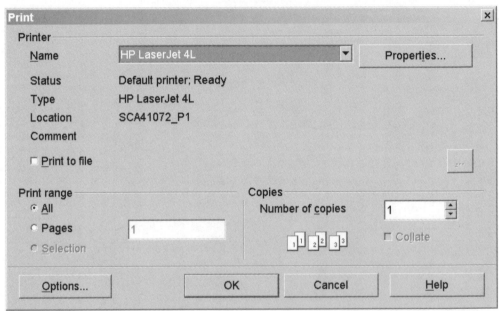

Figure 10. The Print dialog lets you specify which slides to print and which printer to use. To get to most of the interesting choices, click the Options... button.

Most of what you want to set for printing presentations is accessed through the Print dialog's Options... button. Clicking it opens the Printer Options dialog (**Figure 11**), where you choose the items to print, set the quality of print, and more. Note that the Contents section contains check boxes, so you can print more than one format at a time. (This is different from PowerPoint, where you use a drop-down list to choose one item to print.) Be sure to select only the type of output you want. **Table 1** explains what output you get from each choice.

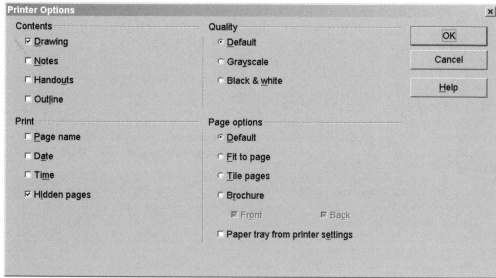

Figure 11. The Printer Options dialog lets you determine which forms of output to print and what to include on each page.

Table 1. You can print a presentation in a variety of formats. The Contents check boxes on the Printer Options dialog determine which items print.

Contents	Prints
Drawings	The slides as they appear in Drawing view.
Notes	Notes pages containing the slide and the notes.
Handouts	Handout pages with multiple slides per page. You can set the format of the pages using Handout View.
Outline	The outline as displayed in Outline view.

Although the Contents choices are check boxes, they're interlinked, so you must have at least one selected at all times. If only one is selected, you can't clear it. Instead, select the format you want first, and then clear the one you want to remove.

You can determine what handout pages look like. By default, they include four slides in a 2x2 grid. To change that, switch to Handout View (click the Handout View button in the buttons above the vertical scroll bar, or choose View | Workspace | Handout View from the menu). Once in Handout View, click Modify Slide Layout to see a list of available layouts. Choose the one you want. Once you choose, you can adjust the layout in some ways, for example, moving the slides around within the layout. You can also add objects to the handout, for example, to put lines next to each slide to take notes. The layout you specify is used whenever you print handouts for this presentation.

The Print section of the Printer Options dialog lets you add items to the printed pages. Select Date and Time to have the date and time printed at the top of each slide. Select Page name to include the name of each slide (as displayed in the Navigator).

The Quality section lets you save on ink. Choose Black and White to print slides in black and white only, omitting any background color.

Summary

This chapter offers the tools for building a basic presentation, running it, and printing it. In the next chapter, you'll see how to add effects like slide transitions, how to include graphics and other objects, and how to build master slides to enforce appearance across an entire presentation.

Updates and corrections to this chapter can be found on Hentzenwerke's web site, **www.hentzenwerke.com**. Click "Catalog" and navigate to the page for this book.

Chapter 12
Presentations with Pizzazz

Once you have a simple slide show working, you will likely want to add graphics and transition effects. In addition, Impress offers techniques that make it easy to create uniform presentations and to show only a subset of the slides in a presentation.

Once you have the basic information in your slide show, the next step is to make it more interesting. Adding graphics and effects gives the audience something to watch while they listen to you. Of course, as with so much else, moderation is a good idea when it comes to "eye candy" in a presentation.

How do I add graphics to my presentation?

There are several kinds of graphic items you may want to add to a presentation: existing graphic files, clip art, and drawing items. The technique for adding each is a little different, but whatever you want to add, you need to be in Drawing View (View | Slide or the Drawing View button above the vertical scroll bar) to add graphic objects to the slide itself.

Adding graphic files

To add a graphic file to a slide, choose Insert | Graphics from the menu or from the Main toolbar. The Insert Graphics dialog (**Figure 1**) appears to let you choose the graphic file. You can insert a copy of the file on the slide or link to the original file so changes to the graphic reflect in the presentation. To link to the original, select the Link check box in the dialog.

Adding clip art

Clip art is stored in the Gallery. (See Chapter 4, "The OpenOffice.org Interface," for more on the Gallery.) To open the Gallery, choose Tools | Gallery or click the Gallery button on the Function toolbar. Once the Gallery opens, you can add an item listed there to a slide by dragging it onto the slide or by choosing Insert from the item's shortcut menu. When you choose Insert, you have two choices: Copy or Link. As with graphic files, choosing Copy makes a copy of the item, independent of the original, while choosing Link ties the item on the slide to the original stored in the Gallery, so any changes to the image also appear on the slide.

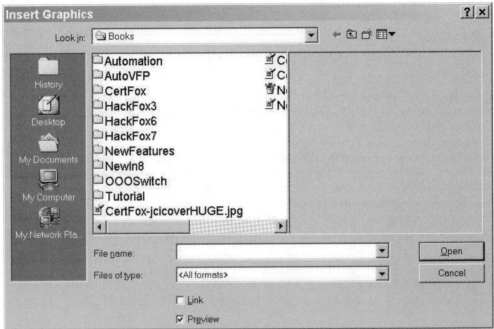

Figure 1. Use the Insert Graphics dialog to navigate to graphic files you want to add to slides. When the Preview check box is selected, the graphics appear in the dialog.

Adding drawings

The Main toolbar contains a number of items that allow you to create drawings. All the items in the second section of the toolbar, beginning with the Text button and continuing through the Connector button, create drawing objects. **Figure 2** shows that section of the toolbar with each button labeled.

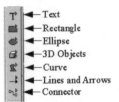

Figure 2. The drawing buttons on Impress's main toolbar let you add shapes and text to a slide.

To add a drawing object to a slide, click the appropriate button. Each of these buttons can either use a default object or open a toolbar of objects of the appropriate type. See Chapter 4, "The OpenOffice.org Interface," for more on this type of toolbar button. Once you choose the appropriate object, click and drag on the slide to insert it. Depending on the object type, you may need multiple clicks.

The drawing capabilities here are the same as those provided in Draw, OOo's drawing program. For more information, see Chapter 14, "Creating Drawings."

Formatting images

Once you add a graphic of any sort to a slide, you can modify it in a number of ways. Click the item you want to format and choose the appropriate operation from the Format menu or the shortcut menu. The exact set of items available depends on the graphic type. The various formatting options are described in Chapter 14, "Creating Drawings."

How do I add transition effects to my presentation?

In some situations, adding effects to the transition from one slide to the next or controlling the appearance of text on an individual slide can enhance a presentation. (On the other hand, overuse of transitions and effects can detract from the content of a slide show.)

You control the transition from one slide to the next using Slide Show | Slide Transition from the menu, which opens the Slide Transition window (**Figure 3**). You can set the transition for a single slide or for a group of slides. To work on multiple slides (or an entire presentation), switch to Slide View and choose the slides that are affected. The transition effects you choose apply when changing *to* the specified slides, but not when leaving them.

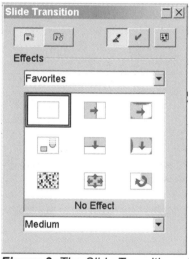

Figure 3. *The Slide Transition window lets you set the effects used when changing from one slide to the next.*

Use the drop-down list to choose a type of transition, and then choose the desired transition from that group. The Favorites group shown in Figure 3 includes some of the most commonly used transitions. You can also set the transition speed using the drop-down list at the bottom of the window. Once you choose the transition and speed you want, click the Assign button (the check mark) to apply the transition to the selected slides.

The Slide Transition window also lets you set up automatic transitions so a presentation can run without user intervention. Click the Extras button to switch to the Extras page (**Figure 4**). The Transition option buttons in the middle of this page determine the behavior of the slide or slides. **Table 1** shows the choices. When you choose Automatic Transition, use the spinner to determine how long each slide displays. Click Assign (the check mark) to save your choices.

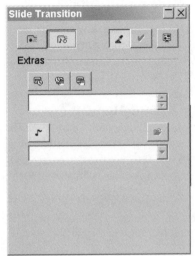

Figure 4. *The Extras page lets you set up automated slide shows and add sounds to transitions.*

Table 1. *You can have a slide show fully automated, automated only within individual slides, or totally manual.*

Icon	Tooltip	Meaning
	Automatic Transition	Run this slide or group of slides totally automatically. No user invention needed. This option is good for situations like trade shows, where you want a presentation to run continuously.
	Semiautomatic Transition	Run any effects within this slide or group of slides automatically, but require user intervention to change from one slide to the next. (See "How do I control the timing of items on a slide?" later in this chapter to set up effects within a slide.)
	Manual Transition	All transitions and effects require user intervention. This choice gives the presenter the most control.

You can combine Automatic Transitions with the Auto setting on the Slide Show dialog to set up a slide show that runs continuously.

You can also associate a sound with movement between slides. Select the Sound check box to turn sounds on, and then choose a sound from the drop-down list or point to a sound file. As with the other choices, you must click the Assign button (the check mark) for your choices to take effect.

The transitions in the Favorites category have sounds associated with them. You can find the same transitions in other categories without sounds. You can also remove the sound after choosing a transition.

How do I control the timing of items on a slide?

Just as you can determine the transitions between slides, you can also determine how and when items on a slide appear. Impress calls these *effects*. You set them using the Effects window (**Figure 5**), accessed through Slide Show | Effects on the menu or using the Animation Effects button on the Main toolbar. You set effects only from Drawing View.

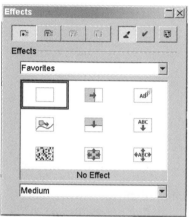

Figure 5. The Effects window controls the appearance of items within a slide. As with transitions, you have many choices.

To add an effect to an item on a slide, select that item (whether text or a graphic), choose the desired effect, and then click the Assign (check mark) button. As in the Transition window, use the Effects drop-down list to choose a category, and then choose the actual effect from the category by clicking it. Set the speed of the effect using the drop-down list at the bottom of the window.

> It's sufficient to click into an outline area on a slide to apply an effect to all the bullet points in that outline. In fact, even if some bullets are highlighted, the effect applies to all bullets.

The Extras page of the window (**Figure 6**) lets you set up two additional features for items with effects. The first set of option buttons determines whether each item changes on the next click after it displays (an "after-effect," so to speak). You can either make it disappear (the Object Invisible button) or you can change its color (the Fade Object with Color button). When you choose to change its color, you can then choose the new color from the drop-down list. For example, the setting shown in Figure 6 indicates that on the next click after the item displays, it changes to dark gray.

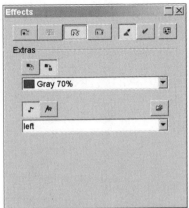

Figure 6. *The extras page of the Effects window lets you determine whether items change on the click after they display and whether a sound is associated with the effect.*

Although you can't choose both the buttons for after-effects, it is possible to turn them both off, resulting in no after-effect. The buttons behave as a combination of option buttons and check boxes. To turn off after-effects, click the currently chosen button.

The second section of the Extras page controls sounds. Select the Sound check box (the note) to associate a sound with the effect (though not with the after-effect). Next choose a sound from the drop-down list or click the folder to locate a sound file. (As with transitions, the effects in the Favorites category already have associated sounds.) The Play in Full determines whether you can interrupt the sound with another click.

The Order page of the window (**Figure 7**) lets you set the order in which the items appear. It lists only items with effects set. Use drag-and-drop to reorganize the list.

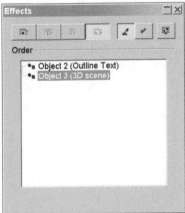

Figure 7. *The Order page of the Effects window lets you set the appearance order of the objects.*

How do I control the overall appearance of a presentation?

Within a presentation, the master slide controls a number of formatting features. The master slide determines the background color or pattern for the slides in a presentation, as well as any fixed text or graphics that appear on every slide. To access the master slide for a presentation, choose View | Master | Drawing from the menu or, while in Drawing View, click the Master View button in the set of buttons to the left of the horizontal scroll bar. **Figure 8** shows the master slide for a new, empty presentation before any modifications have been made to it.

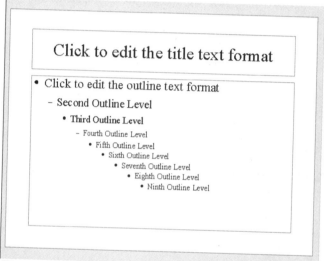

Figure 8. The master slide for a presentation determines the background color, the formatting of text on the slide, and any fixed text or graphics.

Once you're looking at the master slide, you can change the formatting of the items on the slide or add items to the slide. To change the appearance of the title or the outline section, click into that section and use the menu, toolbar, or shortcut menu to change the font characteristics. (You can also change font characteristics and other items by modifying the relevant styles. See "Changing slide appearance through styles" later in this chapter.)

Add fixed items to the slide master using the various drawing choices on the Main toolbar. For example, to put a footer on each slide, use the Text button. Similarly, you can add graphics to the background of all slides using the same tools as you would to add a graphic to an individual slide. (See "How do I add graphics to my presentation?" earlier in this chapter.)

In PowerPoint, a presentation has two master slides, one for the title slide and one for the other slides within the presentation. Impress has only one master slide, which means whatever you put on it appears on the title slide as well as on the content slides.

Changing slide appearance through styles

Like the other OpenOffice.org applications, Impress uses styles for formatting. However, you can't create new styles in Impress. The various components of a presentation use the styles provided. Editing those styles is one way to change the overall appearance of a presentation.

In fact, some changes you make to the master slide actually change the underlying styles. For example, when you change font characteristics for the title on the master slide, the Title style is modified. When you change font characteristics for the outline section of the master slide, the styles Outline 1 through Outline 9 change.

Some items can be changed only by modifying a style. To change the background color or pattern of the master slide, modify the Background style. **Figure 9** shows the same master slide as in Figure 8, but with a text object added at the bottom of the slide, the background color changed, and the font characteristics for both the title and the outline modified.

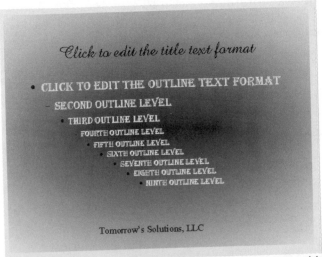

Figure 9. In this master slide, a text item has been added, the background color changed, and font characteristics modified.

When you finish editing the master slide, use View | Slide from the menu or the Slide View button to the left of the horizontal scroll bar to return to the actual slides in the presentation. All slides reflect the changes made to the master slide.

How do I control the format of speaker's notes in a presentation?

As with the overall look of a presentation, Impress offers a couple of ways to control the appearance of speaker's notes. You can modify the location and formatting of notes using the master notes view, accessible by choosing View | Master | Notes from the menu or by clicking the Master View button to the left of the horizontal scroll bar while in Notes View.

The notes themselves are a text object, so you can change the size, shape, or position of the object by clicking the border, and then drag with the mouse. Click inside the text object to format the notes text. The item you will most likely want to change is the font and size. Highlight the text there ("Click to edit the notes format") and set the font and size you want.

You can also format notes text by modifying the Notes style.

To return to Notes View, click the Slide View button to the left of the horizontal scroll bar or choose View | Slide from the menu.

Can I keep many slides in a single presentation and show only those I want?

If you frequently give presentations on a particular subject and have developed a number of slides about that topic, it can be handy to keep them all in a single presentation. However, simply skipping over slides during a slide show gives an unprofessional appearance.

Fortunately, Impress offers a solution, custom slide shows that include only a subset of the slides in a presentation. To work with custom slide shows, choose Slide Show | Custom Slide Show from the menu. The Custom Slide Shows dialog (**Figure 10**) appears, listing all the custom slide shows already defined for this presentation. Click New to define a new slide show—the Define Custom Slide Show dialog appears (**Figure 11**).

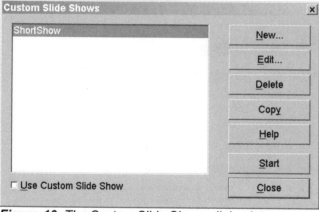

Figure 10. *The Custom Slide Shows dialog lets you manage slide shows for the current presentation.*

Specify a name for your custom slide show. Move items from the list of Existing slides to the list of Selected slides by clicking them, and then click the >> button. (Remove slides from the Selected slides list by selecting them, and clicking the << button.) You can move several slides at once in either list.

Slides appear in the order you add them to the list of Selected slides. To change the order, drag-and-drop slides within the list.

Click OK to save your custom slide show.

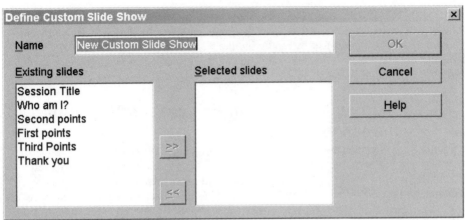

Figure 11. To define a slide show, specify a name, and then choose the slides that should appear.

There are two ways to use a custom slide show. One is to click the Use Custom Slide Show button in the Custom Slide Shows dialog and select the show you want to use. You can also choose a custom slide show using the Slide Show dialog (Slide Show | Slide Show Settings on the menu, Figure 9 in Chapter 11, "Creating Simple Presentations").

How do I make final tweaks to my presentation?

Impress offers a feature called "Live Mode" that allows you to modify a presentation while it's being shown. This lets you see your slides as they will display and make changes right away rather than having to make notes and fix things in edit mode.

 PowerPoint doesn't have anything analogous to live mode.

Enable live mode by selecting Navigator visible in the Slide Show dialog (Slide Show | Slide Show Settings on the menu). Once you're running the slide show, click the Live Mode button (**Figure 12**) in the Navigator to start editing. From this point forward, you can edit the text and formatting of your slides. Edit text directly. To edit formatting, highlight the item you want to change and use its shortcut menu.

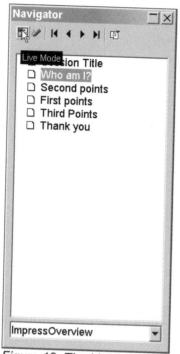

Figure 12. The Live Mode button in the Navigator lets you edit slide contents while the slide show is running.

When you finish editing, click the Live Mode button in the Navigator again to turn off live mode. You must do this before you can close the presentation. When you return to the editing environment, the changes you made in live mode persist and can be saved.

Summary

Impress offers the tools needed to create attractive, customized slide shows. Judicious use of graphics, transitions, and effects in your slides can make your presentations more interesting. Master slides and styles let you apply standards to slides. Custom slide shows let you keep a large group of slides together and show only those you want. Finally, Live Mode makes it easy to give your slides the fit and finish that makes them look professional.

With Writer, Calc, and Impress under your belt, you have seen the major tools of OpenOffice.org. The next few chapters look at the additional applications that are part of the package.

Updates and corrections to this chapter can be found on Hentzenwerke's web site, **www.hentzenwerke.com**. Click "Catalog" and navigate to the page for this book.

Section V
But Wait, There's More

Chapter 13
Creating Web Pages

The growth of the Web can't be exaggerated, and many people who never heard of a web page a few years ago now have the responsibility of managing web sites. OpenOffice.org offers a tool for creating and editing web pages.

OpenOffice.org's HTML Editor is an alternate face for its word processor. As a result, much of what you know about Writer transfers directly to the process of creating web pages. This chapter focuses on the ways HTML Editor differs from Writer, or creating a web page differs from creating other kinds of text documents.

 It's worth noting from the beginning that HTML Editor is simply a text editor capable of producing HTML output. It doesn't include many of the fancier features of Microsoft FrontPage, such as themes or the ability to publish directly to a website. In addition, HTML Editor deals with individual web pages, not with websites as a whole. That means it has no facilities for mapping site navigation, cataloging links, and so forth.

How do I start HTML Editor?

There are several ways to open HTML Editor. If QuickStarter is running, choose Open File from QuickStarter and pick an existing HTML document to open HTML Editor with that document loaded.

If you have another OpenOffice.org application open, choose File | New | HTML Document or long click the New button on the Function toolbar and choose HTML Document to open HTML Editor with a blank document. Choose File | Open or the Open button to open HTML Editor with an existing web page.

Finally, depending on your operating system, you may be able to open Writer from a menu. In Windows, choose Start | Programs | OpenOffice.org <version> | OpenOffice.org HTML Document.

What do I see when I first open HTML Editor?

Not surprisingly, when HTML Editor opens, you may think you're actually in Writer. Although there are some differences, the overall appearance is quite similar. In addition, things you do in Writer, such as docking Stylist or Navigator, affect HTML Editor. **Figure 1** shows HTML Editor as it may look when you first open it.

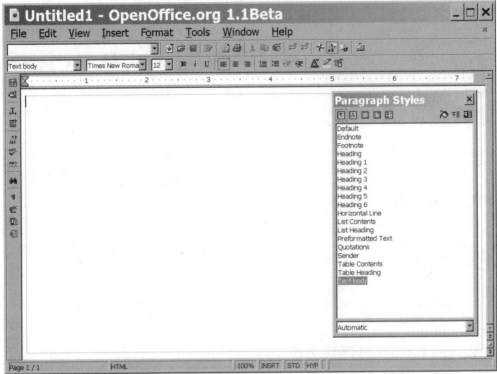

Figure 1. *When you open HTML Editor, it looks a lot like Writer.*

Like Writer, HTML Editor has two toolbars (the Function bar and the Text Object bar) docked under the menu, and the Main toolbar docked at the left. The contents of the Function bar are identical to Writer's. The Text Object toolbar is slightly different—it omits justified paragraph alignment, as that's not a viable option on a web page.

The Main toolbar has several differences. Most significant are two additional buttons that toggle Print Layout mode and HTML Source mode.

How do I create a new web page?

As described in "How do I start HTML Editor" earlier in this chapter, you can create a new web page by choosing File | New | HTML Document from the menu or by long-clicking on the New button on the Function toolbar and choosing HTML Document.

How do I enter text for my web page and format it?

Entering text in HTML Editor is identical to doing so in Writer; just type in the text you want. To format it, apply appropriate styles or format directly from the Format menu. For details on formatting, see Chapter 6, "Creating Simple Documents."

Can I edit HTML directly?

HTML Editor gives you two options. By default, it's a WYSIWYG ("what you see is what you get") editor, where you use menu options or toolbar buttons to add formatting. However, when creating web pages, sometimes it's easier to work directly with the underlying HTML; HTML Editor offers that option as well.

To view or edit the HTML, you must save the web page first. Once you do so, choose View | HTML - Source from the menu or HTML Source from the Main toolbar to switch to HTML view. Once in HTML mode, you can make changes. To return to the normal view, choose the same menu item or button or choose HTML Source from the shortcut menu.

Figure 2 shows a very simple web page displayed in normal view; **Figure 3** shows the same page in HTML view.

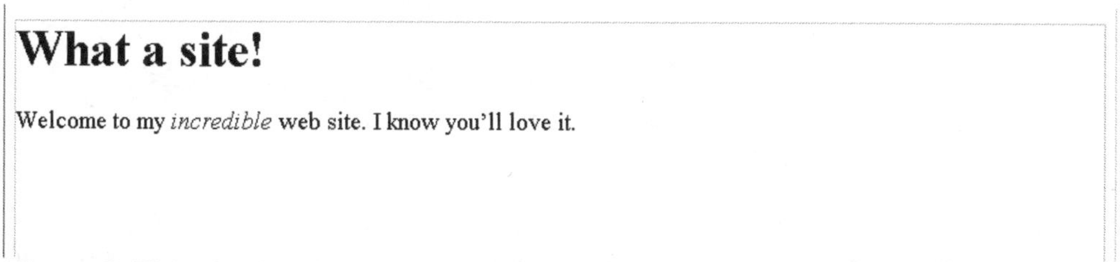

What a site!

Welcome to my *incredible* web site. I know you'll love it.

Figure 2. *This simple web page was created using the tools in HTML Editor.*

```
<!DOCTYPE HTML PUBLIC "-//W3C//DTD HTML 4.0 Transitional//EN">
<HTML>
<HEAD>
    <META HTTP-EQUIV="CONTENT-TYPE" CONTENT="text/html; charset=windows-1252">
    <TITLE></TITLE>
    <META NAME="GENERATOR" CONTENT="OpenOffice.org 1.1Beta  (Win32)">
    <META NAME="AUTHOR" CONTENT="Tamar Granor">
    <META NAME="CREATED" CONTENT="20030415;14370999">
    <META NAME="CHANGEDBY" CONTENT="Tamar Granor">
    <META NAME="CHANGED" CONTENT="20030415;15122425">
</HEAD>
<BODY LANG="en-US" DIR="LTR">
<H1>What a site!</H1>
<P>Welcome to my <I>incredible</I> web site. I know you&rsquo;ll love
it.</P>
</BODY>
</HTML>
```

Figure 3. *You can see and change the HTML underlying a web page.*

How do I add hyperlinks?

One of the key elements of web pages is links to other pages. Adding hyperlinks is easy in HTML Editor. There are a couple of ways to do it.

You can enter the text for the hyperlink, highlight it, and then choose Insert | Hyperlink from the menu. You can also choose Insert | Hyperlink without first entering the text. In either case, the Hyperlink window (**Figure 4**) opens. If text is highlighted, it displays in the Text textbox. If no text is highlighted, you can either type in the text for the hyperlink or you can click back to the document and select the text.

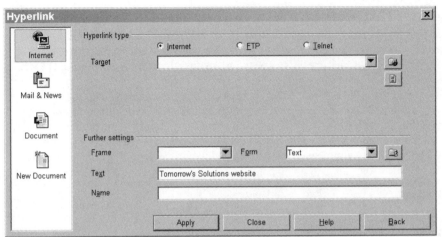

Figure 4. *Specify the URL for a hyperlink as the Target and the text to appear on the web page as Text when creating a hyperlink.*

You can link to a variety of sources. Click the source type in the bar at the left. (In Figure 4, it's a web page.) The dialog changes to reflect the data you need to provide for each type of source. Choose Document to link to another location on the page you're editing.

When linking to a website, click the WWW Browser button to the right of the Target textbox to open the default browser displaying instructions for copying a URL (**Figure 5**).

Transferring Web Addresses

1. Enter the required URL into the URL input line in StarOffice or search for one by using the search functions in the Hyperlink bar.
2. Select the URL that appears in the URL input line (e.g. http://www.sun.com/staroffice).
3. Select the command Edit -> Copy or use CTRL + C.
4. Return to your document. Insert the URL by using either the command Edit -> Paste or CRTL+V.

Figure 5. *When you click the WWW Browser button, this page appears to guide you in specifying a URL.*

 In the analogous dialog in Microsoft FrontPage, you can navigate to a website and have the URL automatically copied with no need to cut and paste.

To specify an e-mail link, choose Mail and News from the bar on the left. The dialog changes (**Figure 6**) to let you specify the address to which the message should be sent and the text that should appear. You can also specify the subject link for the message.

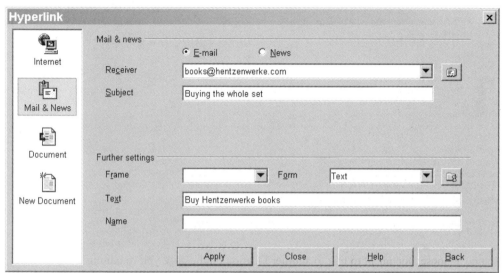

Figure 6. For an e-mail link, you specify the e-mail address and subject line.

Summary

Creating a web page with OpenOffice.org isn't much different from creating any other text document. You use the same features for formatting and entering text, but you have the added ability to look at and edit the HTML underneath the document.

OOo's HTML Editor is a major step above writing HTML in a plain text editor like Notepad, but it still has a way to go before it offers the functionality of a dedicated website tool.

Updates and corrections to this chapter can be found on Hentzenwerke's web site, **www.hentzenwerke.com**. Click "Catalog" and navigate to the page for this book.

Chapter 14
Creating Drawings

Diagrams using shapes, arrows, lines, and the like are useful for conveying information in a natural way. OpenOffice.org's Draw application lets you create such diagrams, which you can incorporate into documents created with the other applications.

Draw is unusual among OOo's applications in that it doesn't have a direct analogue in Microsoft Office. To be more accurate, while you can do many of the same things in Office using the AutoShape functionality, in that setting you're restricted to creating drawings within another application. You can't create and save drawings independently in Office. Draw gives you that option in OpenOffice.org.

How do I start Draw?

You can open Draw in a number of different ways. If QuickStarter is running, right-click it and choose Drawing to open Draw with a new blank drawing. Choose Open File from QuickStarter and pick an existing drawing to open Draw with that drawing loaded. A third choice with QuickStarter is to choose From Template, and then choose a Draw template; that opens Draw with a new drawing based on the chosen template.

If you have another OpenOffice.org application open, choose File | New | Drawing or long click the New button on the Function toolbar and choose Drawing to open Draw with a blank drawing. Choose File | Open or the Open button to open Draw with an existing drawing.

Finally, depending on your operating system, you may be able to open Draw from a menu. In Windows, choose Start | Programs | OpenOffice.org <version> | Drawing.

What will I see when I first open Draw?

The first time you open draw, the Stylist and Navigator may be open. (See Chapter 5, "Making Life Easier with Templates and Styles," for details on the Stylist and Chapter 4, "The OpenOffice.org Interface," for information about the Navigator.) The new drawing is shown with a tab labeling it "Slide 1."

Figure 1 shows a typical appearance for Draw.

Three toolbars are docked by default. As in the other OOo applications, the Function toolbar is docked beneath the menu, containing buttons for common operations like New, Open, Save, Print, Cut, Copy, Paste, and others. The Draw object bar is docked beneath the Function toolbar. It includes controls for formatting lines and areas. The Main toolbar is docked at the left; it includes buttons for adding a variety of drawing objects.

Both the vertical and horizontal rulers display, by default. You can change the unit of measure in the Options dialog, using the General page of the Drawing section. You can turn the rulers off by choosing View | Rulers from the menu or by clearing the Rulers visible check box on the View page of the Drawing section of the Options dialog. In the latter case, your choice affects new drawings you create as well as the drawing you're working on.

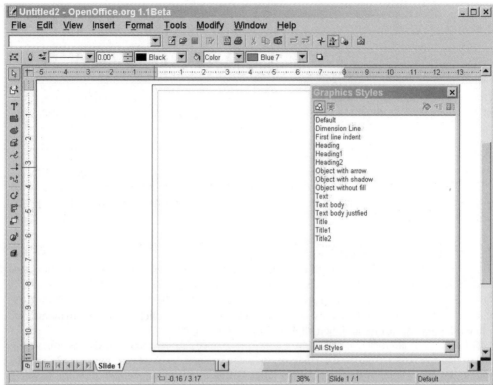

Figure 1. Draw opens with three toolbars docked and both horizontal and vertical rulers displayed.

How do I create new drawings?

As described in "How do I start Draw?" earlier in this chapter, you can create a new drawing in several ways when you open Draw. The same techniques work to create another new drawing once you're working in Draw.

What goes into a drawing?

Draw lets you build drawings from a collection of components, accessed through the Main toolbar. There are seven buttons, shown in **Table 1**; each button can be long clicked to open a toolbar for that type of component. (As with other buttons that offer a long click, once you make a choice, these buttons change to show the item chosen, and subsequent regular clicks allow you to add another item of the same type.)

Table 1. *The Main toolbar in Draw has a button for each type of drawing object you can add. Long click a button for a toolbar of items of that type.*

Icon	Type of object
T▸	Text
▢	Rectangles
◔	Ellipses
▱	3D Objects
⌁	Curves
⟶	Lines and arrows
⌁	Connectors

 Although Draw has a reasonable selection of built-in components, it offers far fewer than Office's AutoShape functionality.

To add a component to a drawing, click the button (or long click for the submenu and click the item you want), and then click and drag on the drawing. Each component has a surrounding rectangle. The location of the original click and the location of the button release form opposite corners of that rectangle. **Figure 2** shows the process of adding a rectangle—at the point shown in the figure, the upper left corner has been set and the rectangle is being dragged to size. **Figure 3** shows the result.

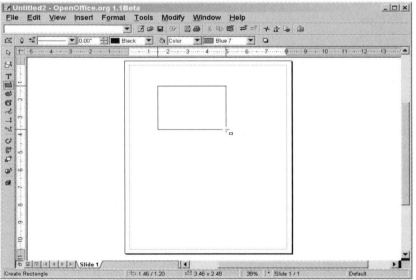

Figure 2. *To add a component to a drawing, choose the item from the Main toolbar, and then click and drag to position it.*

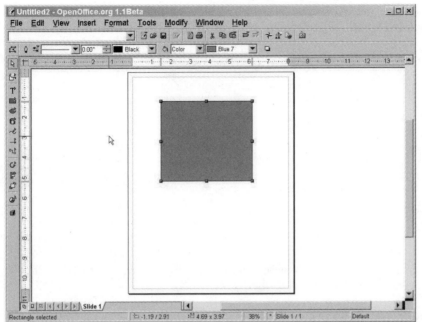

***Figure 3**. Once the item is dropped into place, the default fill color and style appears.*

How do I add text to a diagram?

There are a couple of ways to add text to your drawings. The more obvious way is using the Text objects available on the Main toolbar. You can add a regular textbox, a textbox that fits the text to its frame, or a callout that combines text with a "pointer." **Figure 4** shows one of each type. The text in the "fit to frame" textbox is a different size and shape than its font settings would indicate.

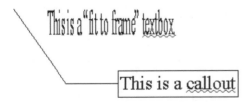

***Figure 4**. One way to label diagrams is using textboxes. Draw offers three types.*

You can add regular textboxes without using the toolbar button. Double-click almost any object (though not a 3D object) to add a textbox at the center of that object. (You can also do this by typing when the object is selected.) Type the desired text. Although the text appears to be attached to the object, you actually have a separate textbox associated with the object. **Figure 5** shows a couple of objects with the textboxes in their default positions.

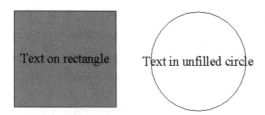

Figure 5. *Double-clicking on an object or typing with the object selected adds a textbox on top of the object.*

Can I change the text?

To edit any text, double-click the containing object. The cursor changes into an insertion point and the text becomes editable.

Is there a quick way to add several of the same component?

If you need to add more than one of the same component, choose the appropriate component from the submenu so it's the default for that button. Next, double-click the button. From that point on, each time you click your drawing, you add an object of that type. To stop adding objects of that type, click the Select button (the arrow) on the Main toolbar.

How do I move an object?

To move an object once you add it to a drawing, click to select it, and then drag it to the desired position. When an object is selected, you can also move it using the keyboard.

If you hold down the shift key while dragging, the object moves exactly vertically or exactly horizontally.

How do I change the size of an object?

To resize an object, click to select it. Green sizing handles appear at the corners and the midpoints of the surrounding rectangle. Grab a sizing handle with the mouse and drag the object to its new size.

How do I format a drawing object?

As in most of the other OOo applications, you can use styles to impose uniform formatting. The objects in Draw use Graphics Styles. You can modify the styles provided or define your own to incorporate the formatting you want to use. See Chapter 5, "Making Life Easier with

Templates and Styles," for instructions on modifying or defining styles. In addition, of course, you can directly format individual objects.

In general, to change the formatting of an object, you first need to click the object to select it. You can format several objects at once by clicking the first, and then Shift-clicking the others. When you do so, the selection box is enlarged to encompass all the selected objects. Draw doesn't support multiple distinct selections.

How do I change the color inside a shape?

Many of the objects are filled with a color or pattern. To change the fill, use the Area Style/Filling drop-down on the Draw object toolbar, or choose Format | Area from the menu or Area from the shortcut menu. When you use the menu or shortcut menu, the Area dialog (**Figure 6**) opens. Choose the desired color or pattern on the Area tab.

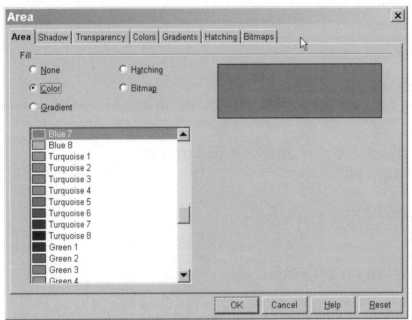

Figure 6. The Area tab of the Area dialog lets you specify a color or pattern to fill an object.

You can fine tune your selection on the other tabs of the dialog. Use the Colors tab to specify a color not listed. Use the Gradients tab to modify the specification for a gradient fill or define a new one. The Hatching tab lets you modify the specification for a hatching pattern or create a new one. The Bitmaps tab lets you choose a bitmap to fill the object, including importing bitmaps not listed.

How do I change the lines around an object?

Most objects have lines surrounding them as well as a fill color or pattern. You can change several characteristics of those lines. The most obvious is the line color. By default, lines are black. To use another color, select the object and choose the desired color from the Line Color drop-down on the Draw object toolbar. You can also change the color by choosing Line from the shortcut menu or Format | Line from the menu to open the Line dialog (**Figure 7**).

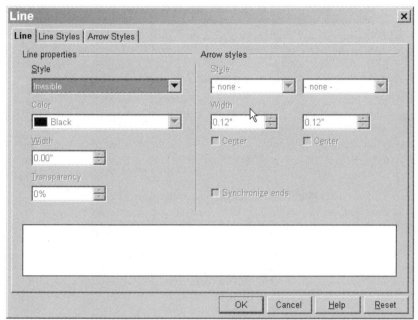

Figure 7. The Line dialog lets you set the color, style, and width of the lines around objects. For line objects, you can also choose arrowheads.

The Line dialog also provides a mechanism for choosing the type of line and its width. Use the Style drop-down in the Line properties section to specify whether the line is visible at all and, if so, whether it's continuous, dashed, or one of a number of other choices. The Width spinner indicates the line width, with the default 0 actually indicating a single pixel.

You can set the line style and width without going into the Line dialog, if you prefer. The Drawing object toolbar includes a drop-down for line style and a spinner for line width.

How do I format text?

You have pretty much the same options for formatting text in Draw as in the other OOo applications. You can choose the font, size, attributes, color, and so forth.

To format the text associated with an object (including a textbox or callout), select the object by clicking it. Next choose Format | Character from the menu or Character from the shortcut menu to open the Character dialog (**Figure 8**). Choose the font characteristics you want and click OK to make the changes.

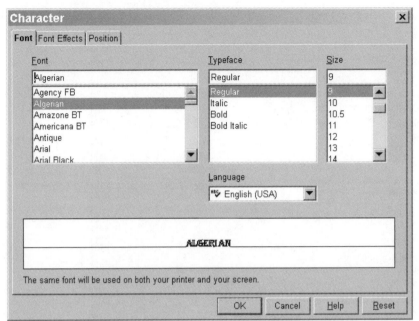

Figure 8. *Just as in other OpenOffice.org applications, use the Character dialog to specify font and other character formatting information.*

You can also change the way text is attached to the containing object. Select the object and choose Format | Text from the menu or Text from the context menu to open the Text dialog (**Figure 9**). The Text Tab lets you determine whether the text displays in the specified font and size or resizes to fill the available space (Fit to frame). For regular textboxes and callouts, you can determine whether the frame around the text resizes to fit the text, as well as specifying a margin around the text. For text that doesn't fill the available space, you can specify which point of the containing object it's attached to. By default, text is centered in the object, but you can attach it to any corner or the midpoint of any side.

The Text Animation tab lets you specify effects such as blinking and scrolling.

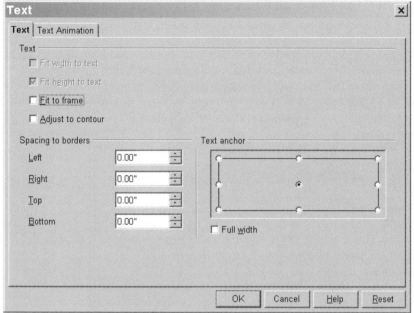

***Figure 9**. Use the Text dialog to indicate where text attaches to an object and whether the text resizes to fit the available space.*

How do I rotate an object?

You change the orientation of an object by selecting it and choosing Modify | Rotate from the menu. The selection handles change color and an indicator of the center of rotation appears. Figure 10 shows a rectangle ready to be rotated.

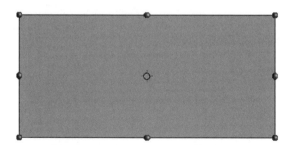

***Figure 10**. When you choose to rotate an object, the handles change from green to red and the center of rotation is marked.*

You can change the center of rotation by dragging the compass icon. To rotate about the center of rotation, position the mouse over any of the corner handles (the icon changes to an open circle with arrows on both ends), and drag the handle.

Dragging any of the side handles fixes the opposite side and rotates about that side, changing the shape of the object. Once an object has been rotated in this way, dragging a side handle fixes a corner point and rotates about that corner.

You can also rotate objects using the Rotation Tab of the Position and Size dialog (**Figure 11**). Select the object and choose Format | Position and Size from the menu or Position and Size from the shortcut menu. Set the center of rotation using the Pivot point settings and the angle using the Rotation angle settings. The Slant & Corner Radius Tab of the dialog lets you change the object's shape by fixing a side or point and rotating about that.

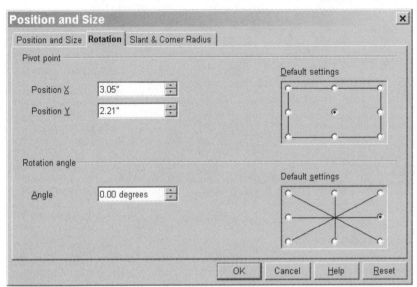

Figure 11. *If you know exactly what you want, you can set rotation using the Position and Size dialog.*

Can I put one object on top of another?

Many objects can occupy the same space in a drawing. Simply drop objects on top of each other or drag existing objects to the same place. Similarly, objects can overlap, which is probably more useful.

When objects are in the same place or overlap, you can determine which is on top and which is underneath. (This setting is often known as the "Z order" of an object because when graphing, depth is usually represented as the Z axis.) You change the depth of an object by selecting it and choosing Modify | Arrange from the menu or Arrange from the shortcut menu. That opens a submenu containing the choices shown in **Table 2**.

Table 2. *You can change the depth of an object in several ways.*

Menu choice	Meaning
Bring to Front	Make this object the topmost object.
Bring Forward	Move this object in front of the object on top of it, making it one object closer to the top.
Send Backward	Move this object behind the object beneath it, making it one object closer to the bottom.
Send to Back	Make this object the bottommost object.
In Front of Object	Put this object on top of the next object clicked. This item doesn't change the horizontal or vertical position of the selected object, only its depth.
Behind Object	Put this object underneath the next object clicked. This item doesn't change the horizontal or vertical position of the selected object, only its depth.
Reverse	Completely reverse the depth order of the selected items. This item appears only when two or more items are selected.

Figure 12 shows two sets of overlapping rounded rectangles. The left set is the original. The right set was copied from the left, and then the rectangle on top was sent to the back.

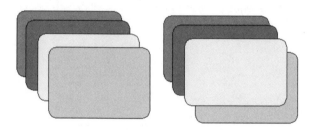

Figure 12. *The Arrange item on the shortcut menu lets you change the depth position of overlapping items.*

The Main toolbar also offers a way to set the depth of items. With one or more items selected, long click the Arrange button to open the Arrange toolbar. It includes buttons for each of the items in Table 2. **Figure 13** shows the left group from Figure 10 after being reversed.

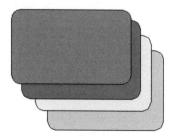

Figure 13. *Choose Reverse to turn a stack of items over, putting the bottommost object on top and the topmost on the bottom.*

What if the shape I want isn't listed?

You can create any shape, although it isn't always easy. To create a shape not included in one of the groups, start with the shape most like the one you want. Next select the object and choose Modify | Convert from the menu or Convert from the shortcut menu. If you want to create a shape containing only straight lines, choose To Polygon from the submenu. If you want the ability to create curves, choose To Curve. Next, choose Edit | Points from the menu or Edit Points from the shortcut menu. The shape appears with handles you can drag to reshape the object. **Figure 14** shows a rectangle that has been converted to a polygon and is ready to be edited. **Figure 15** shows the same object after dragging the upper left and lower right corners.

Figure 14. You can create any shape you want by starting with an existing shape, converting it to a polygon or curve, and editing the points.

Figure 15. This trapezoid was created by dragging the upper left and lower right corners of the rectangle in Figure 14.

You can also add points to an object, allowing you to drag from other positions. When an object is being edited in this way, the Drawing object toolbar changes to include a variety of choices for this type of editing. Choose Insert Points, and then click where you want a handle on the object. To stop adding points, click the Move Points button.

When you finish editing the object, choose Edit | Points from the menu, Edit Points from the shortcut menu, or click the Edit Points button on the Drawing object toolbar to turn off this mode.

Another way to create a shape not directly available is to build it from other shapes. Create, size and, if necessary, rotate the shapes you need, and position them together. Next select all the shapes involved and choose Modify | Shapes | Merge from the menu to turn several shapes into one. **Figure 16** shows a pentagon created from two rectangles.

Figure 16. *You can build the shapes you need by merging the basic shapes.*

Can I save my custom shapes in the Gallery?

When graphics are stored in the Gallery (see Chapter 4, "The OpenOffice.org Interface"), it's easy to use them throughout OOo.

To copy a shape to the Gallery, make sure the Gallery is open and the appropriate item is displayed. Click the shape once to select it. (You will see green sizing handles at the corners and sides.) Now, click and hold the mouse button down for at least two seconds, and then drag the shape into the Gallery and drop it. Unfortunately, there's no visual indicator to tell you when you can safely drag the shape to the Gallery, but if you start dragging too soon, the shape moves in the drawing. (If necessary, use Edit | Undo to return it to its original position.)

Are there any tools to help me get things lined up right?

Draw offers several features to aid in precise positioning of objects in a drawing. The first is simply there. The status bar at the bottom of drawing shows the current mouse position, as well as the size of any selected object. In addition, while you're selecting an object (that is, while the mouse button is still down), the current mouse position indicator shows the upper left corner of the rectangle bounding the object. **Figure 17** shows that portion of the status bar.

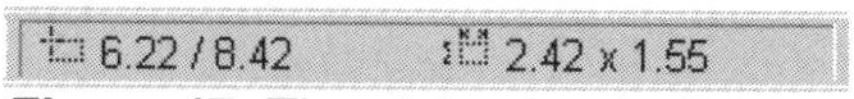

┊⁻┊ 6.22 / 8.42   ┊ 2.42 x 1.55

Figure 17. *The status bar includes position information. The lefthand values show the mouse position, while the righthand values are the size of the currently selected object.*

The second position tool is grid lines. You can turn on faint lines that offer a guide to position. To turn on grid lines, choose View | Grid | Visible Grid from the menu or Grid | Visible Grid from the shortcut menu (when no object is selected).

As initially configured, the grid lines are nearly invisible. You can adjust the settings on the Grid page (**Figure 18**) of the Drawing section of the Options dialog. The Resolution settings determine the distance between grid lines. The Subdivision section specifies how many points are shown between adjacent grid lines. The default setting of 1 is too small, change it to at least 3 in each direction to make the grid useful.

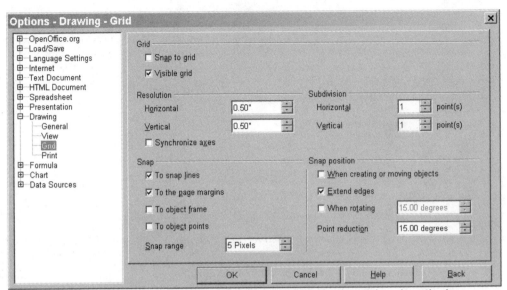

Figure 18. *To make the grid more useful, increase the horizontal and vertical subdivisions.*

Figure 19 shows part of a new drawing with grid lines on, set .5" apart with 6 points shown between lines. If you still find the grid lines too faint to see, consider changing the background color of the drawing to something dark. You can change it back to None before saving the drawing or using it elsewhere.

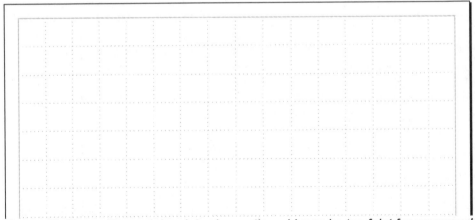

Figure 19. *Even with enough points shown, the grid may be too faint for your needs. Use a dark background color to provide contrast, if necessary.*

If you want to line things up at a particular place, a snap line will probably be more useful to you than grid lines. Snap lines are lines you create and position to give you a guide while designing a drawing. Snap lines do not appear in output. You can set things up so that any object dropped or moved close to a snap line moves to touch the snap line. (Draw also supports snap points, individual points with the same opportunity to grab nearby objects.)

To add a snap line to a drawing, choose Insert | Insert Snap Point/Line from the menu or Insert Snap Point/Line from the shortcut menu (when no object is selected). The New Snap Object dialog (**Figure 20**) appears. Specify either a point or the type of line you want to create and the position of the point or line.

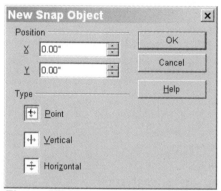

Figure 20. You can add guidelines to a drawing to help you position objects exactly where you want them.

Snap lines appear as dashed lines running from the ruler to the scroll bar in the appropriate direction. Snap points have no visual representation. **Figure 21** shows a drawing with a couple of horizontal snap lines.

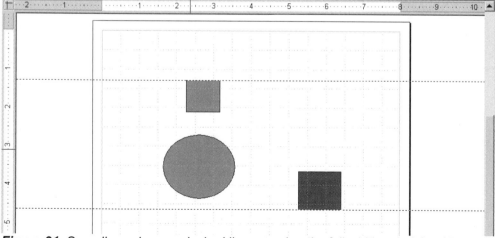

Figure 21. Snap lines show as dashed lines running the full width or height of Draw.

You can move a snap line from its original position by dragging it. However, items snapped to the line do not move with the snap line.

By default, objects "snapping" to snap lines is turned on. You can change the setting using Snap Lines | Snap to Snap Lines from the shortcut menu or View | Snap Lines | Snap to Snap Lines from the menu. The Grid page of the Drawing section of the Options dialog (shown in Figure 18) offers more control over snap lines. Select To snap lines to turn snapping on. The Snap range spinner determines how far away from a snap line or snap point an object can be without snapping. The default of 5 pixels is pretty small; you're likely to want to increase it.

Sometimes you want to line objects up with each other rather than at particular places in a drawing. You can use Modify | Alignment from the menu or the Alignment button on the main toolbar. Long click the button to open the Alignment toolbar (**Figure 22**). Both the menu and the toolbar offer options for both horizontal and vertical alignment. In each case, you can align either edge of the objects or their centers.

Figure 22. The Alignment toolbar lets you line up objects.

How do I use a drawing in another application?

Most often, you create drawings for use in other documents rather than as independent documents. There are a couple of ways to add a drawing to a document.

In Impress, the Main toolbars includes the various drawing objects and you can create drawings directly on a slide. In Writer and Calc, you can do the same, but it's a little harder to find. In those applications, the Main toolbar has a button whose tooltip reads "Show Draw Functions." Clicking that button opens the Draw Functions toolbar, which contains the various drawing objects. When a drawing object is selected in the various applications, the Drawing Object toolbar displays.

You can also add existing drawings to a document. Choose Insert | Object | OLE Object from the menu or choose Insert OLE Object from the Insert toolbar that appears when you long click the Insert button on the Main toolbar. The Insert OLE Object dialog (**Figure 23**) opens. To insert an existing drawing, choose Create from file and point to the file.

Figure 23. To put an existing drawing into a document, choose Create from file and specify the filename and path.

The same dialog lets you open Draw inside the other application. Choose Create new, and then choose OpenOffice.org <version> Drawing from the list. A new drawing object is added to the document and the menus and toolbar change to let you create it. When you finish, click outside the drawing object to return to editing the containing document.

To modify a drawing in a document, double-click it. The menus and toolbars change, and you can modify the drawing. As before, click outside the drawing to return to regular editing.

What formats can I save my drawing in?

In addition to the native SXD format, Draw lets you save drawings in a variety of graphic formats. The list includes BMP, JPG, TIF, and quite a few others. The most intriguing options on the list are PDF and Flash.

To save a drawing in another format, choose File | Export from the menu. In the dialog that appears (a variation of the regular Save As dialog), choose the type you want from the File format list and specify the filename and folder. When you click Save, another dialog may appear to specify options (like resolution and color depth) for that format.

Summary

OpenOffice.org's drawing application is extremely powerful. It gives you the ability to create a wide variety of drawings and diagrams, as well as to incorporate them into other OOo documents.

Updates and corrections to this chapter can be found on Hentzenwerke's web site, **www.hentzenwerke.com**. Click "Catalog" and navigate to the page for this book.

Chapter 15
Building Formulas

Those working in technical fields often need to include formulas and equations in documents to demonstrate ideas, show proofs, and so on. OpenOffice.org's Math application makes it easy to construct equations and use them in other applications.

Math has tools for building formulas using the symbols needed for a wide variety of professions. It's important to understand that, unlike Calc, Math doesn't provide any means for evaluating or solving equations; its purpose is to display them.

 Math is analogous to Microsoft Office's Equation Editor. However, Math can run independently and formulas you create can be saved to files, tasks Equation Editor can't handle.

How do I start Math?

You can open Math a number of different ways. If QuickStarter is running, choose Open File from QuickStarter and pick an existing formula to open Math with that formula loaded.

If you have another OpenOffice.org application open, choose File | New | Formula or long click the New button on the Function toolbar and choose Formula to open Math with a new formula. Choose File | Open or the Open button to open Math with an existing formula.

Depending on your operating system, you may be able to open Math from a menu. In Windows, choose Start | Programs | OpenOffice.org <version> | Formulas.

Finally, you can use Math within other OpenOffice.org applications. See "How do I put a formula into another document?" later in this chapter.

What do I see when I first open Math?

Math has a somewhat different appearance from the other OpenOffice.org applications. The first time you open it, a Command window is docked at the bottom and the Selection window is floating. **Figure 1** shows what Math looks like when you first open it.

In addition to the Command window, two toolbars are docked. The Function toolbar is docked under the menu, containing common items like New, Open, Save, Print, Cut, Copy, Paste, and so on. The Main toolbar is docked at the left; it contains a number of zooming options, plus access to additional symbols.

How do I create new formulas?

As described in "How do I start Math?" earlier in this chapter, you can create a new formula in several ways when you open Math. The same techniques work to create another new formula once you're working in Math. You can also create a new formula from within other OOo applications; see "How do I put a formula into another document?" later in this chapter.

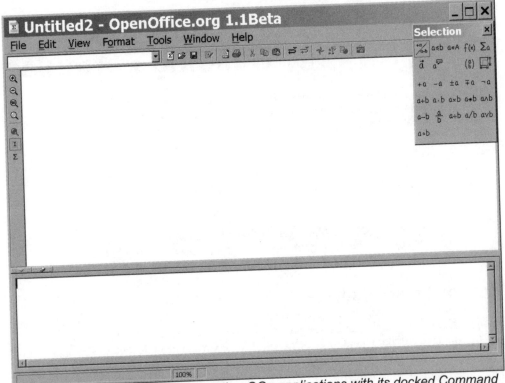

***Figure 1**. Math looks different from other OOo applications with its docked Command window and floating Selection window.*

How do I specify a formula?

Creating a formula is unlike nearly every other data entry activity in OpenOffice.org. In most OOo applications, you simply type in the data you want, whether it's text in a document, bullet points in a slide, or a formula in a spreadsheet. Even in Draw, you drop the objects you want onto the diagram.

In Math, however, you work in the Command window to specify the contents that show in the main window. If you type directly into the Command window, when you pause, the data you type is formatted and displays in the main window. The Selection window lets you specify items you can't type directly from the keyboard, such as subscripts, superscripts, and operators like the Greek letter sigma for summation. Specifying a formula generally involves a mix of choosing from the Selection window and typing on the keyboard.

> *Before digging in any deeper, it's probably useful to define a couple of terms. An* operator *is something that acts on values. For example, the plus sign ("+") is an operator, as is the square root symbol ("√"). Operators work on* operands, *the values to which they're applied.*

How does the Selection window work?

The Selection window (**Figure 2**) is a combination menu and palette for choosing operators to put into a formula. Although it resembles a toolbar, you can't dock or reshape it, although you can move it around. In fact, you can even drag the Selection window outside the Math window.

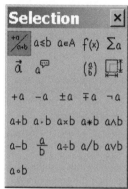

Figure 2. *The Selection window lets you choose the type of operator you need and add the operator to your formula.*

The top two rows contain categories of operators. When you click one of those buttons, the rest of the window changes to show the operators in that category. Figure 2 shows the unary and binary operators (the default, associated with the first button). **Figure 3** shows the Selection window after clicking the Set Operators button (the middle in the first row).

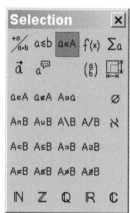

Figure 3. *Clicking a button from the first two rows changes the rest of the Selection window to show the appropriate operators.*

To add an operator to a formula, click the appropriate button. In the main window, you see the appropriate operator with boxes representing the operands. The Command window shows a textual representation of the operator and "<?>" for each operand. In some cases, curly braces ("{" and "}") surround operands. **Figure 4** shows the main window after inserting the absolute value operator, while **Figure 5** shows the Command window at that point.

Figure 4. When you choose an operator in the Selection window, the appropriate symbol appears in the main window, with operators represented by boxes.

Figure 5. In the Command window, operators have a text representation and operands are shown as "<?>."

How do I specify the operands?

While you can simply highlight the "<?>" placeholders and replace them with the appropriate values or expressions, there are two easier, more reliable ways.

Press F2 to highlight the next operand placeholder to the right of the cursor position. Use Shift-F2 to highlight the next operand placeholder to the left of the cursor position.

Using the mouse, you can highlight a placeholder in the Command window by double-clicking the corresponding box placeholder in the main window.

Once the appropriate placeholder is highlighted, you can either type in the operand or use the Selection window to build a complex expression.

Do I have to use the Selection window?

There are two ways to enter operators other than choosing them from the Selection window. First, you can simply type in the textual representation. Unfortunately, Help doesn't appear to offer a concordance table that matches the symbols to their textual representations.

In addition, the shortcut menu for the Command window (**Figure 6**) includes all the operators divided into the same categories as in the Selection window. In many cases, the shortcut menu uses the text representation, so you can also use it as a learning tool.

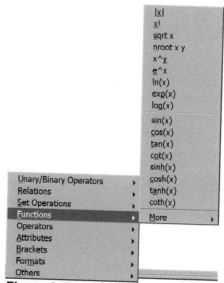

Figure 6. *The Command window's shortcut menu lets you insert operators directly.*

How do I specify summation with bounds?

Some operators need lower and/or upper bounds to make the specification complete. One well-known example is the summation operator ("Σ"), used to indicate that an expression should be totaled.

The operators that take boundaries, including summation, integrals, and limits are all found in the Operators category. (Although this category is called "Operators," in fact, most of the items you insert from the Selection window are operators.) The category also includes three special choices (along the right edge in the Selection window) that let you add the boundary conditions to specified operators. **Figure** 7 shows the Operators category in the Selection window.

Figure 7. *The Operators category includes operators involving boundary conditions.*

To use one of these operators, first specify the operator. Next, as the operand, choose the appropriate boundary condition operator. When you finish, the first operand or operands are the limits and the final operand is the actual expression. **Figure 8** shows how a summation is specified in the Command window; **Figure 9** shows the resulting formula.

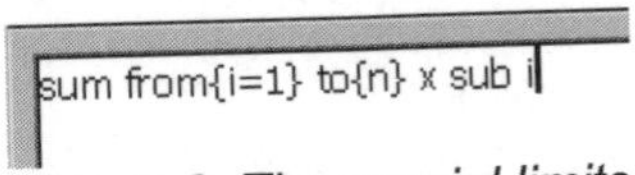

sum from{i=1} to{n} x sub i

Figure 8. The special limits operators let you set up summations and other operators that involve lower and/or upper bounds.

$$\sum_{i=1}^{n} x_i$$

Figure 9. The Command window expression in Figure 8 results in this formula.

Can I change the fonts?

Math has an entirely different way of dealing with fonts compared to other OOo applications. You can't set fonts, sizes, and attributes by simply highlighting something and choosing a menu item. Math also doesn't support styles in the way the other applications do.

In general, fonts and sizes are specified for the various types of components (such as variables or numbers) that comprise a formula; these specifications affect the formula as a whole. In addition, you can override the setting for a particular item; see "How do I change the appearance of an item?" later in this chapter.

To set fonts for components, choose Format | Fonts from the menu. The Fonts dialog (**Figure 10**) opens. The dialog lets you set the font for variables, functions, numbers, and text. You can also set three additional fonts to be used when you explicitly choose them.

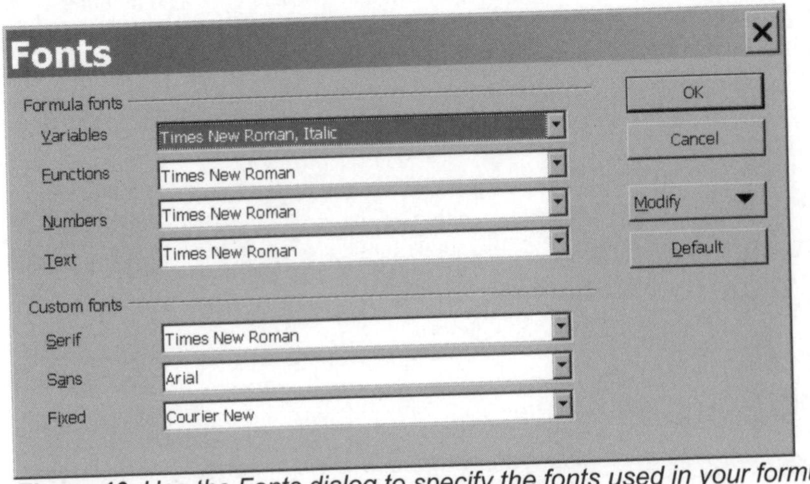

Fonts		
Formula fonts		OK
Variables	Times New Roman, Italic	Cancel
Functions	Times New Roman	
Numbers	Times New Roman	Modify
Text	Times New Roman	Default
Custom fonts		
Serif	Times New Roman	
Sans	Arial	
Fixed	Courier New	

Figure 10. Use the Fonts dialog to specify the fonts used in your formula.

The Fonts dialog works differently than you might initially think. For each type of element, there's a drop-down list of available fonts for that element. Initially, each drop-down list contains only one choice. To add choices to a list, click Modify and choose the element type from the menu that appears. Another dialog (**Figure 11**), also labeled Fonts, opens. In this dialog, choose the font you want to make available. If you want bold and/or italic, select the appropriate check boxes. When you return to the Fonts dialog, the new font appears in the specified drop-down list and, in fact, is the chosen font for that element type.

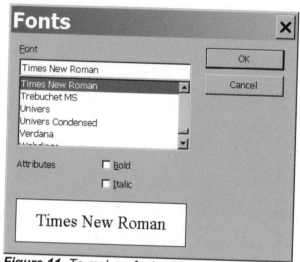

Figure 11. *To make a font available for a particular element type, choose it in this dialog.*

When you choose a font from the drop-down list for a particular element, it applies to all items of the type.

How do I use the custom fonts?

The Fonts dialog includes three specifications for "custom fonts," one each for Serif, Sans Serif, and Fixed. You set these fonts just as you do those for formula elements, but they're not used unless you explicitly select them.

To use one of the custom fonts, type the tag "font" followed by the font type in the Command window. Surround the text to use that font with quotation marks. For example, the following entered in the command window results in the text shown in **Figure 12**.

```
font sans "This is sans serif text."
```

This is sans serif text.

Figure 12. *You add text in whatever format you want by using the three custom fonts.*

How do I set font sizes?

The Fonts dialog sets only the font itself, and doesn't let you set font size. To set font sizes, choose Format | Font Size from the menu. The Fonts Sizes dialog (**Figure 13**) opens. Rather than specifying the size of each element type independently, you indicate a base size, and then specify the others as relative percentages of the base size. Each relative size you specify applies to all elements of the specified type.

Font Sizes ☒

Base size	12pt	OK
Relative sizes		Cancel
Text	100%	
Indexes	60%	Default
Functions	100%	
Operators	100%	
Limits	60%	

Figure 13. You specify font sizes as percentages of a base size.

How do I change the appearance of an item?

The settings you make in the Fonts and Font Sizes dialogs apply to all the elements of a formula. Occasionally, you may need to change the appearance of a particular item within a formula. You do so by specifying the attributes you want it to have before the actual item.

For font, you can specify one of the custom font styles preceded by the keyword "font." For example, this displays the element "xy" using the specified sans serif font.

```
font sans xy
```

For size, use the "size" keyword followed by an asterisk ("*") and the desired size. Size is relative to the default size. For example, continuing the previous case, the following shows "xy" using the sans serif font at twice the normal size:

```
font sans size*2 xy
```

You can also indicate whether the element should use bold and italic. The attributes "bold" and "italic" turn those items on for that element, while "nbold" and "nitalic" turn them off.

How do I control the spacing between elements?

As with fonts, you control spacing globally in Math, but have some ways to override the global settings. Spacing is specified for the different types of elements and the settings you specify apply to all items of the particular type.

To set global spacing, choose Format | Spacing from the menu. The Spacing dialog (**Figure 14**) opens. At first glance, the dialog includes only three items. However, the Category drop-down button lets you change the dialog to offer spacing options for various types of elements. You specify spacing as a percentage of the base font size.

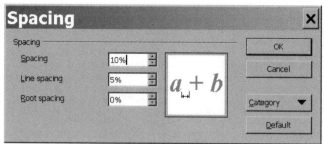

***Figure 14**. The Spacing dialog lets you determine how much white space appears between the various components of a formula.*

When you position the cursor in a particular spinner, the diagram changes to show you exactly what spacing the spinner sets. In **Figure 15**, the dialog shows spacing options for fractions. The cursor is in the denominator spinner, and the diagram indicates that you're setting the space between the divider and the denominator of the fraction.

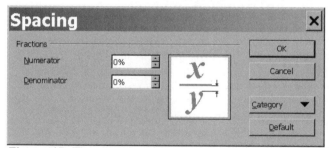

***Figure 15**. The diagram in the spacing dialog indicates the element being set.*

How do I force extra space into a formula?

In addition to the space defined by the Spacing dialog, you can put extra space into a formula. To put a small space in, put the accent grave character ("`"), found to the left of the digit "1" on US keyboards) into the Command window or choose Formats | Small Gap from the Command window's shortcut menu.

Insert a larger space using the tilde character ("~", the shifted version of the accent grave key on US keyboards) or choose Formats | Gap from the shortcut menu for the Command window.

How do I put a formula into another document?

As with Draw, you can either save a formula and add it to another OOo document or create a formula right in another document on the fly.

To insert a saved formula into a document, choose Insert | Object | OLE Object from the menu in the application where you want to insert the formula. When the Insert OLE Object dialog appears, choose Create from file and point to the saved formula, as shown in **Figure 16**.

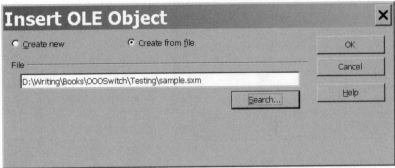

Figure 16. You can insert an existing formula into a document.

To create a new formula on the fly without leaving the other application, choose Insert | Object | Formula. An empty Math formula is added to the document, the menus change to allow formula creation, and the Selection window and Command window appear. When you finish specifying the formula, click elsewhere in the document.

To edit a formula you add, double-click the formula. The menus change and the Selection and Command windows appear.

To move a formula, click it once to select it, and then drag it to the new position or use the arrow keys to move it. The ability to move a formula is constrained by the way the formula is anchored; in some cases, you can only move a formula in some directions. To change the anchoring setting, choose Anchor from the shortcut menu or Format | Anchor from the menu with the formula selected. (See "How do I add pictures to a document?" in Chapter 7, "Dressing Up Documents," for a discussion of anchoring types.)

Summary

OpenOffice.org's Math application provides the tools needed to create equations and formulas you can put into other documents.

Now that you have seen all the individual OOo applications, it's time to move on to some more advanced features. The next chapter examines OOo's Master Document tool, which lets you consolidate multiple documents into a single result.

Updates and corrections to this chapter can be found on Hentzenwerke's web site, **www.hentzenwerke.com**. Click "Catalog" and navigate to the page for this book.

Chapter 16
Using Master Documents
to Consolidate

Some documents, like books, are large enough to make storing them as a single file unwieldy. OpenOffice.org's master document feature lets you store such a document in multiple files yet still produce such features as a table of contents.

Master documents offer a way to consolidate text documents without actually storing them as a single file. They're especially useful in collaborative situations, where different people may be editing different portions of a long document.

What is a master document?

When writing a book or other multi-chapter work, it's convenient to store each chapter in a separate file. It's especially true when multiple authors or editors are involved. However, there are some things, such as page numbering, that apply to the work as a whole.

The master document feature is meant to give you the best of both worlds. It allows you to break a work into manageable chunks, but still tie the whole thing together, with common styles, numbering, and the like.

There are two components involved; the master document and one or more (usually more) sub-documents. The master document contains links to the sub-documents and is the one you use to see the complete work. The sub-documents are text documents of some sort; you can't specify a spreadsheet, drawing, or other document type.

Think of the master document as a container for the sub-documents. While the sub-documents aren't actually stored in the master document, the master document is the one that knows where to find everything and their order.

Should I use a master document?

The answer is a definite "it depends." While master documents have the benefits described above, they are quite finicky. Getting them to behave exactly as you want requires doing things just so.

 Although OOo's master documents are tricky to work with, they do work. Word's master documents are difficult enough to use that most Word experts recommend avoiding them.

 There's no way to create cross-references between the sub-documents in a master document. This removes one of the strongest reasons for using them.

So how do you decide whether to use a master document? First, experiment with a small example to see what works for you and what doesn't. Ideally, structure your example like the document you need to create. Once you do that, evaluate the benefits and the necessary effort and make a choice.

How do I create a master document?

While you can create a master document directly (by choosing File | New | Master Document from the menu), that's not the best approach. Instead, first create a template (see Chapter 5, "Making Life Easier with Templates and Styles") that includes all the styles you want for both the master document and its sub-documents.

Once the template is set up, create a new document based on the template. Save the document as a master document by choosing File | Send | Create Master Document from the menu. Once you specify a file name, the document is saved as a master document. In addition, the Navigator changes to show options related to master documents, as in **Figure 1**. (Figure 1 actually shows the process a little farther along, after creating and adding a couple of sub-documents.)

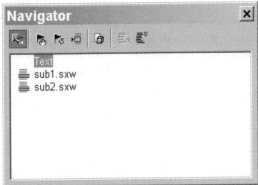

Figure 1. *When a master document is open, the Navigator shows its structure and has buttons for manipulating the master document.*

The leftmost button in the Navigator (its tooltip is "Toggle") lets you switch back to the conventional view, with headings, tables, and so forth.

How do I add sub-documents to a master document?

Things work best when you create the sub-documents from the same template as the master document. (That's why the template should contain all the styles you need.) To set up a sub-document, create a new document based on the template and save the document.

Next, open the master document and, with the Navigator in Master Document view (as in Figure 1), long click the Insert button and choose File, or choose Insert | File from the Navigator's shortcut menu. In the Insert dialog that appears, point to the sub-document.

The chosen file is added in a separate section. (See Chapter 6, "Dressing Up Documents," for an explanation of Writer's section mechanism.) The new section is at the top of the document. Use the Move Up and Move Down buttons to position it correctly. Figure 1 shows the structure of a master document (identified as "Text") with two sub-documents, named sub1 and sub2.

Once you add one sub-document, you have better control over the positioning of additional sub-documents. Each sub-document you insert is placed before the one currently highlighted in the Navigator. This suggests that the ideal order to insert your sub-documents may be back to front rather than front to back.

What goes where?

Conventional wisdom seems to agree the master document itself should contain the "front matter" for the overall work, items like the foreword or preface, the table of contents, and so forth. Typically, each sub-document represents a chapter or major section of the work.

Why doesn't my page formatting stick?

This appears to be a bug. Each time you insert a sub-document into a master document with the initial Text section chosen in the Navigator, the first page (the first "Text" section in the Navigator) returns to the Default page style. If that page uses another page style, formatting related to that style disappears. The solution is to either use the Default page style for that part of your document, or reset the style after insertions.

Fortunately, once you insert the first sub-document and reset the page style, you probably won't run into the problem again.

How do I specify headers and footers?

Unfortunately, it's hard to specify headers and footers in the template used for a master document. Unless you plan to use the Default page style for the entire document, specify the headers and footers in the master document itself.

Don't add headers and footers to the sub-documents; they won't appear when the sub-document is added to the master document.

Can I add text to the master document in between or after the sub-documents?

This is a well-hidden feature you could easily miss. When a sub-document is highlighted in the Navigator and there's another sub-document immediately above it, a Text item is added to the list of things you can Insert (**Figure 2**). When you choose Insert | Text from the shortcut menu or long click Insert and choose Text, a new section is added to the master document allowing you to add text between sub-documents.

To put an additional text section at the end of the master document (for example, for an index or bibliography), insert a text section between the last two sub-documents, and then move that section down, as in **Figure 3**.

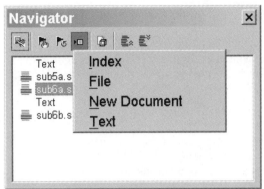

Figure 2. When the second of a consecutive pair of sub-documents is highlighted, the Insert menu includes a text item.

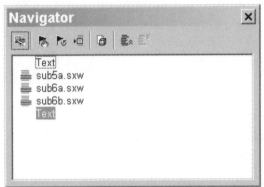

Figure 3. To add a text section at the end, add it between the last two sub-documents, and then move it down.

How do I start a sub-document on a new page?

By default, sub-documents are inserted immediately following the preceding section, which is often on the same page. None of the options for starting a sub-document on a new page are particularly elegant, but they do work.

What appears to be the best approach involves page styles. In the template for the master document, define a page style to use for the first page of each sub-document. You can use the built-in First Page style, if you wish.

Next, define a paragraph style to always use as the first style in a sub-document. You can use one of the built-in heading styles or define one of your own. In the Breaks section of the Text Flow tab of the Paragraph Style dialog (shown in **Figure 4**), select Enable and make sure the Type drop-down shows Page and the Position drop-down shows Before. Select With Page Style and set the drop-down to the your first page style.

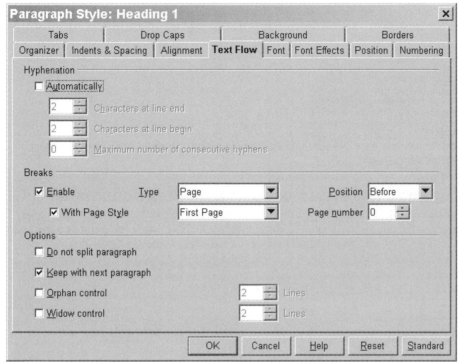

Figure 4. To make each sub-document start on a new page, you need a paragraph style with a page break, linked to a page style.

In the sub-documents, make sure the first paragraph uses the specified style. Don't use that paragraph style elsewhere unless you want to force a page break.

When you add the first sub-document using this technique, you will likely need to reset the page style for the Text section of the master document, as described in "Why doesn't my page formatting stick?" earlier in this chapter.

How do I edit the sub-documents?

The sub-documents within a master document are read-only. That is, you can't edit a sub-document from within the master document. However, you can always open a sub-document in the usual way and edit it.

The Navigator offers another choice. Double-click a sub-document, select the sub-document and choose Edit from the shortcut menu, or select the sub-document and choose the Edit button in the Navigator to open it for editing.

The master document does not immediately reflect changes in a sub-document. Choose Update | Links from the Navigator's shortcut menu or long-click the Navigator's Update button and choose Links to bring in changed content.

How do I edit a master document?

You open a master document for editing just like any other. However, when you open it, you may be prompted as shown in **Figure 5**. If you want to update the master document to show the current contents of each sub-document, choose Yes. If you choose No, the master document opens, showing the sub-documents as they existed when last updated.

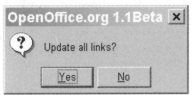

Figure 5. When you open a master document, you can update it to show the latest content from the sub-documents.

Can I change the styles used in a master document?

While you can edit styles in a master document or any of the sub-documents, it's not a good idea. If you need to change the formatting of a style, open the template for editing and make the change there. That way, the changes apply to all the documents, not just to one.

When you change style definitions in the template, the next time you open the master document or any of the sub-documents, you're prompted to update the styles, as shown in **Figure 6**. Choose Yes to make the changes to the document.

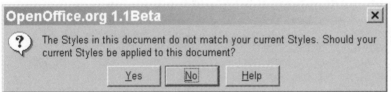

Figure 6. When the styles in the template for a document change, this prompt appears when you open the document.

How do I incorporate existing documents into a master document?

The best way to create a master document is to plan for it from the beginning, but that's not always possible. To take a batch of existing documents and make them sub-documents for a master document is a multi-step process.

First, define a template that incorporates all the styles used in the group of documents as well as any you need for the master document itself. Create the new master document as described in "How do I create a master document?" earlier in this chapter.

Next, one at a time, open each document you want to incorporate, create a new document using the new template, and cut-and-paste the existing document's contents into the new document. Save the new document. It's now ready to add to the master document, as described in "How do I add sub-documents to a master document?" earlier in this chapter.

Summary

OpenOffice.org's master document feature is extremely powerful and can be very useful when dealing with large documents or documents being created by multiple authors. However, making a master document work requires advance planning and caution.

Updates and corrections to this chapter can be found on Hentzenwerke's web site, **www.hentzenwerke.com**. Click "Catalog" and navigate to the page for this book.

Chapter 17
Managing Data with
OpenOffice.org

While OpenOffice.org doesn't include a full-blown database application development tool like Microsoft's Access and Visual FoxPro, it has considerable power for working with data, including the ability to create databases.

Data is everywhere. An address book is data, a spreadsheet is data, a list of errands you need to run after work is data. OpenOffice.org offers a variety of things you can do with data once you make it available. Writer can use data in mail merge (see Chapter 7, "Dressing up Documents"), Calc can crunch data and create pivot tables (see Chapter 9, "Database manipulation with Calc"), as well as graph data to make it comprehensible (see Chapter 10, "Working with Graphs and Charts"). In addition to those uses, OOo offers tools for managing and manipulating data directly. This chapter examines those tools.

How do I work with data in OpenOffice.org?

One window and one dialog form the key tools for managing data. The Data Source Administration dialog lets you make data available to OOo applications, while the Data Source window lets you use it.

A *data source* is any data set you specify. It can be data from a database server like SQL Server or MySQL, data created by a database product like dBase, data contained in a spreadsheet, data available through ADO or ODBC, data in an appropriately-structured text file, data from an e-mail client's address book, or one of several other possibilities.

OOo also allows you to create new databases using the dBase format.

How do I make OOo see my data?

To make data available to OOo, you use the Data Source Administration dialog (**Figure 1**). Open it by choosing Tools | Data Sources from the menu in Writer or Calc. The dialog lists all defined data sources and allows you to add new ones. The Bibliography data source shown in Figure 1 comes with OOo and lists a number of relevant books.

Because an address book is one of the most common forms of data (virtually every computer user has one), the first time you run OOo, it prompts you to set up an Addresses data source, and allows you to point to the address book that provides the data. You can set up additional data sources by clicking New Data Source. Specify a name for the data source and its type, and then point to the actual data.

Once you add a data source, you can examine it in the other tabs of the Data Source Administration dialog. The exact set of tabs available depends on the type of the data source.

Each data source contains one or more tables with the tables containing the actual data. A table is made up of fields (or columns); each field holds one piece of information. You can explore the information in a data source by switching to the Tables tab. Expand the All tables item to see the list of tables. **Figure 2** shows the single table available in a data source based on an Outlook address book.

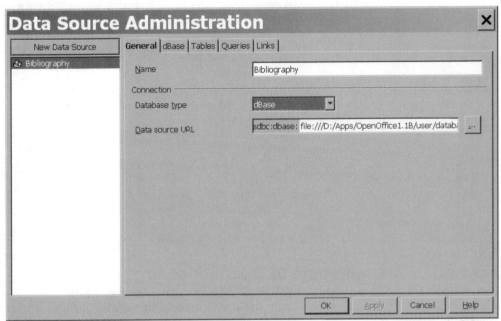

Figure 1. Use the Data Source Administration dialog to make data available to OOo.

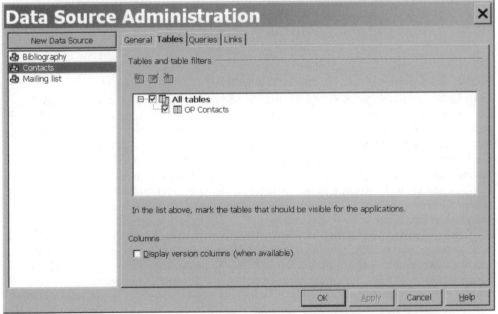

Figure 2. The Tables page shows you the tables that comprise a data source.

Can I create new data sources from scratch?

OOo allows you to create dBase data sources on the fly and populate them. To create a new dBase database, add a data source as described above, specifying its type as dBase. For the Data source URL, point to the folder where you want to store the data.

Next, switch to the Tables page and click the New Table Design button. The Table Designer (**Figure 3**) opens for you to define the structure of the table. Add each field (data item) you want to put in this table. Keep in mind a database can contain more than one table, so don't feel you have to stuff everything into one place. Figure 3 shows fields you might define for a table designed to keep contact information about members of a group.

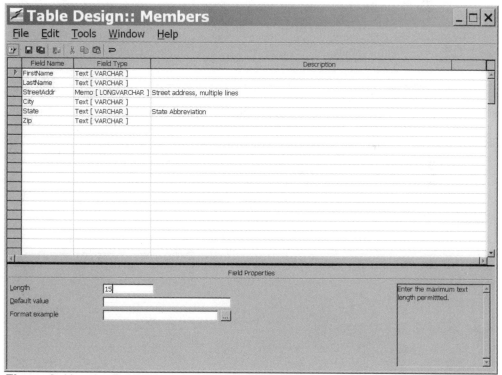

Figure 3. Use the Table Designer to define the fields for a table. Each field is one piece of data.

You must specify three pieces of information for each field and have the option of indicating several others. Every field has a name of no more than ten characters; the name must begin with a letter, and can include letters, digits, and the underscore character ("_").

The second data item for a field is the type; **Table 1** shows the field types available. Data you put in a field is restricted to the specified data type so, for example, if a field is decimal, you can't put alphabetic characters into it.

Table 1. Each field has a type. Choose the right type to help keep data organized.

Field type	Used for
Text	Character data that is never longer than a specified size.
Memo	Character data of any size.
Yes/No	Items that are either true or false.
Decimal	Numeric data.
Date	Date data, such as birth dates, date hired, and so forth.

The final required item is the field size. You specify this in the Length text box beneath the list of fields. Some data types, including Memo, Date, and Yes/No, have predetermined field sizes. The Length text box doesn't appear for fields of those types. For Decimal fields, you specify both the total size of the field and the number of digits to the right of the decimal point. The decimal point counts so, for example, a Length of 7 with Decimal places set to 2 gives you 4 digits to the left of the decimal point.

You can specify additional information for each field, including a default value to fill in when you add a record. For example, if you're working with addresses and most of the records fall in the same state, you might put that state abbreviation in as a default.

Once you specify all the fields you want, click the Save button. A Save As dialog appears for you to specify the name of the table.

A single data source may contain multiple tables. However, OOo doesn't provide a way to specify or take advantage of relationships between tables.

How do I add data to a new data source?

You can't change the data in a data source using the Data Source Administration dialog. Instead, use the Data Sources window (**Figure 4**), which you open by choosing View | Data Sources on the menu or by pressing F4. Like the Stylist and Navigator, the Data Sources window includes buttons to hide itself and to make the document window resize itself. However, unlike those tools, the Data Sources window is docked at the top and can't be undocked or moved to another location.

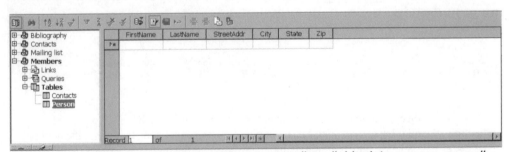

Figure 4. The Data Sources window lets you see all available data sources, as well as add, edit data, and drag data into documents.

To add records to a new data source, drill down to the appropriate table on the left. Click the table so its fields show as columns on the right. (In Figure 4, the Person table is shown before any records are added.)

The list of records on the right side shows an empty record at the end. You can simply type data into it. As soon as you type a single character into the empty record, it's added to the table and a new empty record appears at the bottom. The empty record isn't stored as part of the actual data. You can recognize an empty record that hasn't been added—it has an asterisk to its left.

Adding data in the Data Sources window is fine for a record or two, but for larger amounts of data, you probably want to use a custom data entry form. See "Can I create data entry forms?" later in this chapter.

Can I modify data?

Whether records are part of a new data source you just added or an existing data source, you can edit some data. The ability to edit depends on the data source; the data must have a unique primary key (a field that uniquely identifies each record) for the data to be editable. When you can't edit a particular data source, the Edit Data button in the Data Sources window's button bar (known as the *database bar*) is disabled. Even when a data source is editable, you can turn editing off by toggling the Edit Data button. That prevents you from accidentally changing data.

When data is editable, you simply click in the field you want to change and modify it. To save your changes, either click the Save current record button in the database bar or navigate to another record.

Keep in mind that changes you make to data through OpenOffice.org are reflected in other applications that use the data.

Can I sort data?

You can sort data on any field. The easiest way to sort is to click the field name for the desired field, which highlights that column. Next, click either the Sort Ascending or Sort Descending button. If no column is highlighted when you click one of the sort buttons, data is sorted based on the first field in the table.

If you want to specify more complex sorting (such as last name, and then first name), use the Sort Order button, which opens the Sort Order dialog. **Figure 5** shows how to set up last name, first name sorting.

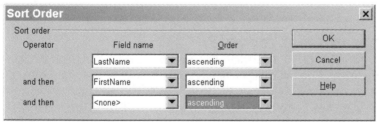

Figure 5. You can sort on up to three fields, specifying ascending or descending order for each.

Whichever way you sort, the records are shown in that order. To turn off sorting and show records in their original order, click the Remove Filter/Sort button on the database bar.

Can I show only some records?

Displaying a limited number of records based on their content is known as *filtering*. The Data Sources window lets you filter data in a couple of ways. The simplest is to click the AutoFilter button. That creates a filter based on the current field (the one containing the cursor) of the current record. It includes all records with the same value for that field.

You can be more explicit about what you want to filter. Click the Default Filter button to open the Default Filter dialog (**Figure 6**). You can specify up to three filter conditions combined using AND or OR.

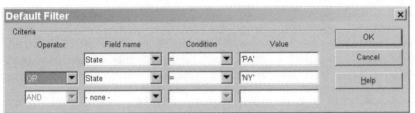

Figure 6. *A filter can specify up to three conditions, combined with AND or OR.*

> The meaning of AND and OR in a filter is more precise than in ordinary language. When you use AND, each condition in the filter must be true independently for the record to pass the filter. When you use OR, any condition can be true. This calls for special care when you work with negative conditions. In Figure 6, the filter limits results to records where the state is PA or NY. If you want to find all the other records, you need to specify State <> 'PA' AND State <> 'NY'.

Once you set a filter using the Default Filter dialog, it's applied immediately. You can turn it off, but leave it defined by clicking the Apply Filter button. Click that button again to turn the filter back on. To remove the filter entirely without leaving it defined, click the Remove Filter/Sort button.

For a more persistent filtering capability, use a query instead. See "Can I define subsets of my data?" later in this chapter.

How do I find a particular record?

At any time, a pointer to the left of the first field indicates the current record. In **Figure 7**, the record for Mary Jones is current. You can navigate through the records in a table by scrolling with the keyboard or the mouse. There's also a set of "VCR buttons" beneath the records. They allow you to move forward or backward one record at a time or jump directly to the first or last record.

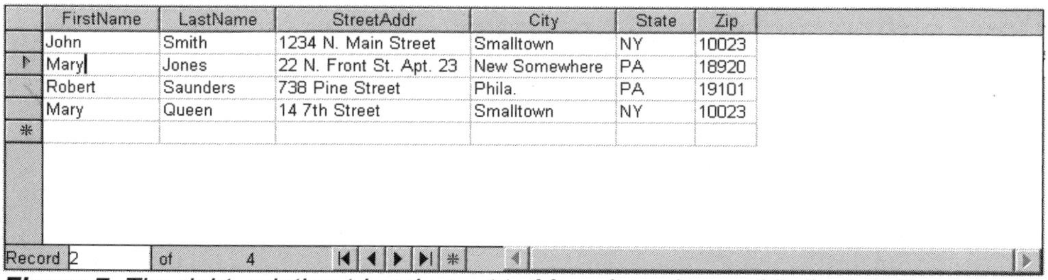

	FirstName	LastName	StreetAddr	City	State	Zip	
	John	Smith	1234 N. Main Street	Smalltown	NY	10023	
▶	Mary	Jones	22 N. Front St. Apt. 23	New Somewhere	PA	18920	
	Robert	Saunders	738 Pine Street	Phila.	PA	19101	
	Mary	Queen	14 7th Street	Smalltown	NY	10023	
✱							

Record 2   of   4   ◄◄ ◄ ▶ ▶◄ ✱   ◄   ▶

Figure 7. *The right-pointing triangle next to Mary Jones' record indicates the current record. The VCR buttons at the button let you move forward and backward one record at a time or to the beginning or end of the data.*

The position of the current record (as well as the total number of records) displays at the bottom of the record list. If you know the position of the record you want, you can simply type it in this area. Be aware that the number reflects the record's position in the current sort order, not any absolute value.

While all of these techniques allow you to move around in your data, more often, you want to find a record based on its contents. To do so, use the Find Record button on the database bar. It opens the Record Search dialog (**Figure 8),** which lets you search for a specified string in one or all fields. When you click Search, the record pointer moves to the next matching record; both the current record indicator in the data and the record number in the Record Search dialog update. (If the search reaches the end of the list, it wraps around to the top and continues.)

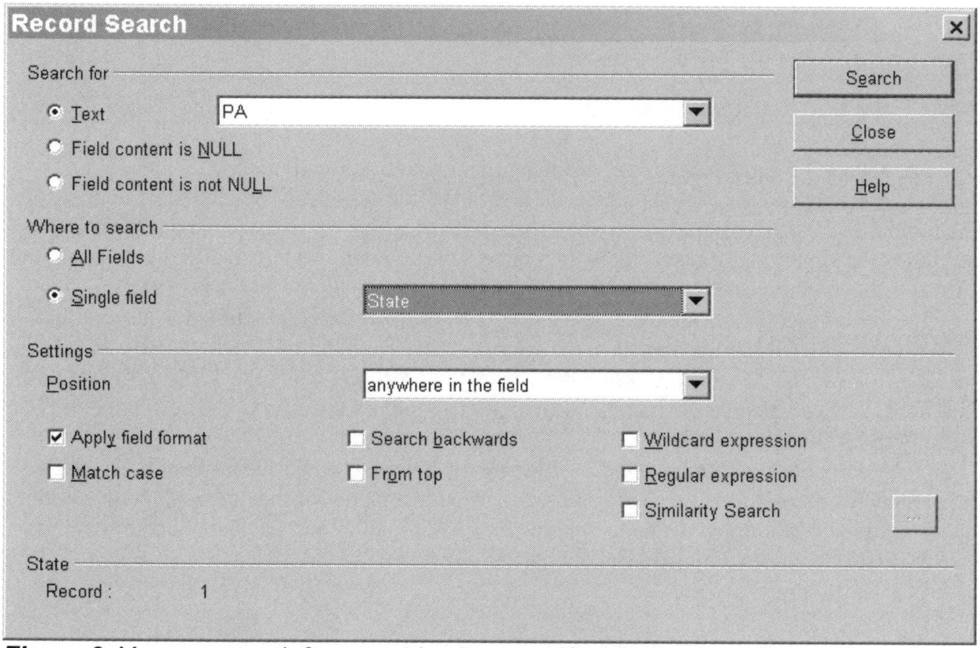

Record Search   ✕

Search for ───   ┌──────────┐
                                                                   │ Search │
  ⦿ Text   [PA   ▼]   └──────────┘
  ○ Field content is NULL   ┌──────────┐
  ○ Field content is not NULL   │ Close   │
                                                                   └──────────┘
                                                                   ┌──────────┐
                                                                   │ Help   │
                                                                   └──────────┘

Where to search ──
  ○ All Fields
  ⦿ Single field   [State   ▼]

Settings ───
  Position   [anywhere in the field   ▼]

  ☑ Apply field format   ☐ Search backwards   ☐ Wildcard expression
  ☐ Match case   ☐ From top   ☐ Regular expression
                                                     ☐ Similarity Search   [...]

State ──
  Record :   1

Figure 8. *You can search for any string in a specified field or in all fields. The string can be at the beginning, end, or anywhere in the field.*

Can I define subsets of my data?

There are situations where you may want to work frequently with a certain subset of the records in a table. While you may be able to use a filter to limit the display to those records, the ability to have only one filter at a time makes this approach less than ideal. A better solution is to define a query that extracts the records you want. Not only can you define multiple queries, but queries can also include only a subset of the fields and offer more sorting and filtering ability.

To define a query, right-click the Queries item for the data source and choose New Query (Design View). (If you're comfortable writing SQL queries, you can instead choose New Query (SQL View).) The Query Designer opens. Initially, the Add Tables dialog (**Figure 9**) appears to let you specify the table to query; it shows all the tables for this data source. Choose one and click Add. The dialog closes and you can work in the Query Designer (**Figure 10**).

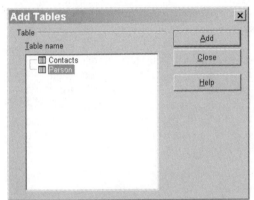

Figure 9. The Add Tables dialog shows all tables in the data source and lets you choose the one to use in the query.

The Query Designer has several sections. Immediately beneath the menu, there's a toolbar. A number of the buttons determine which sections appear below the toolbar. Beneath the toolbar is the Tables area, which shows the table or tables involved in the query. This section is far larger than it needs to be, in most cases. You can make it smaller by dragging the splitter between this section and the one beneath it.

The bottom section of the Query Designer is where you actually define the query. It has one column for each field to appear in the query results. To add a field to the query, use the Field drop-down list. When you move away from the drop-down list, the Table item fills in for that field. You can change the name of a field in the result by specifying the new name in the Alias item for the field.

Once you define a query, save it by clicking the Save button on the toolbar or choosing File | Save from the menu. You're prompted to provide a name for the query. Once saved, the query is added to the list of available queries for this data source in the Data Source window and the Data Sources Administration dialog.

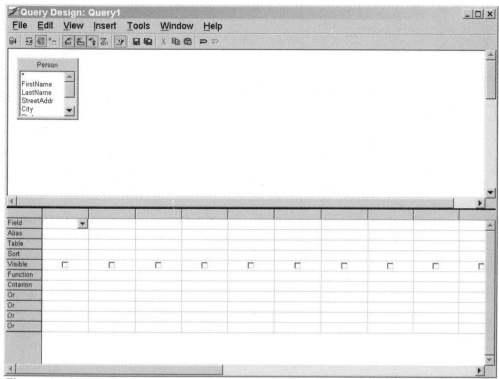

Figure 10. Use the Query Designer to define a query so you can work with all records meeting specified characteristics.

How do I filter data in a query?

You can specify one or more values to match for each field you list. Enter the value to match in the Criterion section for the specified field. **Figure 11** shows a query that extracts the first name, last name, and state for each person and limits results to those living in Pennsylvania. To include records that match one of several values for a single field, list the first possible value in the Criterion item, and put other values in the Or items. **Figure 12** shows the same query, but includes people in Pennsylvania, New Jersey, and Delaware.

Field	FirstName	LastName	State
Alias			
Table	Person	Person	Person
Sort			
Visible	☑	☑	☑
Function			
Criterion			'PA'
Or			
Or			
Or			
Or			

Figure 11. To filter on a particular field, enter the value you want in the Criterion item.

Field	FirstName	LastName	State
Alias			
Table	Person	Person	Person
Sort			
Visible	☑	☑	☑
Function			
Criterion			'PA'
Or			'NJ'
Or			'DE'
Or			
Or			

Figure 12. To match one of several values, list each value in the right column.

> Don't include the quotation marks around the values when you enter them. They're added automatically when you leave the cell.

To use a condition other than equality, include the operator with the criterion. For example, if you want to see all records with last names starting with the letters S through Z, use ">= S". Don't include the quotation marks, but do make sure to leave a space between the operator and the value. **Figure 13** shows this query.

Field	FirstName	LastName	State
Alias			
Table	Person	Person	Person
Sort			
Visible	☑	☑	☑
Function			
Criterion		>= 'S'	
Or			
Or			
Or			
Or			

Figure 13. You can use the >, >=, <, and <= operators in filters.

Sometimes, you want to find records in a range of values. For example, you might want those last names between "L" and "P". You can't specify such a condition in a single column. Instead, you need to include the column twice in the field list and specify each of the conditions for one instance of the column. **Figure 14** shows this example. (The second condition is "< Q" because we want to include all records that start with "P".)

Field	FirstName	LastName	State	LastName
Alias				
Table	Person	Person	Person	Person
Sort				
Visible	☑	☑	☑	☐
Function				
Criterion		>= 'L'		'< "Q"'
Or				
Or				
Or				
Or				

Figure 14. *To combine conditions with AND rather than OR, you need to include the field twice in the field list.*

Of course, in this situation, we don't need to include the last name twice in the results, so the Visible check box is cleared for the second instance of last name. You can do the same thing for any column you want to filter on, but not include in the results.

How do I sort query results?

You can specify the order of the records in a query using the Sort row. For each field in the query, you can specify ascending, descending, or no order. **Figure 15** indicates that the query results should be sorted by last name.

Field	FirstName	LastName	State
Alias			
Table	Person	Person	Person
Sort		ascending	
Visible	☑	☑	☑
Function			
Criterion			
Or			
Or			
Or			
Or			

Figure 15. *Use the Sort row to specify the order of records in the result.*

Sorting is applied from left to right in the list of columns. So, for example, if the first name column in Figure 15 also specified an ascending sort, the results would be sorted on first name first, and then on last name for those records with the same first name. To change the order of sorting, you need to change the column order. You can do so by clicking and holding on the column header (above the field name) and dragging to the new position.

Can I see what results a query will give?

It's convenient to see what the result set of a query looks like as you're working on it. To do this, click the Run Query button on the toolbar. A new section appears showing the query results. **Figure 16** shows the Query Designer after running the query shown in Figure 11 (which filters on State="PA").

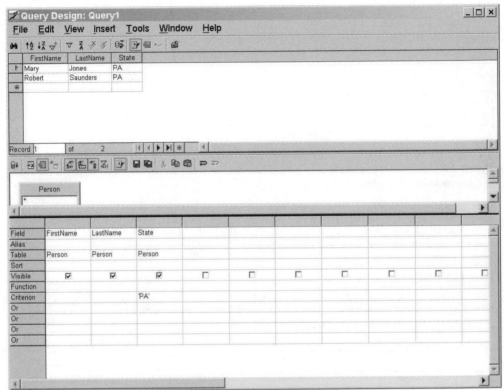

Figure 16. When you run the query, the results section appears at the top of the Query Designer.

You can work with the query results pretty much as you do with table data (described in a number of sections earlier in this chapter), but changes you make to query results don't affect the actual data in the tables. To close the results section, click the Close button on the database bar in the results section.

Can I create data entry forms?

The Form AutoPilot helps you set up custom data entry forms that display the fields you want and provide some control over what is entered. To create a new form, choose File | AutoPilot | Form from the menu. A new text document opens and the Form AutoPilot appears. The first step (**Figure 17**) is to choose a data source and table. When you select the right table (or query), the list of fields in the table appears. You can include as many or as few as you want on the form; specify the fields to include by moving them from the Existing fields list to the Fields in form list. Click the "=>>" button to include all fields. To include a subset, highlight the fields you want and click the "->" button. You can remove fields from the Fields in form list using the "<-" and "<<=" buttons. In Figure 17, all fields from the Person table have been added to the Fields in form list.

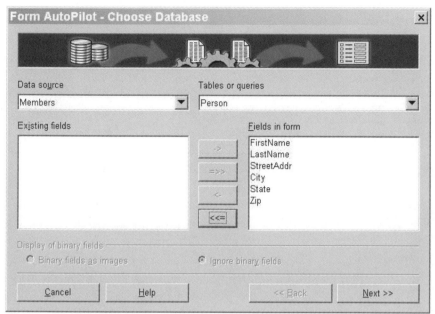

Figure 17. The first page of the AutoPilot lets you specify the table to use and the fields that should appear.

Click the Next button to move to the second page of the AutoPilot (**Figure 18**). On this page, you specify visual aspects of the form—the layout of fields, alignment of labels, and the background. As you make changes, you can see the results on the new form. When things are set as you want them, click the Create button. You're prompted to save the new form; it's a Writer document (SXW), which you can store wherever you want. When the save finishes, the form appears showing the first record from the specified table. **Figure 19** shows the form created by the choices in Figures 17 and 18.

The form includes a database bar, by default, docked at the bottom. The database bar contains controls for navigating, sorting, filtering, and searching, as well as buttons to save the current record, add a new record, and delete a record. The various controls work as they do in the Data Sources window.

New records are always added at the end. To do so, click the New Record button and enter data. (You can also add a new record by clicking the Next Record button while positioned on the last record.) The record isn't actually added until you type at least one character into it. The data you add isn't saved until you click the Save Record button or navigate to another record. The same is true for data you change in existing records.

The Delete Record button deletes the current record after prompting to verify you mean to do so.

Because a form is just a regular Writer document, to stop editing your data simply close the form. You may be prompted to save changes.

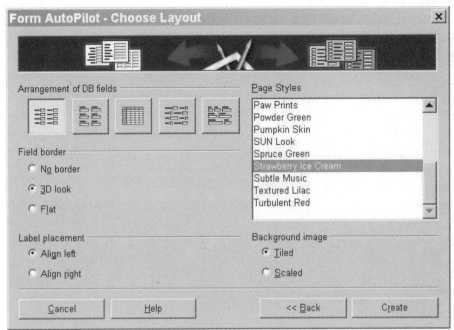

Figure 18. The second page of the Form AutoPilot specifies the layout of fields, the background pattern or color, and other visual aspects.

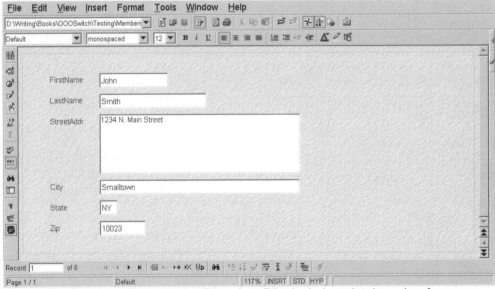

Figure 19. Forms created with the Form AutoPilot include a database bar for navigating, sorting, filtering, and searching.

Can I create reports?

The Report AutoPilot lets you create a variety of reports based on your data. To start, choose File | Report | AutoPilot from the menu. A new text document is created and the Report AutoPilot opens. On the first page (**Figure 20**) specify the data source and table, and then indicate the fields that should appear in the report. Like the Form AutoPilot, the Report AutoPilot uses a two-column mover to let you choose the fields. Use the "->" and "=>>" buttons to add fields to the report; use the "<-" and "<<=" to remove fields.

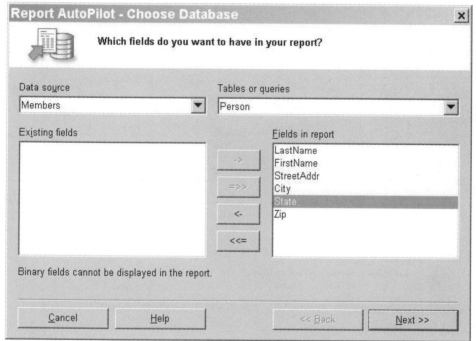

Figure 20. *The first thing you specify in the Report AutoPilot is the data source, table, and fields.*

The report normally displays the fields in the order of the Fields in report list. You can't reorganize that list, so be sure to add the fields in the order you want to see them. When the list is as you want it, click Next to move to the next page.

The second page of the Report AutoPilot (**Figure 21**) lets you specify the column headings used for the fields in the report. Depending on the data source, the field names may or may not be appropriate for a report. If not, modify them on this page. Again, click Next when you have the results you want.

The third page (**Figure 22**) lets you set up grouping in the report. It's common to want to put all records that meet certain conditions together in the report. For example, a sales report might group sales by salesperson, a membership report might group by zip code, and so forth. The Report AutoPilot allows for multiple levels of grouping, using a two-column mover. The final report includes a heading for each group. Click Next when the groupings are set.

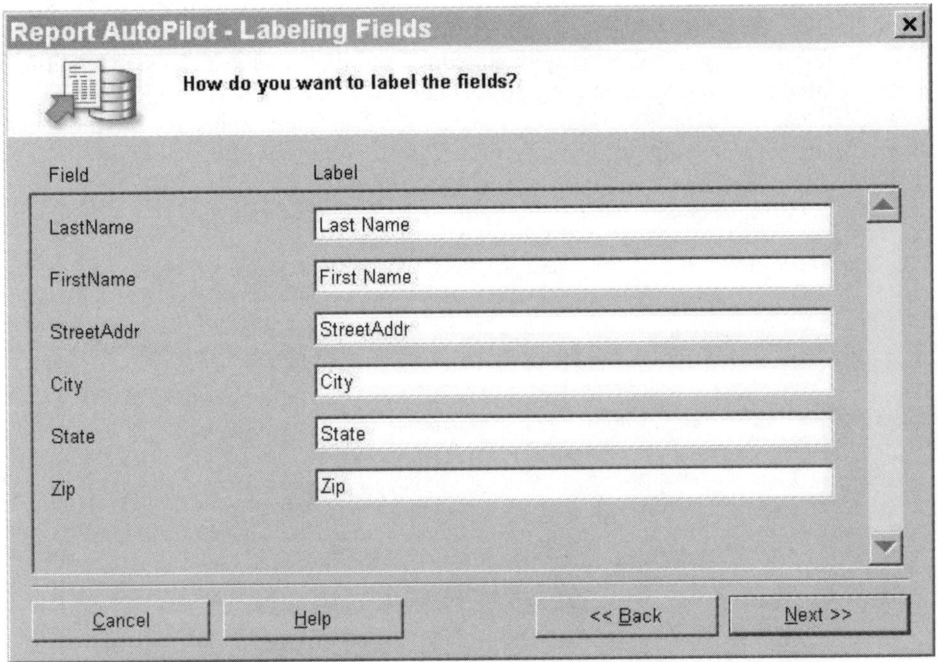

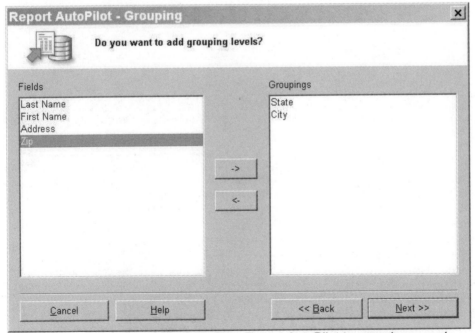

Figure 21. This page of the Report AutoPilot specifies the labels to use.

Figure 22. Use the Grouping page of the Report AutoPilot to organize records by content.

The next page (**Figure 23**) of the Report AutoPilot is for specifying the sort order of the records. You can sort on up to four fields. Fields chosen for groupings aren't included in the list because the report automatically sorts by those fields. Again, click Next after you specify the fields on which to sort.

> *As of this writing, there's a bug in the Report AutoPilot. When you specify sorting, the order of fields in the report changes. Apparently, the AutoPilot assumes you want to see the sorted fields first.*

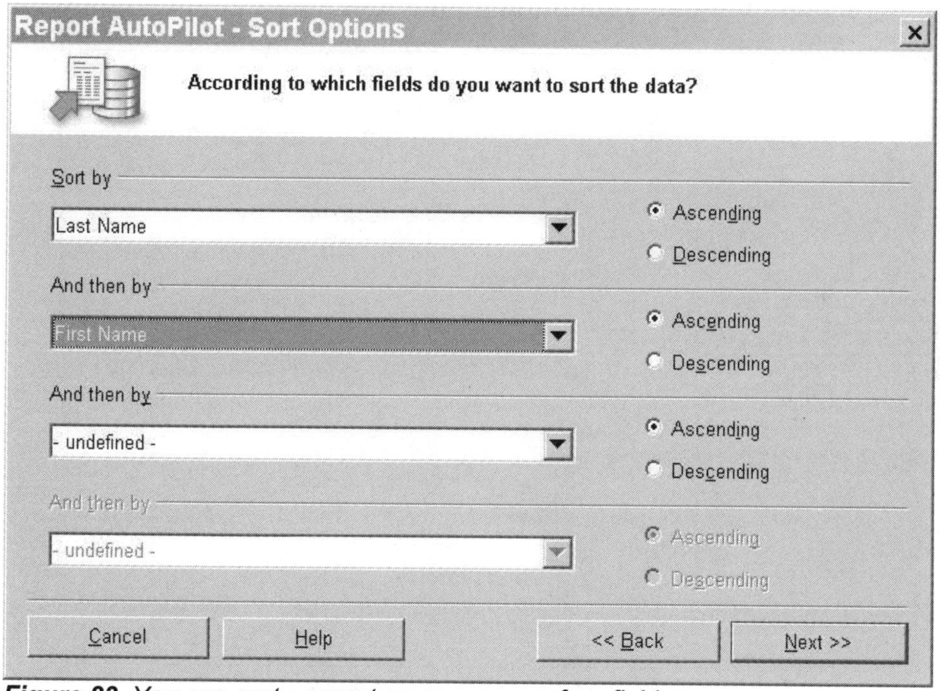

Figure 23. *You can sort a report on as many as four fields.*

The fifth page of the Report AutoPilot (**Figure 24**) addresses aesthetic issues. You can specify the title for the report, indicate landscape or portrait orientation, and choose the layout for the fields and for headers and footers. While the AutoPilot currently handles only columnar reports, there are quite a few choices for their actual appearance. Some of the header and footer layouts also include background graphics. As you make choices on this page, the text document is modified to show the results. Click Next to reach the last page of the AutoPilot.

On the final page (**Figure 25**), you specify whether to create a template or a document. You actually have three choices. You can create a template and open it for editing, you can create a template and immediately create a document based on the template, opening that for editing, or you can create a document directly. When you make your choice, click Create and the template and/or document is created and opened.

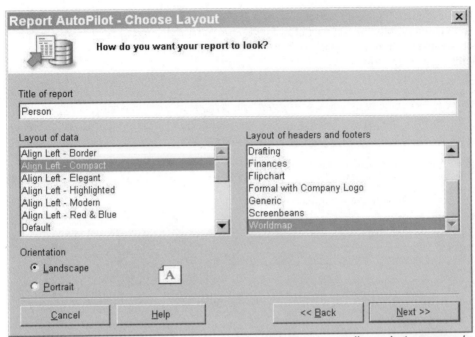

Figure 24. You can choose the layout of the columns, as well as what appears in headers and footers.

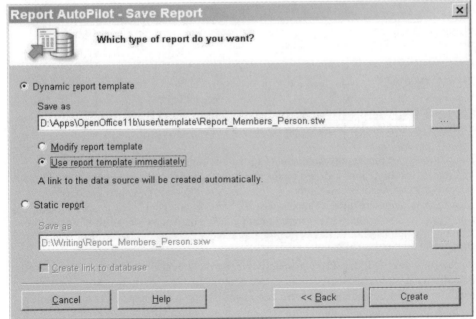

Figure 25. The final page of the Report AutoPilot lets you indicate what to do with the generated report.

If you choose to create a document directly, you can link it to the data source, so each time you open it, the contents update. As noted on the page itself, templates you create automatically link to the data source.

Figure 26 shows part of a report based on the template created in Figures 20 through 25. You can modify some aspects of the report, such as the header and the column headings. Unfortunately, once you create a report, there's no way to move the data around or otherwise reorganize it. For those tasks, you have to start over and create a new report.

Title:	
Author:	Tamar Granor
Date:	5/19/03

State	CA			
City	My Town			
Last Name		*First Name*	*Address*	*Zip*
Johnson		Janice	87 Market Street	90012

State	NH			
City	OurTown			
Last Name		*First Name*	*Address*	*Zip*
Masters		Jason	747 W. Della Street Apt. 27A	01039

State	NY			
City	Smalltown			
Last Name		*First Name*	*Address*	*Zip*
Smith		John	1234 N. Main Street	10023
Queen		Mary	147th Street	10023

State	PA			
City	New Somewhere			
Last Name		*First Name*	*Address*	*Zip*
Jones-Smith		Mary	22 N. Front St. Apt. 23	18920

Figure 26. A report generated using the Report AutoPilot.

Reports and forms you create with the AutoPilot are added to the Links section in the Data Source window.

How do I use my data in OpenOffice.org?

Both Writer and Calc offer opportunities to use data you register as a data source. Writer uses a registered data source to provide the data for mail merge; see Chapter 7, "Dressing Up Documents," for details. Calc can perform a variety of data-crunching tasks; see Chapter 9, "Database Manipulation with Calc." Calc can also graph the data; see Chapter 10, "Working with Graphs and Charts."

Summary

For a suite with no database component, OOo offers a surprising range of database capabilities. It's worth spending some time to learn what you can and can't do.

Updates and corrections to this chapter can be found on Hentzenwerke's web site, **www.hentzenwerke.com**. Click "Catalog" and navigate to the page for this book.

Chapter 18
Forms, Macros, and Automation

Sometimes you need more than what the package natively provides. This chapter looks at three advanced capabilities, custom input forms, macros to speed up or simplify your work, and automation that allows you to use the OpenOffice.org applications from within other applications.

For most users, simply creating documents of the various types and working with them handles their needs. However, some people want or need to go farther.

In some situations, you need to create a document that allows people to enter information without changing certain aspects. Such a document is called a *form*, analogous to the preprinted forms everyone has filled out dozens of times.

There are also times when some task needs to be performed over and over, or when a task is complex enough that doing it manually makes it hard to get it right. *Macros* allow you to save a sequence of operations with a single name so you can do the same thing repeatedly.

Automation is a first cousin to macros. It lets another application control OOo and make things happen without user intervention.

How do I create a form where people can only enter data?

In some situations, you want to create a form that contains some fixed text, but allows users to enter some items and perhaps take some actions on those items. Chapter 17, "Managing Data with OpenOffice.org," looked at one such case—providing a data entry form for a data source. However, you can create custom forms in most of the OOo applications; forms you create without the Form AutoPilot don't have to connect to a data source (though they can—see "How do I attach a data source to a form?" later in this chapter). If the form isn't connected to a data source, information the user enters there is simply saved with the form. (You might do that when you want to send a form to a group of people for them to fill out and return.) Writer, HTML Editor, Calc, Impress, and Draw all support forms.

To create a form, start with a document in the appropriate application. Long click the Show Form Functions button on the Main toolbar. (In some cases, you may have to add the button to the toolbar first; see "How do I customize the toolbars?" in Chapter 4, "The OpenOffice.org User Interface.") The Form Functions toolbar (**Figure1**) appears. The toolbar includes an assortment of controls you can put on your forms, as well as buttons for managing the form as a whole.

Figure 1. The Form Functions toolbar lets you add controls to a document to create an input form.

As with the other toolbars available through a long click, once you make a selection from the Form Functions toolbar, it closes. However, you can drag the toolbar away from the button that opens it and it stays open until you close it. When designing a form involving a number of controls, this can be a very handy feature.

The items in the first row of the Form Functions toolbar are controls. The second row contains a variety of options for working with forms and controls. Most of them are discussed later in this chapter.

To add a control to a form, click it on the Form Functions toolbar. The cursor changes to crosshairs. Click and drag where you want to place the new control. **Figure 2** shows the process of inserting a textbox; **Figure 3** shows the result.

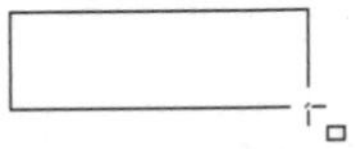

Figure 2. After you choose a control from the Form Functions toolbar, click and drag to place it on the form.

Figure 3. Once you drop a textbox control, it takes on a chiseled look.

Once you choose a control from the Form Functions toolbar, you can continue dropping that type of control. To turn off that control type, either click another control to select it, click the form itself without dragging, click the same control on the Form Functions toolbar, or click the Select button on the Form Functions toolbar.

What controls are available?

OOo offers a wide variety of controls from the general to the specific. **Table 1** lists them.

Table 1. *The selection of controls available for use in forms is extensive. Controls are shown here in the order in which they appear on the Form Functions toolbar.*

Control	Use
Push Button	Used to execute commands.
Option Button	Used, with one or more other option buttons, to allow choice among mutually exclusive options. See Group Box.
Check Box	Used for on/off or yes/no choices.
Label Field	Used to provide labels for other controls. Doesn't accept input.
Group Box	Used to visually combine several controls, as well as create groups of option buttons.
Text Box	Used to enter free-form text.
List Box	Offers a list of choices. User can choose one or, in some cases, several.
Combo Box	Offers a list of choices. User can choose one or enter a new value.
Image Button	Used to execute commands; has a picture rather than a text caption.
Image Control	Displays a picture on the form.
File Selection	Allows user to point to a file.
Date Field	Used to enter a date. Supports up arrow and down arrow to change portions of the date.
Time Field	Used to enter a time. Supports up arrow and down arrow to change portions of the time.
Numerical Field	Used to enter numbers. Optionally has spinner arrows to change value with the mouse.
Formatted Field	Used to enter text applying formatting codes as in Calc.
Currency Field	Used to enter monetary values. Supports up arrow and down arrow to change value. Optionally has spinner arrows to change value with the mouse.
Pattern Field	Used to enter text, applying a specific formatting pattern.
Table Control	Used to display data from a table or query in a grid format.

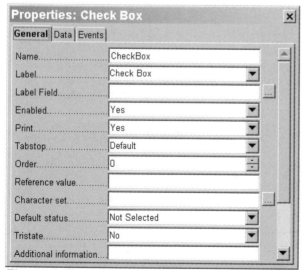

Figure 4. *The Properties dialog for a control lets you specify its appearance and behavior.*

How do I customize controls?

With some controls, you can simply drop them on a form and use them as is. That works for things like a Text Box, Date Field, or Time Field. With others, though, once you add the control, you need to provide additional information. Even for those that work immediately, you may want to customize their appearance or behavior.

To set up a control, click it to select it (green sizing handles appear around the edges), and then choose Control... from the shortcut menu, Format | Control... from the menu, or Control Properties... from the Form Functions toolbar. The Properties dialog for the control appears. The contents of the Properties dialog vary, depending on the type of control. **Figure 4** shows the Properties dialog for a Check Box.

Just as the contents of the Properties dialog vary with the type of control, so does what you need to do to get it working. **Table 2** lists some of the items common to a number of controls.

Table 2. The Properties dialogs for the various controls let you set them up as you want. The properties shown here are common to a number of the controls.

Property	Meaning
Name	Identifies the control. In some cases, including option buttons, assigning the same name to several controls turns them into a group.
Label	The caption that appears on the control.
Label field	Links the control to a Label Field control. Used for controls (like Text Boxes) that don't have their own label.
Enabled	Determines whether the control is available to the user.
Tabstop	Determines whether the control is part of the tab order, that is, whether the user can reach it by tabbing from one control to the next.
Order	Determines the position of the control in the tab order.
Character set	Specifies the font characteristics for the control.
Default value	Specifies the initial value displayed in the control.
Background color	Specifies the background color for the control.
Help text	Specifies the tooltip for the control.

Individual controls have additional properties related to their purpose. For example, a Check Box has a Default Status property that determines whether it's initially checked and a Text Box has a MultiLine input property that determines whether you can put multiple lines of text into the control.

Some controls need certain properties specified in order to be useful. In some cases, AutoPilots are available to help you specify the necessary information. The next few sections consider some of those controls.

How do I create a group of option buttons?

Option buttons (also known as "radio buttons") let you choose one item from among a mutually exclusive group. **Figure 5** shows a group of option buttons (or *option group*) set up for choosing a color.

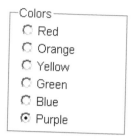

Figure 5. *Option buttons let you choose one among a group of alternatives.*

There are a couple of ways to set up a group of option buttons, but the easiest is to make sure the AutoPilots On/Off button on the Form Functions toolbar is on. (When it's on, it has a thin border around it.) Next, put a Group Box on the form. When you do so, the AutoPilot Group Element (**Figure 6**) appears to guide you through the creation of an option group. On the first page, specify the options to appear in the group. For each, type it in, and then press Enter or click the >> button. When all the items have been entered, click Next.

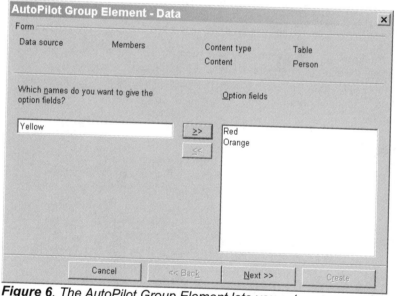

Figure 6. *The AutoPilot Group Element lets you set up groups of option buttons. On the first page, you specify the options.*

On the second page, indicate which item in the list should be initially selected. You can also specify no item be selected. Click Next to go to the third page (**Figure 7**), which allows you to associate a value with each item. Specifying a value is particularly significant when data on the form is tied to a data source. (See "How do I associate a form with a data source?" later in this chapter.) To specify the value for an item, click that item in the list, and then type the appropriate value in the text box. By default, character items are associated with numbers starting from 1. Click Next to move to the Database Field page.

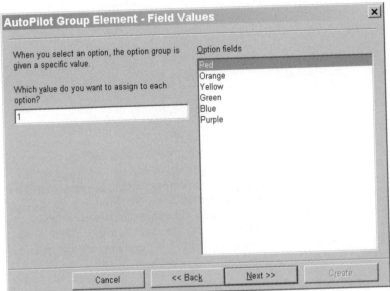

Figure 7. *Each option has a value associated with it.*

The Database Field page lets you automatically save the user's choice to a field in a table. If you prefer, you can specify that the value is available only in the form. Click Next to reach the final page of the AutoPilot. On this page, you specify a name for the option group—the name appears as a caption on the surrounding box. Click Create to exit the AutoPilot and create the option group.

How do I set up a combo box?

Like an option group, a combo box lets a user choose from among a mutually exclusive group of options. However, a combo box usually takes up less space than an option group and also allows the user to type in a value not on the list. Again, the easiest way to configure a combo box is to use the AutoPilot.

Make sure the AutoPilot's On/Off button is on and put a combo box on the form. The AutoPilot Combo Box opens. Combo boxes always draw their contents from a data source. If you haven't associated a data source with the form yet (either by using it for another control or by explicitly doing so—see "How do I associate a form with a data source?" later in this chapter), the first page (**Figure 8**) that appears lets you choose a data source and table for the form. Click Next to move to the Table Selection page once you choose a data source.

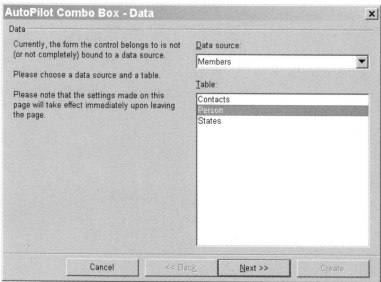

Figure 8. *If the form doesn't have a data source, the AutoPilot Combo Box prompts you for one.*

If the form already has a data source, the AutoPilot opens on the Table Selection page (**Figure 9**). The data you display in the combo box doesn't have to come from the table the form is linked to, and in fact, often comes from another table that contains look-up information. In Figure 9, it's a separate table containing states and their abbreviations. Click Next once you choose the table that contains the list of items to appear in the combo box.

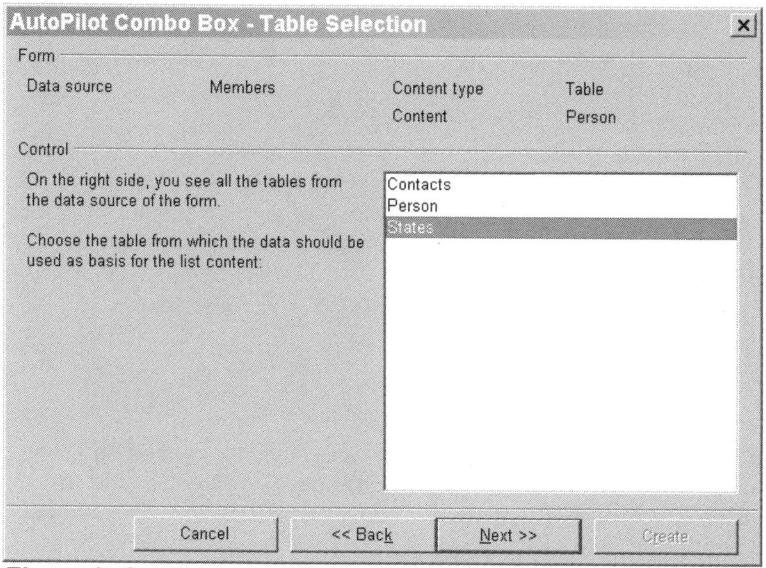

Figure 9. *On this page, choose the table containing the data items for the combo box.*

The Field Selection page (**Figure 10**) lists the fields from the specified table. Choose the one to use in the combo box. The specified field not only provides both the list of items the user sees, but also the value to store based on the user's choice. (With a combo box, there's no way to display data from one field, but store the value from a different field. List boxes do provide that option; see the next section "How do I set up a list box?") Click Next to move to the Database Field page to indicate where to store the user's choice. Click Create to create the combo box.

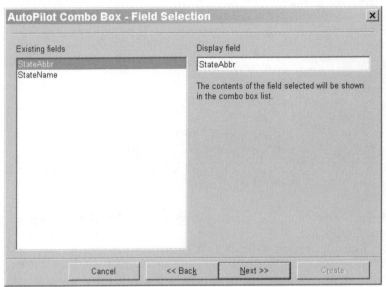

Figure 10. A combo box lists data from a single field.

Figure 11 shows the combo box listing US states created in Figures 8 through 10.

Figure 11. This combo box lists the abbreviations for the US states.

How do I set up a list box?

A list box has a lot in common with a combo box, so it's not surprising the method for specifying a list box isn't much different from that for a combo box. Like a combo box, the easiest way to set up a list box is with the AutoPilot.

A list box must be tied to data from a data source. It draws data from a table and stores its results in a table. Usually, the data comes from one table (a look-up table) and the results are stored in another table. Unlike a combo box, a list box can store data from a different field than is displayed.

As with a combo box, if no data source is associated with the form, the first page of the AutoPilot (Figure 8) lets you choose one. Once you finish and click Next, choose the table that contains the data to appear in the list, as in Figure 9. After clicking Next, the process continues as with a combo box. On the next page (Figure 10), you specify the field to appear in the list box.

At this point, list boxes part company from combo boxes. When you click Next, you reach the Field Link page of the AutoPilot (**Figure 12**). On this page, you link a field from the form's data source table to a field from the list box's table. The link indicates that when the user makes a choice from the list box, the value of the specified field of the list box's table is copied to the specified field of the form's table. In the example, I set the list box up to show the full name of each state (though Figure 10 specifies the abbreviations), but store the abbreviation in the Member table.

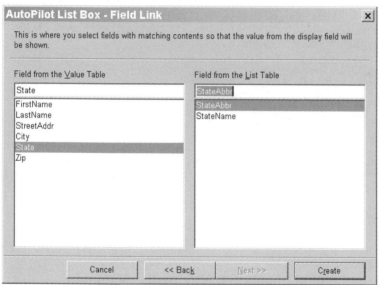

Figure 12. The Field Link page makes it possible to display data from one field, but store data from a different field.

When you click Create, the list box is created. By default, it's a drop-down list that looks like a combo box, but doesn't allow the user to type in a new value. To change it to a regular list box, with a number of items displayed at once, choose Control from the list box's shortcut menu or with the list box selected, choose Control Properties... from the Form Functions toolbar or Format | Control from the menu. Change the Drop-down property to No. **Figure 13** shows the list box of states.

Figure 13. To turn a drop-down list into a regular list, change the Drop-down property to No.

Do any other controls have an AutoPilot?

Most of the remaining controls are simple enough to configure that no AutoPilot is needed or provided. However, the Table control is fairly complex. It provides a grid type display of the data in a table, along with navigation controls. The Table Element AutoPilot (**Figure 14**) lets you choose which fields display and in what order.

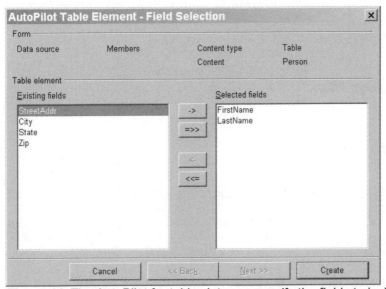

Figure 14. The AutoPilot for tables lets you specify the fields to include.

How do I attach a data source to a form?

As described in the last few sections, using the AutoPilots for some kinds of controls requires you to specify a data source for the form. However, sometimes, you may want to do so even if you're not creating a combo box or list box.

To link a data source to a form, choose Form Properties... from the Form Functions toolbar. Choose the Data tab (**Figure 15**), and then choose a Data Source from the drop-down list. Once you choose a data source, choose a table from the Content drop-down list. You can also specify a query or write a SQL command directly to provide the form data by changing the Content Type, and then specifying the appropriate Content.

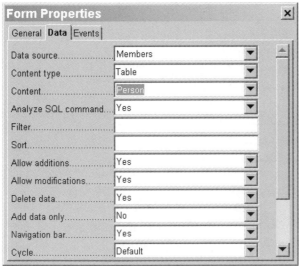

Figure 15. The Data tab of the Form Properties dialog lets you specify the data source for a form.

How do I associate data with a field?

Once the form has a data source, you can link fields to controls. To do so, add the control to the form, and then open its Properties dialog. On the Data tab, choose a field from the Data Field drop-down list.

Be aware that when you link a field to a control in this way, every time you use that control, changes you make are stored in the actual data source.

How do I make something happen in my document?

While editing a data source is one use for forms, you may want to use a form for other things. For example, you might want to add a button to a spreadsheet to perform a calculation or to a presentation to run a video clip.

Each control has a number of events associated with it. An event is something that occurs due to user action. For example, when the mouse is moved, an event fires each time it enters the area of a control and each time it leaves that control's area. Typing a character also fires an event. So does clicking the mouse.

The Events tab of the Properties dialog for each control lists the events available for that control. **Figure 16** shows the Events tab for a text box. For each event, you can specify what happens when that event fires. You do so by clicking the ellipsis button next to the event, and then pointing to the OOo macro that performs the desired action. (For details on writing macros, see "How do I create a macro?" later in this chapter.)

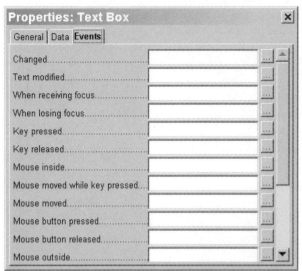

Figure 16. Every control has a number of events that occur as the user interacts with it. You can associate actions with events.

The form itself has events, as well. To access these, click the Form Properties... button on the Form Functions toolbar and go to the Events tab. As with control events, you can assign a macro to any form event.

How do I use the form?

Once you finish laying out a form, you can "run" it by clicking the Design Mode On/Off button on the Form Functions toolbar. When design mode is off, the controls operate as you would expect—you can select and clear check boxes, open combo boxes and drop-down lists, and so forth.

Ordinarily, when you open a saved form, it automatically has design mode off. So, a user opening a form you supply sees it as they would expect. (Be aware, however, that a user can turn design mode on and change the form.) If you're working on a form and want it to open in design mode each time, click the Open in Design Mode button on the Form Functions toolbar before saving the form.

When a form linked to a data source has design mode turned off, the database bar appears at the bottom of the form.

 OOo doesn't have a mechanism to prevent users from changing forms to Design mode. In Microsoft Office, you can protect a form document and give it a password to prevent users from seeing inside.

What else can I do with forms?

A lot. The form capabilities of OOo are significant. When you work with controls, you have options for positioning and aligning them, grouping several controls together, and more. With some experimentation, you can create complex input forms that provide an attractive interface for users.

Can I use macros to simplify repeated actions?

OOo provides two ways to set up macros. The first is to record a macro, where you perform the desired action with OOo "watching." The second choice is to write it yourself using the OpenOffice.org Basic language. Once you define a macro either way, you can assign a keystroke to it and/or put it on a toolbar to make it instantly available.

The ability to record macros was added in OpenOffice.org 1.1. Earlier versions have no macro recorder.

Can I use my Office macros in OOo?

Unfortunately, OpenOffice.org uses a different version of Basic than Microsoft Office, so macros created in Office won't work in OOo. At this time, no mechanism exists for converting Office macros to OOo macros. There's some discussion of creating one, but due to the complexity of the task, it's not likely to happen any time soon.

How do I record a macro?

Before recording a macro, make sure your document is set up as you want it, including putting the cursor where the action you're recording begins. Choose Tools | Macros | Record Macro from the menu. The Recording toolbar (**Figure 17**) appears.

Figure 17. When you start recording a macro, this toolbar appears. Click the Stop Recording button when you're done.

Now, perform the action exactly as you want it recorded, including any cursor movements, choices from the menu, shortcut menu or toolbars, and so forth. (Remember to leave the cursor positioned where you want it to be once the macro finishes. For example, if you record an action to apply to a series of words, lines, or paragraphs one at a time, make sure you leave the cursor at the beginning of the next word, line, or paragraph.) Once you perform all the actions that constitute the macro, click the Stop Recording button.

The Macro dialog (**Figure 18**) appears for you to name the macro and indicate where to store it. Type a name for the macro—the name may not include spaces or a variety of other punctuation characters.

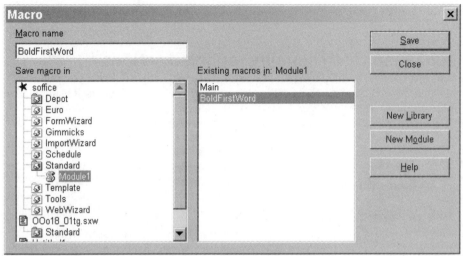

Figure 18. *The Macro dialog lets you save recorded macros, as well as organizing existing macros.*

You can store macros with OpenOffice.org itself or with individual documents or templates. By default, macros you record are stored for all of OOo in the Module1 module of the Standard library of OOo. (See "How are macros organized?" later in this chapter for more information on the hierarchy used for saving macros.)

To store a macro with a document or template, find the document in the left list of the dialog, and click the Standard item for that document. The first time you save a macro to a particular document or template, you are prompted to specify the module; either accept the default Module1 or supply a meaningful name. Once you save one macro with a particular document or template, you can choose the Module1 module to save additional macros there.

How do I use a macro?

Once a macro is defined (whether by recording it or creating it with code), there are a number of ways to run it. The most obvious is to access it from the menu, using Tools | Macros | Macro... to open the Macro dialog. Navigate to the macro you want to run and click the Run button.

You can use a keystroke to run a macro (see "How do I assign a keystroke to a macro?" later in this chapter) or put a button to call the macro on a toolbar (see "How do I put a macro on a toolbar?").

A formula in a spreadsheet can use a macro directly. The formula should refer to the macro by name and pass any required parameters. In this case, the macro must return a value appropriate for use in a spreadsheet. In addition, the macro should be stored in the spreadsheet itself, so it's always available. For example, if you have a macro that computes the cube root of a number, assuming it's called CubeRoot, a formula could use it like this:

```
=CubeRoot(D37)
```

It's likely a macro you can use in this way is one you write yourself (see "How do I create a macro other than recording it?" later in this chapter) rather than one you record.

You can also run a macro when an event occurs on a form. See "How do I make a form do things?" earlier in this chapter. Macros can also be called in a variety of other places, such as during validation in a spreadsheet.

How do I assign a keystroke to a macro?

Assigning a key combination to a macro is like assigning a key combination to anything else. (See "How do I set up custom keystrokes?" in Chapter 4, "The OpenOffice.org User Interface.") You use the Keyboard tab of the Configuration dialog (Tools | Configure on the menu).

In the top section, choose the keystroke you want to assign. Next, in the Category list of the bottom section, find the module containing your macro. Macros stored with OOo are listed under OpenOffice.org BASIC Macros. Macros for the current document are listed under <Document name> BASIC Macros. Both of those items are at the bottom of the Category list.

Click the "+" to show the list of libraries and then click "+" for the appropriate library to find the module. Click the module name; the list of macros displays in the Function list.

Choose the macro you want and click the Modify button.

How do I put a macro on a toolbar?

As with assigning keystrokes, putting a button for a macro on a toolbar is the same as creating a button for any other command. (See "How do I customize the toolbars?" in Chapter 4, "The OpenOffice.org User Interface.") Use the Customize Toolbar dialog. To open that dialog, either choose Customize from the shortcut menu of any toolbar, or click Customize on the Toolbars tab of the Configuration dialog.

Find the toolbar to which you want to add the item in the Toolbars drop-down list. In the Available buttons list, find your macro, navigating down through the document, library, and module as needed. The Available buttons list includes each open document, along with an entry for OpenOffice.org BASIC Macros.

When you find the macro, you can add it to the specified toolbar by clicking the Add button or by dragging it to the position where you want it and dropping it. Once you add the button, you can move it around on the toolbar using drag-and-drop or using the Move Up and Move Down buttons.

Use the Icons button to specify an icon for the macro. If no icon is specified, the name of the macro appears on the button.

How do I create a macro other than recording it?

You can define macros by writing the actual code needed. OpenOffice.org uses a variant of the Basic programming language. While the documentation calls it OpenOffice.org Basic, it appears to be equivalent to the StarBasic language used by StarOffice.

OpenOffice.org Basic is different from Visual Basic for Applications (VBA), the programming language used by Microsoft Office. While both are based on Basic, the object models are quite different. The object model of a macro language is the part that provides access to documents and their components.

The remainder of this section assumes at least some familiarity with simple programming concepts. An introduction to programming is beyond the scope of this book; check the Appendix for a list of materials to get you started writing macros.

How are macros organized?

OOo uses a multi-level structure for storing macros. There are some macros available throughout OOo. In addition, any document or template can have macros stored with it; such macros are available only when that document or template is open.

Macros are organized into modules and libraries. A module is a group of macros, presumably with related functionality. A library is a group of modules, again presumably related by their function. For example, you might create a library of macros related to interest calculations. In that library, one module might contain macros related to mortgage amortization, while another might have macros for computing simple and compound interest.

Both libraries and modules can have meaningful names. Names must begin with a letter and can use letters, digits, and the underscore character ("_"). It's a good idea to use names that indicate the purpose and contents of the module or library.

What tools are provided for writing macros?

OOo offers an interactive development environment (IDE) for writing, editing, and testing macros. It's analogous to the Visual Basic Editor (VBE) provided by Microsoft Office. To open the IDE, choose Tools | Macros | Macro... from the menu. The Macro dialog opens; in this version (**Figure 19**), it contains buttons for working with existing macros.

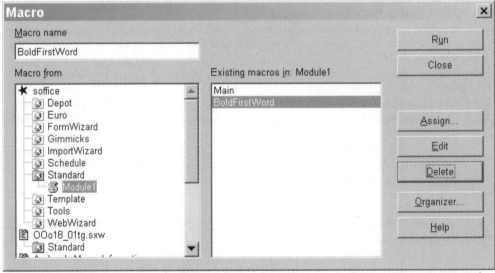

Figure 19. When you open the Macro dialog from the menu, it lets you manage and edit existing macros.

Find the library and module you want to work on and click the Edit button. When the selected library contains no modules, the Macro dialog includes a New button; click that to create a module and open it for editing.

When the IDE opens, the macro highlighted in the Macro dialog is displayed. When you create a new module, OOo adds two empty macros by default. One is called Main and the other is Macro1. You can delete or rename these, and then create the macros you want. **Figure 20** shows the IDE as it opens when clicking Edit in Figure 19.

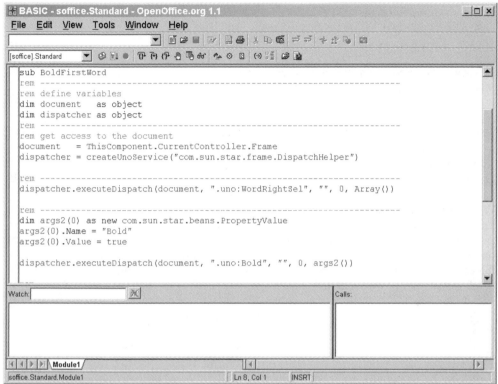

```
BASIC - soffice.Standard - OpenOffice.org 1.1                              _ □ x

File   Edit   View   Tools   Window   Help

          ▼  🗎 🗁 ■  🗏  🗏 🖨  🖾 🗎 🗎  🗎 🗎  🗎 🗎 🗎  🗎

[soffice].Standard   ▼  🗎 🗎 ●  🗎 🗎 🗎 🗎 🗎 🗎  🗎 🗎 🗎  🗎 🗎  🗎 🗎

sub BoldFirstWord
rem ----------------------------------------------------------------
rem define variables
dim document   as object
dim dispatcher as object
rem ----------------------------------------------------------------
rem get access to the document
document   = ThisComponent.CurrentController.Frame
dispatcher = createUnoService("com.sun.star.frame.DispatchHelper")


rem ----------------------------------------------------------------
dispatcher.executeDispatch(document, ".uno:WordRightSel", "", 0, Array())


rem ----------------------------------------------------------------
dim args2(0) as new com.sun.star.beans.PropertyValue
args2(0).Name = "Bold"
args2(0).Value = true

dispatcher.executeDispatch(document, ".uno:Bold", "", 0, args2())



Watch:           🗶                                    Calls:




◄ ◄ ► ► \ Module1 /                          ◄                              ►
soffice.Standard.Module1              Ln 8, Col 1      INSRT
```

Figure 20. *The IDE for editing macros shows the Basic code and offers a variety of tools for editing and testing it.*

The IDE has a number of components. The Function toolbar is docked below the menu. Be aware that it's the regular function toolbar used in all the OOo applications. So, for example, clicking the Open button lets you open a document, and clicking Save saves the current document.

The Macro toolbar is docked beneath the Function toolbar. It contains controls for testing macros, and offers access to various dialogs and tools for macro construction.

When you click the Run button on the Macro toolbar, the first macro in the Module runs. This is different from Office's VBE; in that environment, the Run button executes the macro at the cursor's current position.

The main macro-editing window is below the Macro toolbar. It shows the code currently being edited. The macro is color-coded to represent its syntax and aid in getting it right. To the left of the code window, a narrow window provides a place to set and remove breakpoints. Double-click next to any line of code to set a breakpoint on that line; double-click it again to remove the breakpoint.

By default, two windows are docked beneath the code window. The Watch window lets you track the value of variables as code executes. To watch a variable, type its name in the

Watch text box and press Enter. To remove a variable from the Watch window, click it, and then click the Remove Watch button next to the Watch textbox.

 The Watch window in Microsoft Office accepts expressions as well as variables. OOo's Watch window handles only variables.

The Calls window shows the call stack, that is, the list of routines that have been called. The most recently called is at the top and is numbered 0. The list shows the parameters passed to each routine as well.

There's a tab at the bottom of the IDE for each module of the chosen library. Click a tab to switch to another module. You can rename a module using the shortcut menu for the tab itself.

What does the object model look like?

The OOo object model is quite different from the object models for the Microsoft Office applications. The objects in OOo are organized into *services*. Services, along with other things like constants, are combined into modules. To access an object, you may need to drill down through the module to the service.

For many things you want to do in a macro, you need to create an instance of a service. You do so using the createUnoService() function, passing the completely specified name of the service. Once you have a reference to a service, you can address its properties and methods.

Table 3 lists some of OOo's key services and the modules that contain them.

Table 3. OOo's object model uses a hierarchy of modules and services. You're likely to use some services quite often.

Service	Module	Used for
Desktop	com.sun.star.frame	Opening existing documents and creating new ones.
TextDocument	com.sun.star.text	Working with text documents.
SpreadsheetDocument	com.sun.star.sheet	Working with spreadsheets.
ChartDocument	com.sun.star.chart	Specifying data and other characteristics of a graph.
PresentationDocument	com.sun.star.presentation	Working with presentations.
DrawingDocument	com.sun.star.drawing	Working with drawings.
FormulaProperties	com.sun.star.formula	Working with formulas.

You can use the Desktop service's loadComponentFromURL method to open existing documents or create new ones. For example, the following code opens a new Writer document:

```
dim oDesktop as Object
dim sURL as String
dim mNoArgs()

oDesktop = createUnoService("com.sun.star.frame.Desktop")
sURL = "private:factory/swriter"
oDesktop.loadComponentFromURL(sURL, "_blank",0,mNoArgs())
```

A couple of keywords give you quick access to the OpenOffice.org application object and to the active document. Use StarDesktop to get the application object and ThisComponent for the document object. For example:

```
Dim oApp As Object
Dim oDoc As Object

oApp = StarDesktop
oDoc = ThisComponent
```

 OOo doesn't have a feature like Office's IntelliSense to provide you with help as you type code. You need to know the available properties and methods and their parameters. To make matters worse, the Help file doesn't include information on services, objects, or properties and methods. There's no equivalent to the VBA Help files provided with Office.

Without IntelliSense or a Help file for the macro language, how do you find out what objects are out there and what properties and methods they support? There are a variety of resources, but the best place to start is with a document known as "Andrew's Macro Document," available at **http://www.pitonyak.org/AndrewMacro.sxw**. This document, created by Andrew Pitonyak, contains an introduction to writing OOo macros, along with dozens of useful macros. At this writing, the document runs about 200 pages; it's updated pretty regularly. Andrew's Macro Document points to a variety of other resources for macros; some are listed in the Appendix, "Resources," as well.

Can I automate OpenOffice.org from other applications?

One of the most powerful features of Microsoft Office is the ability to call on its functionality from other applications. For example, a custom database application might call on Word to perform a mail merge, or use Excel for complex computations. Fortunately, you can also automate OOo. Once you're comfortable writing macros, you can apply the same knowledge to run OOo from other applications.

To start an automation session, create an instance of the Service Manager, com.sun.star.ServiceManager, in the application you're automating OOo from. You do this using the appropriate mechanism of the client language (the one doing the automating). For example, using Microsoft Visual FoxPro, that line would look like this:

```
loServiceManager = CreateObject("com.sun.star.ServiceManager")
```

Once you have an instance of the Service Manager, use its CreateInstance method to instantiate the other objects you need, referring to them using their module and service names. For example, in Visual FoxPro, you create a desktop object, like this:

```
loDesktop = loServiceManager.CreateInstance("com.sun.star.frame.Desktop")
```

Once you create objects like a desktop, you can use them just as you would in a macro.

In Microsoft Office, one of the best ways to figure out how to automate a particular task is to record a macro for it and then examine the macro code. Unfortunately, OOo's macro recorder is really just a sophisticated keystroke recorder. The code it generates calls on the executeDispatch method of the Dispatcher service to perform each action in turn rather than using methods of the document services.

You can find documentation for automating OpenOffice.org at **http://udk.openoffice.org/common/man/tutorial/office_automation.html**.

Summary

For long-time Microsoft Office users, forms and macros may be the biggest barrier to switching to OpenOffice.org. Individuals or companies with a large investment in custom forms or macros may find such a transition difficult.

OOo has strong capabilities in both areas, although the Help system is weak in these areas, especially with respect to OpenOffice.org Basic. Some community-based documentation helps to fill in the gaps. No doubt it will improve as time passes.

Updates and corrections to this chapter can be found on Hentzenwerke's web site, **www.hentzenwerke.com**. Click "Catalog" and navigate to the page for this book.

Appendix
Resources

While this book should give you the basics and more, eventually, you're likely to want to do something with OpenOffice.org that isn't covered here. This appendix offers a list of places to go for more help.

Where do I get documentation for OpenOffice.org?

The first place to look for help is on the Help menu. Choose Help | Contents to open the OOo Help system (**Figure 1**). The Help system is a mixed bag. In some areas, it provides excellent information and good step-by-step instructions. In other areas, information is sparse. Worse, for some topics, Help describes the StarOffice functionality rather than the OOo functionality, and is actually wrong.

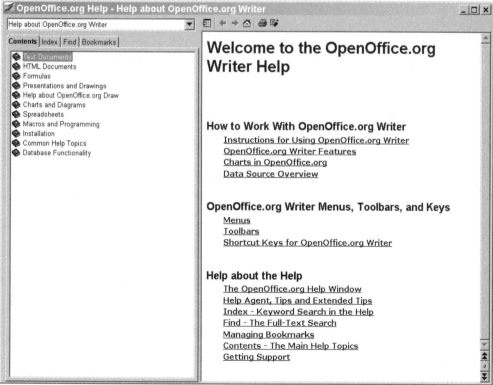

Figure 1. The built-in Help system has a lot of information about OpenOffice.org, although it has some weaknesses.

Despite these weaknesses, try Help first because it often can solve your problems. In addition, the Help system improves with each new version, as the members of the documentation project have a chance to correct and improve the text.

Strange as it may seem, the next source to try is the StarOffice documentation. You can find a complete set of manuals online at **http://docs.sun.com/db/coll/999.2?q=star+office**. You're most likely to be interested in the StarOffice 6.0 Software User Guide. You can download this PDF file from the site above (watch out, it's nearly 4 MB). Because this documentation is for StarOffice, be aware that it may not be exactly correct.

Where do I get help online?

There are two kinds of online help available—documents you can read and interactive discussions. Many sites offer both kinds of help.

For documents, including how to's and FAQ's (frequently asked questions), there are several sites to visit. The first is the home site for OpenOffice.org—**www.openoffice.org**. On that site, click the User Help link to find user documentation. The site also lists other sites with documentation.

Another place with online documentation is **www.openofficesupport.com**. This site includes tutorials as well as FAQ's.

There are several places where you can ask questions and get answers from other OOo users. OpenOffice.org runs a number of mailing lists, which use e-mail to send messages among a group of subscribed users. Click the Mailing Lists link on the OpenOffice.org home page for more information. You'll probably find the Users list the most useful.

If you're interested in joining one of the lists, but don't like to use e-mail for this purpose, you can also read the OpenOffice.org lists in newsgroup format. The newsgroup server is news.gmane.org. Look for lists with openoffice in the name; the Users list is named "gmane.comp.openoffice.questions."

Several sites run web forums devoted to OpenOffice.org. Check out **www.ooodocs.org**, **www.oooforum.org**, and **openoffice.ballsome.com**.

With all of these sites, keep in mind that the people who answer questions are volunteers, not paid staff. Ask one question per message, provide as much information as you can to help people understand what problem you're running into, and understand you're not entitled to an answer. If someone can help, he or she will. Finally, after you get some help, it's polite to stick around and help some others.

If you're not in a big hurry for an answer, you may want to spend some time looking over the lists before asking a question. It will give you a feel for how things work. As with most communities, you will find "regulars" who check in every day (or many times per day), one-time visitors just trying to get help with a single problem, and everything in between.

What else is available?

A number of web sites offer templates, macros, and other things that make it easier to work in OpenOffice.org. If you don't find what you're looking for on this list, search the web because new resources become available frequently.

The official OpenOffice.org site, **www.openoffice.org**, has the product itself, including localized versions for a variety of languages. The dictionary download page, **lingucomponent.openoffice.org/download_dictionary.html**, offers dictionaries (for spell checking, hyphenation, and thesauruses) in varying numbers of languages, as well as instructions and tools for working with dictionaries.

OO Extras, **ooextras.sourceforge.net**, includes templates and artwork. The templates are offered in several languages.

The definitive guide to writing macros in OpenOffice.org is Andrew Pitonyak's macro document, available at **www.pitonyak.org/AndrewMacro.sxw**. You can find additional macro information at **www.darwinwars.com/lunatic/bugs/oo_macros.html**. The home site for macros and automation is **api.openoffice.org**. The How To section at **documentation.openoffice.org** includes a good introductory document on using macros.

You can find instructions for installing OOo on the official site (**www.openoffice.org**) as well as at **http://www.hypermax.net.au/~settantta/ooo/default.html**.

If you still can't find what you're looking for, try using one of the search engines. Google, in particular, turns up a lot of information on OpenOffice.org.

Finally, don't forget to check the Hentzenwerke website (**www.hentzenwerke.com**) for updates and corrections to this book, as well as answers to frequently asked questions.

Index

Note that you can download the PDF file for this book from **www.hentzenwerke.com** (see the section "How to download files" at the beginning of this book). The PDF is completely searchable and will provide additional keyword lookup capabilities not practical in an index.